Chasing Nirvana

Chasing Nirvana

A Seeker's Story of Loss and Liberation

PRIYA HUTNER

SWP

SHE WRITES PRESS

Published in 2026 by
She Writes Press, an imprint of The Stable Book Group

32 Court Street, Suite 2109
Brooklyn, NY 11201
https://shewritespress.com
The Library of Congress Control Number is available upon request.
ISBN: 979-8-89636-088-9
eISBN: 979-8-89636-089-6

Interior Designer: Adrian Morgan

Printed in the United States

Names and identifying characteristics have been changed to protect the privacy of certain individuals.

This book is a memoir and reflects the author's present recollections of experiences over time. She has recreated certain incidents, conversations, and behaviors as accurately as her memory, notes, or research have allowed. Timelines may be slightly altered, and some names have been created or changed to protect privacy.

For my sons,
Hanuman and Ganga Das,
I am so proud of you both.
May you always seek truth,
question everything,
and know that love is the way home.
I love you with all my heart.

Contents

Are you looking for me?
I am in the next seat. My shoulder is against yours.
You will not find me in the stupas, not in Indian shrine rooms, nor in synagogues, nor in cathedrals: not in masses, nor kirtans, not in legs winding around your own neck, nor in eating nothing but vegetables. When you really look for me, you will see me instantly—you will find me in the tiniest house of time. Tell me, what is God? He is the breath inside the breath.

—**KABIR**

1

The Sounds of Silence

I PLACED THE HUMAN-SKULL CUP FILLED with the blood of the Hindu goddess Kali to my lips. The sweet taste of Manischewitz wine trickled over my tongue. The moon was full, and the fire burned bright. I bowed down and kissed the feet of my guru after they were bathed in yogurt, rose water, and honey. My heart was full. I was committed.

I'd chanted with hundreds of people around an RV in the middle of the woods with a dead body in it. I'd eaten the salt that once preserved the body of a deceased Tibetan lama. I'd meditated on my own funeral pyre. I didn't question these rituals at the time. I thought it was normal.

Florida might not be the first place you think of finding an ashram, but that's where the guru planted herself. You never knew when a palmetto bug the size of a small rodent would find its way skittering across your bed or stepping on a mound of fire ants could present serious and painful repercussions. It was important to check your shoes before putting them on, or you might find a coral snake nestled in the toe. Scorpions, rattlesnakes, water moccasins, and brown recluse spiders were only some menaces that could be encountered on the ashram. I rarely wore shoes.

We were a tight-knit spiritual community in the middle of a small town in central Florida, not far from the Atlantic Ocean. In the center of the eighty-acre property was a pond called the Ganga, which was home to the ashes of the dead. Ornate carved temples with life-size bronze statues of dead Indian saints and Hindu deities surrounded the pond, along with five communal houses. Each house was a warren of rooms where twenty or more people resided. I lived with my two sons and fifteen others on the southernmost part of our property next to a cow pasture.

Ma was the guru, the dispeller of darkness, the one who shone the light on our inner spiritual landscape. Every evening, she gave a class called darshan. When I entered the temple for Ma's Thursday night teaching, the room was dark. Candles flickered, illuminating the multitude of Hindu and Tibetan statues that occupied altars and shelves throughout the temple. Massive photos of long-dead Hindu saints hung from the eaves, their watchful eyes inspecting and observing my every move. The scent of sandalwood hung heavy in the air.

I settled into a cross-legged position amid a sea of 150 other cross-legged people. A bronze statue of Ganesh, the elephant god, sat to my left. He offered me the opportunity to remove the obstacles in my life. Across from me, the monkey god, Hanuman, reminded me that service and devotion were the path I'd chosen.

A life-size statue of the black goddess Kali stood like a sentry in the back of the room. Blacker than the night, she was fierce, with a lolling red tongue, a skirt of human arms around her waist, and a necklace of skulls that cascaded over her naked breasts. One foot rested on her consort, Shiva.

In her many hands, she wielded several objects. Each was a reminder of her ability to free me of my ego-self, to help me let go of my worldly attachments and ultimately experience freedom. In one hand, she held a curved sickle; in another, a trident; in her third hand, she cradled a skull cup filled with blood; and in her fourth hand, she clutched the severed head of a devotee. Each symbolized the gifts and boons I desired, including the prospect of nirvana, liberation, and enlightenment. White plaster skulls scattered at her feet; their hollow stares were a constant reminder of my own impermanence. I believed she would slice through my attachments and decimate my ego for a price. She was my patron deity.

I closed my eyes. The whine of the harmonium, the deafening beat of the drums, and the tinny sound of hand cymbals clanged. A woman wrapped in a thin white shawl with *Om* mantras printed on the edges began a devotional chant in Sanskrit to the Hindu deity Shiva.

"*Om Namah Shivaya. Om Namah Shivaya.*" ("I bow to the lord of destruction to clear the path for rebirth.") The beat intensified. Our voices rose louder and louder, responding to the call of the lead chanter. Half of the devotees in the room clapped. Some swayed back and forth, while others sat with their eyes closed.

We came from different backgrounds. The long-haired, stocky man wearing a white button-down shirt who sat beside me was a psychologist. The heavyset blond woman off to my right was a massage therapist. The tall man next to Ma's couch was a lawyer who, at one point, had run the ashram. Our differences didn't matter in that moment. We were all waiting for our guru to enter the room. With every chorus we chanted, we beckoned her to come out to us. We called to her with our hearts, and with each word we enunciated, we chanted like our lives depended on it.

I opened my eyes. As I sang, I watched. I needed to make sure nothing was out of place. I scanned the room. If anything was awry, I'd be the one to answer for it.

The door to the back hall swung open, and like a hurricane, Ma entered through it with a group of attendants following her.

Everyone in the room stood. Our singing had reached a high-pitched crescendo, almost on the verge of screaming. It was like the ocean of devotees were desperately thirsty, willing to drown in the moment of what was about to unfold.

All I wanted was to drop into the deep, rich space of silence, feel the essence of God, and be immersed, enveloped, and transported into a mystical, magical place. I thought I could only attain this state of being when I was in darshan or looking deeply into Ma's eyes.

Ma sat on the custom-made love seat covered with faux leopard skin. A large black sheepskin was draped over it. A chilled bottle of Perrier and a box of tissues sat on a small table next to her. The children lined up for a hug and a lollipop. With a wave of her hand, Ma gestured for the chanters to stop.

"Namaste, my children," Ma said, placing her hands together in prayer.

Breathing in deeply, I looked at her to see if I could sense her mood. I checked to see what she might see. Was there anyone in the space who might be an issue? It could be a familiarity that set her off, someone with their legs sprawled open or their feet pointed toward the guru. Or someone who might lack awareness, speak out of turn, or say something that Ma perceived as disrespectful. Was there a guest who was energetically "off"? Ma scanned the room and observed us as I attempted to read her and what was about to occur.

Her long, black hair flowed down her back and around her face. The large diamond in her nose caught the light and sparkled. Her trademark red dot with three white lines smeared across her forehead accentuated her penetrating glare. Gold bangles ran up her arm and jingled with every move she made. A large pendant of her long-dead guru, Neem Karoli Baba, or Baba, as he was affectionately called, hung from her neck along with a gold necklace that read "Brooklyn" in script.

A quiet hush rippled over the bodies in the room.

"When you die with awareness, you will master your own beautiful death. All you need to do is go to the brightest light. There will be many lights, but the brightest one is the one to choose," she whispered.

A flicker of tension ran through me, tugging at my gut. How would I know which light to go to? I took a long breath in and slowly exhaled out. I held my breath out, visualizing it suspended over the top of my head.

"At the moment of death, you will make the right choice. And although it is hard to conquer the power of thought, your thoughts can be your greatest asset or the most horrible of karmas."

Her last few words offered a small wave of relief, except for the part about the horrible karmas. Who knew the rules of dying were so complicated? I didn't think I'd be making a ton of decisions when I died.

"I will be there, waiting for you," she finally said. "You don't need to worry. Close your eyes, my children, and let me show you what death will feel like."

Thank God, Ma was going to take us into a deeper space. I rolled my shoulders back and down, straightened my spine, tucked my chin, and allowed my breath to slow down. I closed my eyes and fell into the darkness.

"Focus way over the head, breathe in the breath. Feel the spirit, like smoke rising." Ma's voice was smooth, like warm, melted chocolate. Her cadence lulled me deeper.

"Let go, my children; this is what you live for."

I surrendered to the moment, feeling as if I were no longer in my body. There was nothing but stillness around me. I was gently being coaxed deeper into meditation. My body vibrated. The top of my head tingled. Heat rose from the base of my spine and up my back. My insides were on fire, and my skin was burning hot. As my body became lighter, I lost myself in the space. I felt like I was floating and weightless and could barely hear her words any longer. Yet

I was aware. My breath was guided to where it needed to be. The long pauses between Ma's words led me into a delicious silence.

"Conquer the grossness of sleep," Ma said sharply.

My spine snapped straighter. Someone was nodding. I could hear snoring behind me. I wondered what would happen if you did that during the death process? Would you end up choosing the wrong light? I felt as if a heavy blanket was weighing me down. Part of me wanted to fall deeper into myself. My head jerked. *Do not nod, do not nod*, I reminded myself, pinching the web of my hand between my thumb and index finger.

"Keep the body straight." Ma's tone was sharp. "If you can't hold this Shakti,[1] you don't belong here."

The snoring stopped. Ma paused. There was no sound, no movement, no breathing behind me. I dropped back into the stillness, into a long, deep, endless space of nothingness.

"*Samadhi* means uniting with everything that is, everything that will be, becoming total bliss. Remember, death is only an interruption of life," Ma said in a low, hushed tone. The room remained exceptionally quiet. "Death, I call you to me. In this space of love, you must be acknowledged. In this space of love, the fear of death disappears."

Her words were poetry leaking into my soul. Why would anyone fear death if this is what death felt like?

Another long, deep silence ensued. And then, with a sharp clap of her hands, she slipped back into her clipped Brooklynese. "Sit up, sit up, wake up, come back to me. Open your eyes."

I didn't want to breathe. I didn't move. The room around me slowly came to life.

"Daughter, that means you, too."

I felt her gaze on me. I resigned myself and opened my eyes. Ma's long, black hair melted into her black sweater, which melted into the black wall behind her. There was a smoky haze around her. I closed my eyes again. I felt like my whole being had been rearranged; my cells felt charged, as if a thousand volts of electrical current coursed through me. I opened my eyes again.

Ma was looking at me. “How’d you like that, daughter?” She grinned.

I nodded, unable to form words.

“Namaste, my children. I love you all,” she said, and jumped up.

I wobbled, getting up to stand as she left. Leaning back on the railing behind me to balance myself, I breathed in the essence that remained in the room.

It was this part of the teaching that moved me forward. I wanted to experience this every night. I wanted the endless ability to drop into the depth of my being all the time. I wanted to be enlightened. I wanted my guru and Mother Kali to decimate my ego.

2

Free Falling

I LEARNED TO MEDITATE WHEN I WAS TWELVE. My father began practicing Transcendental Meditation in his search for happiness. We lived in the suburbs of Bucks County, Pennsylvania. The split-level houses were all the same, with their brick and white shingle exteriors, their windows all framed with black metal shutters, and their entryways graced with black, wrought-iron columns. Everyone had manicured lawns and a two-car garage. Thick, lush woodlands and creeks spread out behind the cookie-cutter neighborhood. It was a bit too perfect on the outside. Only a few miles away, old stone homes hundreds of years old rested along the main road. My childhood friends lived in homes where George Washington once prepared for battle, the Underground Railroad hid fugitive slaves, and ghosts of the past were rumored to haunt the halls.

My parents called a family meeting without my eight-year-old brother. I sat on my twin bed between them and looked around the room. In the corner was a hand-painted tree, its far-reaching branches dotted with green leaves my mom had applied with sponges. She had painted a swooping, swirling, colorful rainbow across the robin's-egg blue walls.

My dad looked serious. His bushy brows knitted together. I couldn't tell if I was in trouble.

"Your mother and I are learning to meditate, and we think it might be good for you," he said. My mother smiled. Her sleeveless, white-and-blue-flowered button-down blouse puckered as she leaned in toward me.

"Do you want to learn how to meditate?" my dad asked. "If you agree, you need to take it seriously."

I looked at my socks while kicking my feet back and forth on the edge of the bed. "Sure," I agreed. I asked no questions. I just thought it would be cool to learn.

A week later, we drove to Center City Philadelphia to the Transcendental Meditation Center. We were greeted by a thin white man in a white-collared shirt. He had curly brown hair, wiry sideburns, and a mustache that curled down over his upper lip. My parents led me into a small room and left me there with him. I sat across from him, on a beige metal folding chair, the kind you'd find at a school assembly or the Knights of Columbus Hall at an all-you-can-eat spaghetti dinner. The cold metal seeped through the seat of my pants. On a table next to the man was a glass of water and a small photograph of an old man in a white robe, with long, straggly, black hair and a beard streaked with white.

The teacher rested his hands on his thighs. "Your parents tell me you want to learn how to meditate."

"Yes." My pigtails bounced up and down.

"I am going to give you a word to repeat called a *mantra*. This word is yours, and no one else's. You mustn't tell anyone your mantra. Okay?"

"Okay." My hands gripped tightly to the edges of the chair.

"Your mantra is Enga. Can you say it?"

"Enga." I repeated it perfectly.

"Great. Repeat the mantra for fifteen minutes in the morning and again at night before bed. Think you can do that?"

I nodded and thought, *Of course I can do this.*

The following day, I sat on the edge of my bed. I closed my eyes and repeated the mantra over and over. For the next year, I meditated for fifteen minutes twice a day.

I don't know how my parents' meditation practice was going, but during those years, my dad's tight, curly hair grew longer and became more 'fro-like. He grew a mustache, and thick sideburns crawled down the sides of his face. He took up the electric guitar, and "House of the Rising Sun" vibrated through his amplifier. "The Wind Cries Mary," "All Along the Watchtower," and "Ruby Tuesday" pulsed from his stereo.

I knew our family was different. I knew I was different. I read well beyond my sixth-grade level, often sneaking into my dad's room to borrow his books, which rested on the shelf in the headboard of his bed. When he wasn't home, I'd tiptoe in and peer into the rows of books. My small fingers slid the lattice doors open to reveal a treasure trove of paperbacks: *2001: A Space Odyssey*, *In Cold Blood*, *Goldfinger*, and *Dianetics*. I read them all.

I was a sixth-grade vegetarian, meditating with a mantra. My mother fed us walnut meatloaf, vegetarian casseroles, and thick-ground peanut butter and banana sandwiches, layered between two slabs of cardboard-like brown bread with raisins and honey.

Years of practicing yoga, eating healthy food, and meditating did not seem to help assuage my father's unhappiness. He yelled at me during homework. He yelled at my mother when he couldn't find his shoes. He found solace in the arms of other women.

It was in early 1975 when my father met his spiritual teacher, Joya Santana. I didn't think anything of their new interest; my father was always chasing new pursuits. He learned yoga and took sailing lessons. He considered purchasing a spring-water company in New Hampshire and a health-food store in New Hope. My mother bowed to his whims as my brother and I were loaded into the car to explore his latest desire. My parents traveled to New York to attend Joya's classes and weekend retreats, drawn by her promise of taking them to God. My brother spent weekends with my grandparents while I stayed with friends. The woods behind my house became my sanctuary, my friend, my refuge. Without any real supervision, at fourteen, I started dropping acid and smoked pot and drank. I spent a lot of my time in the converted garage of my best friend's house.

One weekend, when my parents left for a retreat with Joya in Montauk, I walked to my friend Sherri's house along the edge of the thick, matted woods. I tapped on the door before entering. Sherri's older brother, Johnny, and his friends were shooting pool. One of them handed me a small, square piece of paper, and I popped it in my mouth without hesitation. The idea of a new experience enticed and excited me.

"Just let it dissolve under your tongue," Johnny said. Bad Company's "Shooting Star" blared from the stereo. Johnny and his friends were the popular kids in school, the bad boys of the neighborhood whom everyone wanted to be friends with. No one knew I had a crush on my best friend's brother.

"How long does it take?" I asked.

"Not long."

I leaned back in the chair and waited. Something almost imperceptible was percolating, a fluttering of something I couldn't quite put my finger on. Maybe it was my imagination? Waves of light emanated from the fixture above. We sat around in chairs and couches on the edge of the room. I fanned the fingers of my right hand; colorful trails of light sprung from my fingertips. Things in the room started moving, but my body was plastered to my seat. I looked at Sherri, and she took the form of an alien from another planet. Closing my eyes, I drifted off into the wild, colorful, geometric images of my mind.

A knock on the door shot us all to rigid attention. The door burst open, and my mother stood on the threshold. Her sun-bleached, blond mane was wild, askew in every direction. Her fair skin was tan. She looked like a lion. She was excited to see me.

Jolted out of my psychedelic state, I shot out of my chair. "Mom, what are you doing here?"

She smiled with outreached arms. "I just got home and wanted to see you."

I nudged her out the door. "You can't be here right now."

My mom was in her hippie-loving God space after a week with Joya, and I was tripping my ass off. The two of us were meeting on very different psychic planes.

"I'll be home soon," I told her.

She left, somewhat confused.

After I came down from my trip, I returned home. My mother was still awake. She didn't ask me any questions.

"How are you?" my mother asked, and patted the couch next to her.

"Fine." I was just glad I wasn't in trouble.

"Your father and I went to Montauk to be with Joya. We meditated and sang with hundreds of other people sitting on the beach with Joya. She told us that God is in the sharing and took us into the silence. It was a beautiful experience."

I watched my mother as she glowed with excitement.

3

You Are Like a Hurricane

THE FIRST TIME I MET MA, who was called Joya then, I was fourteen. My dad thought it was time for my brother and me to attend a class, so we piled into his white Lincoln Continental and drove to Queens, New York. The lights of the city came into view and cars whizzed by as we merged onto Grand Central Parkway and exited into Forest Hills. Bright lights, horns blaring, cars darting—the energy of the city enlivened my senses. I was more excited to be in New York and mildly curious to see what all the fuss was about this Joya woman who had captured my parents' attention.

My father pulled up to a large, turreted house that resembled a castle.

"Okay, we're here."

He motioned for my brother and me to get out of the car. Men with long hair and beards, who were wrapped in white shawls and wearing drawstring pants, and women with long, flowing skirts and peasant tops loitered in the front yard. A lengthy queue of people spilled out the front door.

We filed in. The house smelled spicy, a mixture of brewing herbs, exotic oils, and incense. My parents guided us into a large room. The door to the kitchen was slightly ajar as we passed by. A group of women were laughing. One had flowers in her long, wavy brown hair, and she stirred something steaming in large metal pots. Her eyes twinkled as she mixed the brew on the stove. To this day, the aroma of Celestial Seasonings Red Zinger and Roastaroma tea reminds me of this time in my life.

We entered a large, open room that was filled to capacity. People sat cross-legged on the floor, knee to knee, meditating. My father found us a spot in the middle of it all, and we sat down. He closed his eyes. There was only one other teenager in the room. She sat like the others, erect and deep in meditation. Sandalwood and Nag Champa incense unfurled in slow, curling ribbons that misted through the room, flooding my senses. The man next to me lifted his arms and clapped his hands; I recoiled. The combination of body odor and patchouli oil made me gag. I scooted toward my mother. The room was packed; bodies of strangers pressed against me. I felt alone in this foreign, curious, and weird world.

Muffled sounds came from another room, and a heavy, tanned woman entered from a side door. She spun like a tornado. Chaos and noise not only followed her but also preceded her. I shifted on the pillow. What was happening? I wondered why there was so much pandemonium around this woman. A group of young men in white cotton yoga pants accompanied her. A bearded man with dark, curly hair, wearing a scarf with elephants, held her hand and led her to a couch at the front of the room. The entourage of handsome men sat in front of her. Her long, black hair fell below her waist. She was dressed in a tight, red bodysuit with multitudes of gold bracelets running up both forearms. Her eyes were dark, opaque. I couldn't quite pinpoint the shade of blue on her eyelids; it was darker than a robin's egg and bluer than the sky, a kind of vibrant blue I'd only seen when my black light was on. She gazed into the sea of people through thick, black, fake eyelashes.

"Whaat dah fuck are you all doing here?" She laughed and then pointed at a man swathed in peach, with long, stringy hair and a brown beard. "It's time for you to move into one of my houses. Move to Shyam's house. Talk to my Raghu." She nodded to the man sitting at her feet. Finished with this person, she moved on to another.

"Did you bring me my mun cake?" she asked a woman.

The woman smiled. "Yes, from the best bakery in town."

Joya's finger landed on a man sitting a few rows in front of me. "I name you Tough Tony."

What kind of name is that? I thought.

She told people things about themselves they hadn't even asked about. Some people laughed and others cried.

I fidgeted in my seat.

Joya's gaze fell on a man sitting in the middle of the room. "Sing for me," she said.

The man stood, nodded, and belted out "Amazing Grace."

Tears rolled down my cheeks. The room stilled. Joya's back went rigid, her spine straightened, and her eyes fluttered shut. Not one muscle moved. It reminded me of a hypnotist with his patient or a psychic communicating with spirits. She sat like that for what seemed like hours. The stillness was broken by the jangle of her bracelets.

When she spoke again, it was as if a different person had taken over her body. Her voice became slow and deliberate, melodic, and meditative. "God is in the sharing. If you want my truth, you must also take my insanity," she said.

When it was over, she left just as she had come in with a whirlwind of shrieking, laughter, and calling out to people. She yelled to them to pack, move, or meditate more.

My insides were shaken. What had just happened to me? Tears fell down my freckled cheeks.

"It's just your heart opening. That's how Joya works with you. She has a lot of energy," my dad explained.

I didn't understand what he was talking about, but I knew something big had shifted inside me.

The following year, my dad quit his job as a tax accountant and my mother quit her job as a dental assistant. My grandparents and aunts and uncles were concerned. My mother's brother and wife begged my parents to let my brother and me live with them. Instead, we moved into one of Joya's houses in Forest Hills, Queens.

The beautiful Tudor house was narrow and tall, squashed between two other Tudor houses across from St. Luke's Episcopal Church. Joya named our house Arunachala after the holy mountain where the saint Ramana Maharshi taught his students the path of self-inquiry.

Freed from the boredom of the suburbs, I embraced the living, breathing wildness of my new environment. Although I lived with a group of strangers, I knew the moment I hit the streets of New York, I was home.

4

Come as You Are

We may have moved into a beautiful Tudor home, but not everybody lived in luxury. In the basement dwelt ten students, all somewhat odd and a bit reclusive. They didn't have much money and were relegated to the lower level. Curtained-off areas with colorful tapestries, hanging beads, and sheets created a catacomb of small, makeshift rooms. A mattress or foam pad usually rested on the floor along with a meditation altar holding a photo of Ma and Baba.

I rarely went to the basement. Incense drifted up to the ground floor, where there was a galley kitchen and a dining room with a big wooden table and seating for at least fifteen. The living room was bright with a large, cozy sectional couch and plenty of room on the floor for yoga practice. My room was on the second floor of the house. It was big and bright with two large windows that overlooked Greenway South. My parents were across the hall. My younger brother, Durga Das, had a small room on the third floor.

A gay hairdresser and a beautiful woman from California who reminded me of a '60s flower child also lived on the third floor. She was one of my favorite people among the group of God-seeking hippies whom I now lived with in the house.

On my first day of tenth grade at Forest Hills High School, I arrived in ripped jeans and a black Rolling Stones T-shirt with the *Sticky Fingers* red tongue emblazoned across my chest. My feathered bangs hung in my eyes. I stood amid the long rows of lockers, lost in the endless hallways of a school that was three times the size of my previous one. The other girls my age were all well-manicured. They had Farrah Fawcett hairdos and wore tight, designer Jordache jeans, high heels, and Louis Vuitton handbags. Boys drove fancy Mustangs. *I'm in the wrong school,* I thought. I loved rock and roll. There would be no KC and the Sunshine Band song uttered from my lips.

I made one friend that first week. Cheryl and I had a few things in common, including our clothes and music. Late one night, pulling my coat tight around me in the frigid New York air, I walked up Burns Street to visit my new friend. Station Square seemed quieter than usual as I walked along the cobblestones. Cheryl was hanging out with her much-older boyfriend, Willy, who looked tough, with his long, greasy hair and mustache. I took him to be about twenty-five. I had no doubt he was part of a gang and lived on the other side of the tracks. He and Cheryl were entangled on the old couch in the basement of her apartment building. I was young but not stupid. I didn't stay long.

I began the long walk home. Pulling my coat tighter, I stuck my free hand in my pockets. The dim streetlights cast a hazy, yellow shadow. I quickened my pace. The railway tracks above me were silent. When I approached the square, the stillness was shattered by screeching sirens, flashing lights, cars parked askew, and people running around with flashlights as they searched for something. The street was blockaded.

I slowed to see what all the commotion was about.

A policeman stopped me. "You need to go home. You shouldn't be out at this time of night. There's a murderer stalking young women, and you fit the description."

I wasn't afraid. I walked these streets at night all the time, but tonight I hurried home all the same—it was cold out. That night, the serial killer Son of Sam had claimed another victim.

Jennifer and I were the only two young teens living in Joya's houses. We went to Joya's class every second week and often were charged to babysit the younger kids on the other weeks. We generally did what Joya told us to do, but we were both concerned about one of Joya's rules—the celibacy rule, which she said was the fastest path to God. Surely, at sixteen, we should be exempt from the rule, we reasoned, as we had never experienced sex. Our sixteen-year-old selves prepared our case. We decided to write Joya a letter. We worded it carefully, acknowledging how unfair it was that everyone else had already had sex, and we were still virgins. We asked for dispensation from the celibacy rule.

It was our turn to attend class, and we sat among hundreds of yogis on cushions in a warehouse-like loft in the city. I picked at my jeans while everyone chanted, waiting for Joya to arrive. Jennifer sat next to me, her back erect and her eyes closed.

Joya entered the room with a group of men, one leading her to her seat. "Where's my Jai Laxman?" she asked.

"I'm here."

"Sing for me."

There were questions and personal interactions.

"Where are my girls?"

My back went rigid. Jennifer's eyes shot open. We raised our hands, weakly. I swallowed hard. I knew this was trouble. I knew what was about to occur.

"Stand up, my girls."

Shaking, I stood and looked around at a sea of bodies and felt three hundred pairs of eyes staring at us. I refocused my gaze to the front of the room, where my teacher sat with her trademark false eyelashes, blue eyeshadow, and rows of bangles up her tanned arms. She flapped a piece of paper in her hand.

Fuck me.

"So, you ladies wrote this?"

We both offered a mute nod.

"I'd like you to recite your letter to the class."

My insides turned liquid. I felt like a mouse being tossed about in the paws of a very dangerous alley cat. I looked at Jennifer, and she looked at me.

"Go ahead," I pleaded.

She stuttered and began. "Dear Ma . . . Most of the other people in the satsang have already experienced sex. They have had their fun and we haven't. We are asking for dispensation . . ."

We spit out the letter word by word, taking turns reciting the lines. We stood, our souls laid bare before the crowded room. The song "Killing Me Softly" thrummed through my head. I heard the adults choke back their laughter. The contents of my stomach rose to my throat. I stood at attention, but I wanted to run.

Ma nodded to both of us and said, "Just be careful, my girls."

We were happy to be freed from the celibacy rule, but our freedom came with great embarrassment.

I didn't connect with the kids who attended Forest Hills High School. The girls were stuck-up, and the guys only cared about their new cars. They came from affluent families, and I lived with a group of God-seeking hippies. I transferred to Hillcrest High School in Jamaica, Queens. I made friends who were more like-minded. I cut school lunch to eat across the street at Smile of the Beyond, a vegetarian restaurant where Carlos Santana and Ravi Shankar hung out. I found my tribe. We gathered at Flagpole Park when we weren't in school. Led Zeppelin, Eric Clapton, and the Rolling Stones blared from the radio as we sat on the benches in a cement circle.

Near the end of the school year, I met Chris. He went to Catholic school and lived in an apartment in Rego Park with his alcoholic mother, his younger sister, and a bunch of cats. He was from the Austin Street Park, where a rougher, tougher crowd of teenagers hung out. I noticed him hanging around our park, with his long, dirty-blond hair and bright blue eyes. He was a drummer in a band, and he was funny. I fell hard for him. We started to spend time together.

Parked on the street in Chris's friend Todd's car, we drank Seagram's 7. Todd popped in a mixtape with The Alan Parsons Project's "I Wouldn't Want to Be Like You" and Carlos Santana's "She's Not There." I'd been with other guys and done almost everything, but I was still a virgin. I was just tipsy enough to gather my courage, so I leaned over and whispered, "I'm going home. I'll leave the door open." Chris smiled, revealing his dimple. He knew exactly what I was saying.

When I arrived home, the house was dark. The door creaked as I entered. All of the adults were in the city at Ma's class. The stairs groaned as I climbed the two flights to my room and waited.

Chris arrived ten minutes later. He tiptoed into my room, kissed me, and then slowly guided me toward the bed. He pulled my top off over my head.

"Are you sure?" he asked.

"Yes, absolutely." I helped him unzip my skintight jeans. He tugged them off and laid me back onto the mattress. He was gentle. I gasped when he entered me.

"Are you okay?" he asked.

I nodded. I finally was relieved of another teenage burden.

I knew this wasn't his first time. He'd told me he'd lost his virginity to an older girl in a pew of the Catholic church he attended. He had a reputation for sleeping around, among other things. My peace-loving Flagpole Park friends had warned me about him. He had blown up a district attorney's car after the DA pissed him off.

Chris rolled with a gritty, partying crowd. He was a bad boy . . . apparently, just the type I was attracted to.

I heard the front door open. It was late.

"Oh my God, my parents are back." I bolted upright. There was no way Chris could leave the house at this point. My parents slept across the hall.

"You'll have to sleep here." I grabbed his hand and led him out to the hall, where I opened a small, square panel door just large enough for a body to slide through and lie down. He peered in. It was lined with red and black silk and satin materials, and shelves with candles and photos lined the wall. It was a meditation space that a former devotee had created before he left. We kissed good night, Chris slid into the tiny space, and I went back to my room.

I woke up with the sun, crept out to the hall, and opened the door. "Hurry up and come out. We'll go downstairs and pretend you've come for breakfast," I told him.

Downstairs, I opened the front door, pushed Chris out, and closed it in his face. Then I knocked on the door and let Chris in.

"Mom, this is Chris. He's here for breakfast." My mother, still in her robe, made us breakfast. She didn't ask him much and left us to eat in the kitchen.

Chris and I were together for almost a year before our young teenage relationship started to unhinge. It was his best friend, Massimo, who told me Chris was cheating on me. I didn't break it off with Chris right away, but I was devastated. I cried, and Massimo listened. He became my best friend and confidant.

One warm August night, Massimo walked me home. He took my hand, led me around the side of the old stone church across from Flagpole Park, and kissed me. I leaned my back against the cold concrete of the old building. He unzipped my pants and slid his hands down, his fingers finding their way into me. I wanted him. He wanted me. He pulled my pants down to my ankles. My heart pounded. I touched his olive skin and jet-black, shoulder-length hair while his chiseled Italian body rubbed against me. He smiled.

"I've wanted this for a long time," he whispered. "Chris doesn't deserve you."

We kissed while struggling to stay upright. His hands slid my underpants down. He propped me up and then entered me. I moaned. My breath was ragged. We slid down the wall and onto the sidewalk. It was dark, yet I could see the outline of his body as he moved in and out of me. My breathing was heavy. I wanted to moan. I wanted to scream out, but I was afraid someone would hear me. What if someone was praying inside? I wondered what the parishioners would think of finding two teenagers fucking their brains out against their hallowed walls.

The next afternoon, Massimo found me sitting with friends on the bench at the park. He smiled as he walked toward me. "Here, you left this," he said as he pushed his long, jet-black hair from his eyes and handed me my brown leather belt rolled into a tight bundle.

I took my belt from his hand. It was as if giving it to me in front of everyone, including Chris, was a declaration of war, letting the rest of our friends know his conquest or his intentions. The heat burned my freckled face.

"Thank you," I choked out.

Massimo grinned, his dimple rooted in his dark skin. My insides melted. I felt like I'd been caught like a thief stealing from one of the big, dark houses in the neighborhood. No one said anything, but everyone understood what had occurred the night before.

The next day, I broke up with Chris. We'd been fighting ever since I'd confronted him about sleeping with another girl. He was mad, really mad, but I stood my ground. I didn't want to be with someone who was sleeping with my friends.

My heart was confused. I was in love with Massimo and felt guilty breaking up with Chris. I lived in two worlds, the spiritual one and the teenage one. I was adrift, lost in a sea of yogis, who were lost in a turbulent sea of seeking, desperately meditating and chanting to find themselves. None of my friends understood this part of my life.

5

Papa Don't Preach

Joya and a small group of devotees moved to Florida shortly after we had moved to New York. Her Catholic Italian husband hated the yogis. She flew back to New York to teach in the city on weekends.

We drove to the industrial loft where Joya taught one Friday night. I sat in the back of the room. Numerous "houses" had sprung up in San Francisco, Oakland, Berkeley, and Boulder. She moved people who had lived in New York most of their lives across the country to California or Boulder. She relocated people from the West Coast to the East Coast. Students continued to be moved around all the time from house to house. I thought this was normal. I was told that it was what each person needed for their spiritual growth.

The teaching grew, and Joya became Ma. One afternoon, my parents sat my brother and me down at the dining table.

"Ma has asked your mother to move to Florida with her," my dad said.

"Why?" my brother asked. His big, brown eyes welled.

"Sometimes Ma needs to be taken care of. When she is in God, she is like a child," my dad explained.

My mother and a few other students packed up an old, beat-up Ford and drove to Florida. Not long after, my brother was sent to be with my mother. Looking back, I'm surprised by how little I reacted to all the changes. I honestly didn't think much of it. Life with Ma was like that; people were moved all the time. I loved living in New York and definitely didn't want to move to Florida. So I stayed behind with my dad and a group of Ma's students. A woman named Ananda Ram was charged to help take care of me. She was kind and sweet and had no ability to control me or my wild nature.

Without my mother, I spent more time in the parks and streets of the city with my friends. My straight A's plummeted to C's as I cut classes to hang out with friends. I rarely came home except to eat dinner, and then I went back to hang out in the park. It didn't seem to matter what time of year it was; my friends and I found a place to be together. We huddled in alleyways, doorways, or parks that sheltered us from the elements. I experimented with drugs and made love to the city. Yet somehow, I seemed to stay in control of my paradoxical life. I was confident, responsible, practical, and trusted by my friends. If someone had too much to drink, they handed me the car keys to drive.

When spring arrived, I realized I was pregnant. I calculated my cycles and the last time I had slept with Chris, and I knew it was his baby.

I walked to my dad's office on the corner of Austin Street and Continental Avenue. I passed A&J Pizza, the smell of the grease distracting me for a moment. Horns blared, and sirens screeched in the distance.

The light turned green and I crossed the street, inching closer to my dad's office above the bank. No space was wasted in the city. The door was open, and I climbed the stairs of the dank building.

The stench of age filled my nose, old food smells clung in the hall, paint peeled off the beige walls, and the linoleum steps were chipped from years of feet pounding upon them. I climbed each step with increasing dread.

"Dad, do you have a moment?"

With the phone to his ear, he swiveled his chair around to face me, extended his index finger, and nodded for me to sit and wait.

"To what do I owe this visit?" he asked, hanging up the receiver.

"I'm pregnant," I said.

My father's furry brows came together, and he shrugged a disapproving shrug. "You better call your mother." He handed me another phone and guided me to a hallway.

I dragged the phone and cord outside the door, sat on the cold floor in the dimly lit hall, and dialed my mother.

"Hi, pumpkin. How are you?" my mother asked.

"I'm pregnant," I choked out.

"Oh my God. I need to tell Ma. You need to come here to have the baby. Ma will want you to have the baby."

My mother knew Ma would never condone an abortion. Ma had adopted her grandson when her son, Jimmy, had gotten his sixteen-year-old girlfriend pregnant.

My throat tightened. I wasn't ready to move to Florida. I loved living in New York. Hiccupping a sob, I hung up the phone as tears streamed down my face.

After much discussion, I convinced my parents to let me remain in New York and finish school, and I moved in with my best friend and her mother. A month later, my father also moved to Florida to be with Ma. At seventeen and four months pregnant, I was really on my own.

6

It's a Nice Day for a White Wedding

I BEGAN TO SHOW. I STOPPED PARTYING AND DRINKING. My friends continued with their teenage lives. I promised my mother I'd come to Florida to have the baby after I graduated. But I didn't graduate. I said goodbye to Massimo and moved to the ashram. He didn't care I was carrying another guy's baby. He wanted me to stay.

I settled into life on the ashram. I kept in touch with friends, but absence and time had a way of changing all of us.

I waddled into the kitchen of the main house. My mother was blending a green concoction of supplements for Ma.

"Chris wants to come to Florida. He wants to be part of the baby's life." I leaned in, staring at the green sludge.

She stopped what she was doing and faced me. "I am not sure that is a good thing for you and the baby."

"The baby needs a father."

"He's bad news. Maybe you should have the baby and write 'father unknown' on the birth certificate. He'd have no rights to the baby. What if he wants to take the baby?"

"That doesn't make any sense," I said.

My mother and I met with Ma about Chris coming to Florida. Ma agreed that the baby would be better off with a father.

I was seven months pregnant when Chris moved to Florida. Ma decided we should get married.

The massive living room of the A-frame house doubled as the meditation hall, and for some, it was where they slept at night, their snoring bodies neatly tucked in different corners of the room. But on this night, the room was filled with flowers and candles. The chanting began. I peeked in the room from the kitchen. My dad and I waited for the signal to enter. The door opened.

"Okay, Ma's ready." The woman waved us in.

I walked down the aisle of humans sitting cross-legged and kneeled before Ma. The candlelight shone on Ma's tanned skin. She reminded me of Morgan le Fay from *The Mists of Avalon*, a powerful sorceress with magical powers. Hundreds of Ma's students crammed in around us. Sweat dripped between my swelling breasts. My white, flowing, satiny gown strained against the bulge of my belly. Someone adjusted the tiara of white flowers on my head.

Ma took our hands in hers. "This marriage is a triangle—both of you were born to be with Ma, as will your newborn baby."

My heart exploded. Ma's words were a gift, a boon, and offered me certainty of who I was to her. The baby and I would always be protected by her. Ma had always reminded my family that each of us was born to serve her.

As Ma's words filled the space, the moment took on more meaning. It felt as if I was making a deeper commitment to Ma, creating a bond that would never be broken.

"Do you want this marriage?" Ma asked.

We both nodded.

"In the name of my guru, Neem Karoli Baba, I pronounce you married to each other and your Ma."

She put her hands together. People clapped and threw flower petals. My heart was full of love for Ma, and I was grateful to be married to her, too.

Cake was cut and served after darshan. Chris and I prepared for our honeymoon. Everyone had chipped in to send us on a cruise to Bermuda. My father drove us to Vero Beach to meet the bus in the parking lot of a Sambo's Restaurant. He waited with us.

As the sky darkened, a man ran toward us. "Oh, thank God you are still here," he gasped. "Ma wants you to really think about what you are doing." He looked at me.

"I don't understand," I said, but I did.

"Leaving The Mother's feet," he explained, as his eyes fell on my swollen belly, "is a karmic mistake."

The satsang often referred to Ma as The Mother. She was not only the guru, but she was also our mother. A karmic mistake? My throat tightened. With only a couple of months left before I gave birth, a fear clawed at me. *What will happen if I decide to go? What karmic things will befall my unborn child?* I crumbled down onto the curb and sobbed. I looked at my father and then at my teenage husband, who was clueless about gurus and karma.

Would it really matter if I went away on a honeymoon? Would something happen to my unborn child? Ma's messenger had instilled a spark of fear in me, causing me to doubt and question myself. It was hard to argue with the unseen and the unknown.

Ever since I was a young teenager, my parents had reminded me that Ma was a liberated being, one of the very few. Her gold bracelets helped keep her grounded when she was in a godlike state. I believed them, and I believed that Ma was someone extraordinary with magical, mystical powers and the ability to make our lives better, heal us, and change our destinies.

In the end, I believed the messenger. I believed my enlightenment was at stake. I believed if I left on this trip, my karmic actions might potentially endanger my baby. I was afraid that my choices would come back to haunt me, and something grim and unseen would occur.

"I can't go. Ma is my life. I don't want to make a mistake." I turned to Chris.

"What do you mean? What are you talking about? We're only going away for a few days. How can that be wrong?" Chris shook his head and turned to my father. "What is she talking about?"

"Well, it seems as if Ma feels that leaving at this point in time will have karmic implications," my dad explained.

I kicked the parking lot with my toes, digging them into the asphalt, which was still warm and gooey long after the sun had set. The three of us deliberated for hours. I was paralyzed by indecision. The bus came, and I watched as it pulled away. My dad drove us back to the ashram. I should have known then the marriage was doomed.

Chris and I moved into Laxman House, one of the communal houses. We slept on the floor with fifteen other people in the large, carpeted living room that doubled as the community dining hall. My dad purchased a forty-foot, baby-blue trailer for us to live in after the baby was born, and Ma ordered the ashram men to refurbish and overhaul the inside. When the time came, I would give birth in Ma's rooms—a home birth. I was determined to have the baby naturally.

It was early December and I was three weeks late when I went into labor. People whirred around me while I played cards at the kitchen table. Contractions came and went. Three days later, I still hadn't given birth. Ma asked the satsang to go to the Hanuman Temple and sing the "Hanuman Chalisa," a forty-verse hymn to the deity Hanuman, the god of service and humility. This was to help the baby arrive.

In the back room, my mother, Ma's healer, and a few of Ma's attendants ran in and out of the room while I screamed and called out for Ma. "Get the fuck down here and get this baby out!" I cried.

Ma came marching down the stairs and told me to "calm the fuck down."

Finally, it was time. Dr. Harry, Ma's personal doctor, who was enlisted to deliver all of the ashram babies, peered in between my legs. Sweat poured from his forehead as Ma carefully watched him. Parvati, one of Ma's "girls," reminded me to breathe. I pushed and heaved. Surrounded by Ma, my mother, Chris, and a handful of women, I gave birth to a beautiful baby boy. I knew my baby would always be protected by the guru. The doctor handed Ma my newborn son. She cradled him. "I name you Hanuman," Ma said, handing him to me. His ears were folded up, but other than that, he was beautiful and perfect. "You'll need to tape his ears back so they flatten out," Ma sighed as she pressed his ears back. Ma and her girls left the room. I dozed off with the newborn in my arms.

Chris and I decided to add "Brian Christopher" to the birth certificate.

When Ma found out, I was called to her rooms.

"You need to change the birth certificate. Baba saved this baby. He was going to be born with a birth defect. Baba fixed that. That's why it took so long for him to be born. I made a bargain with Baba that he be named Hanuman. The only thing wrong with him is his ears."

Ma reminded us in darshan that Baba was with her and spoke to her all of the time. She told us she could feel him and see him as if he were still alive in the flesh.

All of the what-ifs and fears flashed before me and roiled around in my mind. What if I didn't change his name? What would happen to my newborn son? Would he die if I didn't change his name?

The next morning, Chris and I drove to a small beige government building.

"I need to change the name on my son's birth certificate," I explained to the heavyset woman behind the counter. The clerk slid a form through the window. I filled it out and handed it back. Her eyes narrowed. She knew where I was from.

Chris and I moved into the old, blue mobile home my father had bought for us. I nursed Hanuman and learned to be a mother. There were a few other mothers on the ashram who had recently given birth, too, but they were much older than me. I was a child raising a baby.

"If you don't have enough breast milk, use goat milk and never use formula," one of the mothers told me.

Chris and I took Hanuman to the local health department for his first checkup. The nurse took one look at the three of us and scowled.

"His skin is yellow. He's jaundiced," she said, thrusting him back into my arms. "You need to see a doctor." She knew we were from the ashram. She knew I'd had a home birth.

I didn't have a clue what jaundice was.

We climbed into the car. "Is he going to be okay? What's wrong with him?"

Chris turned the key in the ignition. "Let's go talk to your mother."

"That woman was such a bitch." I pulled the blanket around the baby.

We found my mother. She called one of the ashram women who practiced natural medicine. She examined Hanuman.

"He's fine. Sit in the sunshine with him. That will cure him."

Weeks turned into months, and Chris became restless. He loved and respected Ma, but he wasn't committed like the rest of Ma's students. He was there because of me and the baby.

One night, Chris got home from work and sat down at the small folding table in the trailer.

"I want to move back to New York," he said.

I sat down across from him. I knew he wasn't happy. "We'll need to find a place to live," I said.

"I'll find a job and it will be okay."

As much as I loved Ma, I was married. I missed my friends and living in New York.

"I'll talk to Ma."

The next morning, I was called into Ma's rooms.

"I understand you want to leave," she said.

"Yes. Chris and I are going to move back to New York."

She looked at me with such love in her eyes. "Don't leave."

I shifted my body. "I need to go."

"Stay. Don't go. You can teach in the school."

Tears welled in my eyes. "I can't stay. I've got to go."

"This marriage will fail. You will only suffer."

I hugged her and said goodbye. It would be many years before I returned to the ashram.

7

I Heard It From a Friend

Chris and I were driving north on I-95 in an old, beat-up, blue Chrysler when the car thumped and rattled beneath us somewhere in Georgia. We pulled off to the side of the interstate and stood on the side of the road. I held Hanuman in my arms and assessed the rear tire. Chris pulled out the spare tire and started to fix the flat. I pondered, *Is this a bad sign?*

Ma told me everything would go to shit if I left the ashram. Her words, "This marriage will fail," roiled around in my brain.

I returned to New York a teenage mother, but I no longer felt like a teenager. I had always been somewhat older than my age, but now with a baby I was catapulted into adulthood. I no longer fit into any category. My friends were either in college, working, or hanging out.

Chris and I found an apartment in Kew Gardens not far from my old Forest Hills neighborhood. We put down the first and last month's rent along with a security deposit, leaving us virtually broke. Chris found a job at a furniture store. My days were spent changing dirty diapers, making homemade baby food, and taking Hanuman to the park.

It was a warm summer evening when I returned home to cook dinner. I set a pot of water on the stove to make pasta and tossed the salad. I looked at the time. It was 6:00 p.m. I wondered where Chris was. I finally fed Hanuman, put him to bed, and ate dinner. At 10:00 p.m., Chris barreled through the apartment door.

"Where were you? You were supposed to be home hours ago." I could smell him from where I was standing. His breath reeked of liquor.

"Out."

"Out where?"

"I had a beer with Nick and a few people." He stepped toward me, straightening to his full height, his eyes narrowed. I caught the faint scent of Kiehl's Chinese Flowers on his work shirt.

"Fuck you!" I yelled, poking my finger into his chest. He grabbed my wrist. I pulled away, rubbed my wrist, and stormed off to Hanuman's room and slammed the door shut. He banged on the bedroom door. "Go away. You'll wake the baby," I said. I'd talk to Nick tomorrow to find out what was going on. I knew Chris was cheating on me. I remembered Ma's prophetic last words: This marriage is destined to fail. It felt as if it was coming true.

The next day, I loaded up Hanuman in the stroller and went to the park. Mothers much older than me sat on park benches while their children played on the monkey bars. Most of my friends were in college or working during the week. A few of the older neighborhood guys played Frisbee nearby. I placed Hanuman on a blanket with a few toys. He was adorably dressed in a red, button-down Hawaiian shirt and cute shorts. At ten months old, his long, curly hair dipped down to his collar. I gave him a cut-up apple, and he happily gnawed on it.

Late in the afternoon, a few friends showed up after school. They played with Hanuman.

As I started home, Massimo walked us down the street. "Chris is up to no good again," he said.

"I figured. He's been coming home late almost every night."

"Rumor has it he's sleeping with Amy."

Tears rolled down my face. "He's a lowlife and she's a fucking bitch."

I walked home prepared for battle. I'd confront Chris and his cheating self. What made me think he'd change?

Chris walked through the door, and I stood up to his six-foot frame. "You motherfucker, you've been out partying every night and now I find out you're fucking Amy. Get the fuck out!" I screamed. My knees shook. There was heat in my face.

"Go fuck yourself." He raised his hand toward me.

I stepped back. I heard the baby in the bedroom and stormed off, slamming the door behind me. Rocking Hanuman back to sleep, I wiped my tears from my son's forehead.

A few nights later, I met Massimo. As the Long Island Rail Road rumbled by, we sat in the dark in my car parked across from the railroad tracks.

"I'm sorry for leaving you." I took a deep breath. "I thought marrying Chris was the right thing to do."

He stared hard at me. "What do you want?"

"I don't know anymore. I know I wanted to say I was sorry for everything."

Things seemed so much more complicated. I was married, and Massimo was seeing my best friend, Lori. He leaned over and kissed me.

My body remembered everything about him. I knew this wasn't going to end well. "I need to get back. Do you need a ride home?"

"No," he said. "I need to walk."

We were quiet for a moment.

"I'll call you," he said, and he got out of the car. He looked at me through the window and smiled. I turned on the car with tears streaming down my face. My heart ached. I had chosen the wrong guy. My fairy tale of happily ever after was crushed. I despised Chris.

Weeks later, a large group of friends met in the city for a birthday party at Captain Nemo's restaurant. It was one of my favorite restaurants. I sat next to Chris, and Massimo was across from me. His dark, brooding eyes stared at me.

I felt like I was naked, and I sucked in a sharp breath as his foot slid up my leg. He wanted me to leave Chris. I was trying to figure out how. I returned the gesture, my foot reaching back before pulling my leg away. It was too dangerous. But it did not go unnoticed.

When Chris and I got back into the apartment, he grabbed my neck. "You fucking bitch, you're with him again!"

"What are you talking about?" I wasn't about to admit anything to him, especially after he'd been drinking.

He went to the bedroom and slammed the door shut.

I tiptoed to the kitchen and called Massimo. I sat on the floor and whispered into the phone, "He knows. Someone told him." I held my hand steady.

"It's going to be okay."

I wasn't so sure. Chris and I had been fighting for months. He drank every night. The small apartment had become a battleground. I needed to leave Chris for good.

Massimo and I were whispering about a solution when the door to the bedroom opened. I bolted up as Chris ran toward me. He grabbed the phone out of my hand and ripped the cord from the wall. I stepped back. Foam formed at the corners of his mouth as he lifted the receiver above his head and headed toward me. I backed up, screamed, and ran, locking myself in the bedroom.

In the weeks that followed, Chris and I barely spoke. He seethed when he was home. We continued living together. Massimo helped me figure out a plan to leave Chris. I needed to find a job. I wanted to be with Massimo. We continued to secretly meet. He and Hanuman were the only things that mattered.

A few months later, I started feeling ill. I went to the drugstore and bought a home pregnancy test, but the strip only confirmed what I already knew. At nineteen, I was pregnant yet again. I had a thirteen-month-old baby and no idea who was the father.

Chris suspected it was Massimo's baby, and I realized the chances were high as I'd stopped sleeping with Chris months ago. I had no idea what I would do, but I knew I couldn't stay with him any longer.

I was down to my last $3 when Chris burst through the door while I was in the bathroom.

"I need some money for beer. I'm going out."

"I only have three dollars, and it's for milk."

"Give it to me." He lunged toward me. I could smell the alcohol on his breath as he shouted at me.

I stood up tall, my growing belly between us. "No."

"Bitch." He pushed me.

I felt myself lose my balance. My hands swirled in the air, and I fell backward into the empty porcelain bathtub. I heard the thump before I felt the pain.

"Get the fuck out!" I yelled.

He turned and left the bathroom, and then the apartment door banged shut. I pushed my heavy body up from the floor of the tub and sat on the edge, one hand on my belly and the other on my head. My life was falling apart. I swore under my breath and vowed that Chris would never touch me again.

8

I Got You Babe

Things were changing back at the ashram as well. It was the time of "the rampage." I didn't know much about it at the time—my mother and I hadn't been in touch very much while I was living in New York—but I had heard unsettling stories from people who left during this period. It was an era in the ashram's history when Ma kept people up all night chanting. She had her students move furniture at all hours of the night. People went without sleep, attending to the urgent task of affixing faux fur to musical instruments and the walls and ceilings of the temples. Students were moved out of their rooms into different ashram houses. In some cases, Ma ordered people to have their heads shaved by other students and accused people of stealing her jewelry.

I visited once during the rampage. Seated in the middle of the temple during darshan, Ma's eyes landed on me.

"What is it you want?"

I shrugged.

"You need to leave and think about what you want. My children are here because they want nothing more than to be at the feet of this Ma. You want the world."

I cringed. Wanting the world meant never attaining liberation, never being close to Ma, never knowing God. I left the next day.

Years later, this era's devotees relayed their stories with nostalgic longing. They were given tasks by Ma that offered an intimacy with her they hadn't had. Ma explained her wildness during this time was freeing her *chelas*[1] from their egos and attachments. I was grateful that I had missed living on the ashram during this time.

I called my mother to tell her I was pregnant. I told her things weren't going well and that my plan was to leave Chris after the baby was born. She said she'd ask Ma for prayers.

A few weeks later, my mother called to check in on me. "Hi, babe, how are you?"

"I'm doing okay. Starting to show." I looked down at the small bump in the middle of my skinny frame.

"How far along are you?"

"Almost four months now."

"When are you due?" she asked.

"October. I'm planning on a natural birth at a birthing center in the city with a midwife." I wrapped the cord around my arm. Hanuman waddled by with a red ball in his mouth.

"Are they prepared to deal with any problems if something happens?"

"Yes, of course." I looked at the paperwork on the kitchen table. I read through the agreement that explained what would happen in the event of an emergency.

"Are things okay with you?"

"It's been hard. Chris is drinking a lot and not home much. We fight. He drinks and it gets ugly. I'll leave and find a place to live after the baby is born."

"I am concerned. Do you need anything?"

"I'm okay. Massimo is helping me."

She paused. "I have something I'd like to discuss with you."

"Sure, what's up?"

My mother explained how happy Ma and her new husband, Soo See Cho, a Korean ninth-degree taekwondo master, were. The ashram called him Sa Bum Nim.

"They would like to have more children. It's important to Ma. And being a mother will help keep her grounded. She spends so much time 'in God.' It's difficult for her when she leaves her body and goes into samadhi and then 'comes down,' returning back to her physical body. It causes her great pain," my mother explained.

"Ma had always said that coming back into her body felt like thousands of knives stabbing her," she added.

Ma and her husband had adopted several other children. One couple became pregnant and explained to Ma they were unprepared to have a child. Ma offered to adopt their child.

"I know life is challenging right now," my mother said. "I thought I'd call and offer you something to consider. Ma would be open to raising your baby as her own."

My hand slid down over my swollen belly as I tried to process what was being asked. Was my mother really asking me to give Ma my unborn baby?

"Are you asking me if I want to give my baby to Ma?"

"Well. It's not quite like that. It's more like doing something very special for someone who can't conceive any longer. She would raise the baby in their family. It would be well cared for with numerous other brothers and sisters."

"But you are asking me to give my baby to them." I clenched my jaw and twisted the phone cord tighter around my arm. "How many other people have you asked?"

"Why don't you think about it and call me back."

"No, I don't need any time. I'm not interested in giving my baby to Ma or to anyone. I'm going to raise my child."

"Ma just wants you to know that you have options if you change your mind. She wants you to know how much she loves you. Give Hanuman a kiss from her as well. I love you."

I placed the phone back in the cradle and sat at the table. I knew that no matter how bad my marriage was, no matter how hard my life was, I was not going to give my child to anyone.

If I was going to leave Chris, I needed to make more money than working at a Gristedes supermarket.

9

Money—It's a Gas

THE AIR WAS COOL AND THE LEAVES WERE CHANGING the evening I went into labor. Paper witches and pumpkin decorations adorned the doors of the apartments. Chris and his friend Nick lay sprawled out drunk across the bed in the living room. I called my friend Nancy, who lived upstairs.

"Could you come down? I'm in labor."

She was at my door minutes later.

"Please stay here with Hanuman. They're drunk." I pointed to the two bodies passed out on the bed. She sat at the old yellow Formica table and said she'd take care of everything.

I called my aunt Vicki, my father's sister, who was to meet me in the city at the birthing center on the edge of Harlem.

I grabbed the bag I'd packed a few days before and called a cab. Then I nudged Chris. "I'm in labor. I'm leaving for the center."

He groaned and rolled over.

"You're a fucking asshole." I slammed the door and walked downstairs into the large courtyard. The air was cold and crisp, and the time between contractions had increased.

When the cab arrived, I lowered my body into it. At nine months, I was barely one hundred pounds. I laid my head back and began counting contractions as the driver sped through the city.

Vicki and my great-aunt Muriel greeted me at the door. As night gave way to dawn, I walked the halls. I kept it up for thirteen hours and into the afternoon. At 2:00 p.m., I gave birth to a beautiful baby boy with black hair and olive skin. I couldn't help but wonder if he was Massimo's child, and my guess was so would all of our friends.

After I was cleaned up, I called my mother to tell her.

"Ma named the baby Ganga Das," she said. I knew she would give the baby a spiritual name, but it didn't roll off the tongue easily. I wondered if I should add another name that would be easier to live with. My thoughts flashed back to what had happened with Hanuman's birth certificate. In the end, I added "Arjuna." It was still Hindu. I thought it rolled off the tongue better. I never told anyone.

Five hours after giving birth, I returned home. My maternal grandmother and aunt came to help me. Two weeks later, with a twenty-two-month-old toddler and a two-week-old newborn, I left Chris to start a new life. One without a drunk, cheating husband. I had heard somewhere that I needed to leave a place setting on the table if I left the household, so I did.

I was a single mother and on my own. I found an apartment not far from the old one, and my friend Suzy moved in with me. Massimo and I were free to be together.

Money was tight. I needed to figure out how to support myself and my two children. I came across an advertisement in the *Daily News* for bartending school. I decided that this was what I could do to make a living. I called my dad, who had relocated to Santa Fe, New Mexico. We had limited contact, but I needed to ask him if he'd lend me money to go to school. He hemmed a bit. He was always tight around money. I told him I'd pay back the $200 it cost for the training. In the end he sent me the money, I learned how to make cocktails, and shortly after I finished the course, I took a job in an Irish pub in Maspeth, Queens.

But I still wasn't making ends meet, so I called my dad yet again to ask for help.

I tugged on the cord of the phone, praying he'd help me. I knew he had ties to people in New Mexico who sold weed.

"Dad, I need to make some money."

"I'll make some calls," he said.

My dad arranged for me to meet his friend Tom in Manhattan. I sat on the molded plastic seat as the subway rattled into the city and met Tom at a bustling coffee shop in Midtown. He was sitting on a stool by the window. He was thin, and his long, greasy hair left a yellowish stain on the collar of his once-white shirt. Even his mustache was oily. His eyes were bloodshot and barely opened. I sat, leaving a stool between us. I tried not to stare. *Does my dad really do business with a guy like this?*

"You Rudra Ram's daughter?" His chin lifted toward me.

"Yes."

"You've grown up," he said, while his eyes moved down toward my hips. I shifted in my seat. What a sleazebag. I didn't bother to order anything.

A large, black duffel bag rested at the base of the stool. Tom nodded at the bag and slid it toward me. "Take it and be careful."

"Thanks." I bent down, picked it up, and then felt his eyes on me as I hurried out of the coffee shop.

With the large, heavy duffel bag over my shoulder, I walked toward the subway. My insides shook as I passed a group of police standing on the corner. I tried to look normal as I navigated what felt like carrying a dead body through the crowded sidewalks. Finally, I hit the subway steps and raced to catch the incoming E Train. As the train lulled along the tracks toward Queens, I kept vigil over the bag stuffed between my feet.

Once behind the locked door of my apartment, I closed the peephole and unzipped the bag. I'd never seen so much pot and hash in my life. I pulled out some Ziplocs and started my new business, which helped me get by. I sold weed and hash to people I knew and friends I made working at the bar. But though it helped me support myself for a short while, it was dangerous. Instead of dealing, I realized I needed a better job.

A French crepe restaurant in Forest Hills hired me, and I started as bartender and was quickly promoted to manager. Chris's mom and my friends helped me take care of the kids. Things were looking up.

10

It's Just a Shot Away

IT WAS A CRISP AUTUMN NIGHT WHEN THE PHONE RANG. "You fucking bitch. How could you?" His words were slurred, but I understood.

"Chris, you're drunk," I said, and sucked in a breath.

"I'm done. I'm going to end it. I've got a gun." The line went dead.

I called Massimo. "I'm heading over to Chris's. He's drunk and has a gun. I think he's going to kill himself."

"Don't go," Massimo said.

"I need to go."

Massimo was quiet for a moment.

"I need to go," I repeated, and hung up the phone. I turned to my roommate, Suzy.

"Can you watch the kids?" She nodded. I called a cab and drove to Kew Gardens.

I climbed the stairs to my old apartment and rang the doorbell. There was no response. I peeked into the peephole and turned the knob. The door was open. Chris was sprawled back on the couch with a rifle pointed at his neck.

"Chris, put the gun down so we can talk," I said.

He struggled to sit up. "Fuck you. You bitch."

"Please put the gun down," I said a bit more firmly. I was shaking. This wasn't a good scene. Chris was drunk and angry. The apartment was dark and dank and smelled of stale cigarette smoke. Maybe Massimo was right. Perhaps I shouldn't have been there. Deep down I didn't want Chris's death on my conscience or to leave my kids without a father.

"Put the gun down and let's talk," I said again.

I watched as he leaned forward and laid the rifle on the floor. As soon as it hit the ground, I jumped forward, grabbed the rifle, and ran.

Chris swore.

I ran out the door and down the long hallway, my heart pounding. Footsteps were gaining on me. At the end of the hallway, I jumped down the first flight of stairs and hit the landing hard. He was close, but I didn't dare look behind me. I took all twelve steps of the next flight and hit another landing, then I jumped down one more flight. I was in the lobby.

Racing to the entrance, I heaved the front door open and ran into the courtyard. Massimo stood waiting. I wanted to run into his arms. I was grateful that he'd shown up. Chris was only a few feet behind me. I tossed the rifle to Massimo. And like a scene out of a lousy police drama, he caught it and threw the gun into his friend Kevin's slow-moving car, which sped off.

Chris and Massimo squared off. Fists flew. They swore at each other. People yelled from the windows above us. There were sirens in the distance getting louder.

"We need to go!" I yelled, tugging on Massimo's shirt. He grabbed my elbow, and we ran down the street. We arrived at Annie's, the bar we hung out in at Station Square. Kevin was already there waiting for us. He handed me the rifle with his jacket draped over it. Massimo and I looked at each other. We couldn't be out on the streets with a rifle. We hailed a cab, and Massimo and I climbed in the back. I sat with the gun between my legs and Massimo's jacket draped over it.

Chris's father called a few days later, requesting that I return his rifle. Ridiculous that he would ask such a thing. Did he not understand that Chris had threatened to kill himself only a few short days ago? Chris never did kill himself.

Over the next few months, Chris's mother asked to spend time with the kids. She would often take Hanuman overnight. Chris rarely showed up. One Saturday morning, I dropped Hanuman off for a weekend visit. Sunday arrived. I waited for Chris or his mother to bring him home. Hours passed. It got later and later. Nobody showed. I started to worry. I kept calling, and no one answered.

"They won't return my calls," I cried to Massimo. I was hysterical. Rocking Ganga Das, I walked back and forth across the dank basement apartment, the cold cement leeching through my socks.

"Fucking loser. I can't believe he'd stoop to this," Massimo said.

I didn't sleep that night, and I called his mother's number every hour. In the morning, I finally called the police.

"What do you mean you can't do anything?" I wailed into the receiver.

"No crime's been committed," the voice on the other end said.

"He stole my son and isn't returning him. That's a crime!" I screamed into the phone, the cord tightening around my arm.

"Come down to the precinct and file a report," the woman on the phone said.

Two weeks later, I met the police at the Rego Park apartment. The police officer banged on the door, but no one answered. I heard movement in the room. They did, too, and they broke the door open. There Hanuman stood, with nothing on but a dirty diaper.

Chris stood up with his chest puffed up.

The apartment reeked of cat piss. Dirty dishes were stacked everywhere.

"I've never seen anything like this. No child should be in this environment," the officer said as he handed me my son. I glared at Chris as I walked out the door.

A few weeks later, I was served with papers. I handed the documents to Massimo. "He's suing me for custody of Hanuman." I bit my lip. I had grown thinner over the last few weeks. "He says I'm an unfit mother and living with a drug dealer."

I wanted to kill Chris. In that moment, I had never hated anyone so much in my young life. I wished he would just disappear. My mother had been right; I should have never put his name on the birth certificate.

I called my dad. He knew a lawyer in the city who was a student of Ma's.

I took the subway to the city to meet the lawyer at his brownstone office. He asked me to sit. I relayed my story about Chris and Massimo and the last few months, telling him about the kidnapping and the fighting and Chris threatening to kill himself.

His mouth opened wide and then shut closed. He leaned in. "What were you thinking? This is what happens when you sleep around." He leaned back in his cushy chair and shook his head, muttering, "Tsk tsk."

I held back my tears. *I am not a slut*, I said to myself. *I am not a slut.* I wanted to tell this fancy lawyer to fuck off, but instead, I sat back quietly in the chair. I needed his help.

A few weeks later, I walked into the courthouse. The building was big, and I felt small. As my insides rattled, I chewed the nail on my thumb. Spotting the lawyer, I walked over to him.

"It's going to be okay," he said as he placed his hand on my shoulder and guided me toward the courtroom.

I wasn't convinced. We found seats in the courtroom and waited for the judge to call the case. Chris had one of our friends show up as a witness. They told the judge I was a drug addict (not true) and my boyfriend was a coke addict (not true) and he was living with me (not true) and was dealing drugs (somewhat true). They claimed I didn't take care of the children (absolutely not true).

My lawyer stood. He buttoned his jacket. "Your Honor, this is clearly a case of revenge and spurned love." He explained the details of Chris's erratic behavior as a father. Not showing up for visitation. The condition of the apartment. The police report, the kidnapping, and the gun incident.

Chris's eyes darkened, and anger shot from them. I met his glare. He wasn't going to win. I wasn't going down without a fight.

It was my turn to speak, and I stood as prompted. "Your Honor, I love my children. I've done a good job raising both children. They are well cared for. I don't drink or do drugs."

The judge couldn't quite understand why Chris only wanted one of the children. He asked how it was that if I was unfit, Chris wasn't asking for both children. Chris didn't have an answer. In the end, the judge voted in my favor.

It would be years before I allowed Chris to see Hanuman.

11

She's Leaving Home

I STOOD BEHIND THE SMALL SERVICE BAR of the French restaurant I managed, preparing for a busy New Year's Eve. We were booked solid. After cutting up lemons and limes for the evening, I reached up on my tippy-toes to grab a blender from the shelf above my head. A train rumbled by on the tracks behind the restaurant. Everything shook, including the glass blenders on the shelf, which started to tumble toward my head. It was one of those moments that happens so fast yet occurs in slow motion. I lifted my hands to protect my head. The two blenders crashed together, glass shattering everywhere. Heads turned. I felt a searing heat in my left hand and looked down to see blood, fat, and bone. Grabbing a paper towel, I covered the wound. My head felt woozy, and I thought I might throw up. I knew it was bad.

Massimo picked me up from the restaurant, and we spent New Year's Eve 1986 in Jamaica Hospital; the tendon in my left hand was severed.

Over the next few months, I underwent several surgeries to repair my ring finger. I was exhausted, overwhelmed, and out of work. My mother suggested I come for a visit. I flew to Florida with the boys, who were five and seven at the time.

I was called into a small temple called the Lion Kuti for a private meeting with Ma. My mother, always present, sat nearby.

Ma leaned in close and whispered, "My daughter, it is time. Before you know it, your life will be over. You're in your twenties, thirty will come and go, and then you'll be forty, and then fifty. It will all happen in the blink of an eye. Your life will pass you by, and so will any chance of enlightenment. Come home."

I trembled at her words. It felt as if she was looking deeply into my soul. It was as if she could read my thoughts. No one knew me at the depth of my core like she did. I knew in that moment I needed to move back to the ashram. I was unwilling to waste my life and any chance of my enlightenment. I wanted my life to matter.

On my brief return home to New York, I told Massimo it was time for me to go. He was devastated. Once again, I would leave him. But in my heart, I knew he wasn't ready to settle down and marry a single woman with two young boys. He was still living at home with his parents and going to college.

My parents had divorced a few years earlier. My dad had moved to New Mexico. My aunt told me that my father had asked my mother if she wanted to leave, but by that time, she was deeply devoted to Ma. She and my uncle said they thought my dad left because Ma wanted money from the sale of my parents' house.

My brother, Durga Das, who had remained on the ashram and served as Ma's driver and bodyguard, flew to New York to help me drive to Florida. We stopped at Flagpole Park to say goodbye to Massimo. The kids and I hugged him. He stood in the middle of the road and watched as we pulled away. I watched as the kids waved goodbye out the back window. Then I looked at Massimo one last time as he stood alone on the cobblestone street. Tears dropped to the floor of my Honda Civic as I left my life in Queens and the boyfriend I loved to begin a new life on the ashram. I was twenty-five.

12

Fat Bottomed Girls

It was my first summer living on the ashram. The boys were adjusting to life in community. There were forty-some-odd kids growing up on the ashram, and they had a built-in friend group. I got a job managing a restaurant at a posh private country club on a golf course in Vero Beach.

We gathered in the temple for one last darshan before Ma left for her annual summer retreat to Sanibel Island. There were a few new people in darshan. Ma entered the temple and settled in. She surveyed the room.

"Don't be sad. I'll be back before you know it. My kids get this way whenever I leave. They miss me," she explained. I looked around, and there was a palpable sadness.

"I grew up on the streets of Brooklyn. I got married at fifteen. My Italian husband Sal worked, and I sold hot goods to make ends meet." Everyone's eyes were glued on Ma.

"I loved food. I'd hide a loaf of Italian bread behind the toilet, and after dinner, I'd take a bowl of Italian dressing and dip the bread in it. One night, Sal opened the door. He caught me red-handed and said, 'Eat much?'" Ma took a sip of her Perrier.

"Sal told me I was fat. I went to Jack LaLanne and signed up for yoga classes the next day. I learned a breath that promised weight loss. I practiced it every night. One night, Jesus Christ came to me. He told me to teach all ways, for all ways are mine. This is why I sit before you tonight."

Ma's need to lose weight was part of the fabric of our lives. I remembered visiting my mother when I was fifteen. Ma had all of her students on the Cursio Diet. It consisted of blended salad, unpeeled fruit, steamed potatoes, and rennet-less cheese.

People's hands atrophied and became gnarled. They developed boils. It was as if every person was suffering in some state of dietary detoxification. I looked around and wondered why anyone would do this.

Ma left with her family, her attendants, and a few of her close students. Meanwhile, the ashram felt empty without Ma's energy and teaching. I watched as some of her students appeared lost and directionless. Occasionally, Ma would call and give darshan over the phone during the summer.

The satsang was thirsty for any message from Ma. Every so often, the pay phone in the house would ring incessantly. Most people who lived in the house walked by and ignored it. Whoever answered it knew they might be sent on some ridiculous and often impossible errand, whether it was to find a resident, go to the store, or be asked to clean the kitchen by someone in charge. Answering it was a gamble, because it might be a message from Ma.

If it *was* a message from Ma, someone would run from house to house banging on bedroom doors and, in a breathy, almost panicked voice, yell like a town crier, "Phone Call Darshan in an hour! Be in the Dattatreya Temple at six o'clock sharp!"

People hurried out of their rooms, and those eating dinner promptly finished. Plates were tossed in the sink while people scurried and maneuvered, jockeying for a place in line for the three bathrooms. People wrapped in towels with their toiletries in hand lined up in the hallways, waiting for the showers. In the Eastern tradition, being clean before entering a temple or seeing the guru was important.

We gathered in the temple, seated on our meditation cushions around the speaker attached to the blue rotary house phone. Eyes closed, cross-legged, in meditation, we waited.

The phone rang. Eyes popped open.

The speaker crackled. "Hi, my children. How I miss you." Ma sounded so far away.

"Hi, Ma," we answered back in unison.

She invited the satsang to come to Sanibel. Most of the 150 students living at the ashram arranged to take time off from work to be with Ma. We packed our cars with sleeping bags, food, and beach gear and piled in, sometimes six to a vehicle; money was tight for many. It was difficult to make money in our small, rural town unless you had a profession. Many cobbled out a living house-cleaning or waiting tables. The people who worked on the ashram didn't earn a salary; they were "supported." They received room and board and a stipend of $20 a week and often struggled to make ends meet. People who worked for the ashram often held a second or third job to do any extracurricular activities like going to the movies or taking a trip to see Ma.

I gathered the boys and piled into a car with another family and their kids. We made the four-hour trek south on I-95 to Sanibel Island. The only place to be in August in Florida was at the ocean, where you might be afforded a cool breeze. Once we arrived, I corralled Hanuman and Ganga Das and lugged towels, toys, and snacks, moving us toward the beach. The palm trees offered little shade. A haze rose from the sand. The ocean lapping at the shore was like a tepid bath.

The sun beating down on them, Ma and my mother sat on chaise lounges in a designated area. Behind them, on towels, was a group of Ma's closest students, her "girls." A third row of towels included Ma's children, their caregivers, and more people from her inner circle. It was as if an invisible fence surrounded Ma, protecting her from the impending onslaught of "us." The rest of us found spots as close as possible to the sacred area where Ma was sunning.

My boys took off and ran to the water, romping in the lapping waves. I slathered myself with oil, lowered my body onto my beach towel, and closed my eyes. Ten minutes later, a shadow loomed over me.

I opened my eyes. One of Ma's girls hovered above me. "Ma would like to see you." Her finger extended toward Ma.

I took a sharp breath and rocketed up to a seated pose. "Oh, okay," I sputtered to the woman with a batik sarong tied around her waist. She waited for me to get up. My heart pounded.

Whenever someone was called to Ma, there was apprehension. One never knew what to expect when the guru called them to her. In this moment, a stomach-churning anxiety brewed inside me along with an anticipated excitement.

I brushed off the sand and grabbed a towel. *What does Ma want? Am I in trouble? Am I going to receive a unique teaching?* Thousands of thoughts raced through my mind in a matter of seconds. The hot sand erupted between my toes and the bottoms of my feet burned as I walked toward the invisible perimeter of the close students who surrounded and protected Ma.

My mother saw me approach and nodded. She leaned in to whisper to Ma.

"Hi, Ma," I greeted her as I entered the sacred circle. It was still early in the formation of the ashram and the teaching, and we had yet to adopt the formal "Namaste" that would come soon after. Respect was essential to Ma. Her head lifted from the chaise. Her face was the color of coffee with a hint of cream. Her black hair, slick with oil, was pulled back in a firm ponytail, stretching her face taut.

"What the hell happened to you?" Her eyes peered at me just above her Coco Chanel sunglasses.

I was unable to formulate a sentence. What was she talking about?

"How did this happen?" Her brows darted toward each other, scanning my body. "I can't believe how heavy you are. Really, tell me how this happened?" She waited for me to answer.

I had no idea I was heavy.

"Didn't you see this?" Ma turned to my mother, but she didn't wait for an answer. "You need to get that weight off immediately," she said, pointing at my body. "I don't want you to struggle all your life like I did. Do you understand me?" Her face softened for a nanosecond, but it no longer mattered—the axe had swung.

"Yes, Ma." My words came out slow and shaky. I'd never thought about my weight. All the years I'd lived in New York, I'd never dieted or worried about my body.

"I mean it. Get that weight off or you will be asked to leave this teaching."

I stood at attention while my insides churned. My mother sat stoic next to Ma, watching.

Ma wasn't finished. "You can eat whatever you want this weekend, and when you get back to the ashram, you are to begin a diet. Your Ma has struggled all her life with weight. I don't want that to happen to you. You're too young."

My face burned. Where was my beach blanket? I wanted to wrap it around my fat, bathing suit–clad body. Nodding, I moved the sand with my foot. My mother remained silent. She rarely interfered when Ma was "working" with me. It would be perceived as too attached. I wanted her to look at me to tell me I was okay, but she kept her eyes on Ma. I knew my mother couldn't help me.

"I love you. I only want what's best for you," Ma said, and with a slight nod, her eyes returned to the Danielle Steel novel in her lap. I was dismissed.

Waves of nausea roiled in my belly. *Get it together*, I told myself. *She was only doing this for my own good, for my growth and well-being*. I returned to my blanket, my head low. Who could eat anything after that?

"So, what did Ma say to you?" asked Shanti, the woman who lived next door to me, her eyes gleaming.

Did I need to tell her? Why was it if Ma spoke to you, everyone was privy? Was there no privacy? I dug my nails into my palms. The satsang was like cawing seagulls hungry for any tidbit from Ma. Somehow, we all were fed through this method. Our lives were open books, and we all learned from each other's experiences with Ma. I relented and relayed my story to Shanti.

"Ohh, you are so blessed! What a beautiful gift Ma gave you. You are so lucky," she cooed.

Christ, the last thing I felt was blessed. I felt like shit. I felt like a fat pig led to slaughter. I fell back on my blanket, covered my face with a towel, shut my eyes, and cried.

We returned to the ashram with me feeling a shame I never had before.

After Ma spoke to me, I realized the gravity of my situation and committed to my first diet. The Body Type Diet was the current diet Ma was doing to lose weight. The test in the book determined what kind of body type you had and how to eat to lose weight. The results: I was a "T" type like Ma. This meant no sugar, which was fine, since no sugar was permitted on the ashram, but it also meant no bread or fruit.

Initially, I was overwhelmed. I went from eating anything I wanted and not caring to becoming very disciplined and concerned about my body. I remained on the diet for a year—the beginning of a long battle with my body image, weight, and shame.

From the time I moved to the ashram until I left, there was a significant emphasis on food and dieting. I don't recall a time when Ma wasn't on a diet.

13

Dancing in the Dark

OCTOBER ARRIVED. We were preparing for the first day of Durga Puja[1] and the ten nights honoring the divine goddess. On my way around the lake, people were busy doing different jobs to get ready for the evening. I passed a woman sitting by the temple, who had several bowls of colored rice around her. There was a design outlined in chalk that bordered the firepit. She placed small amounts of yellow rice around the lip of the cement square, preparing for the evening's tantric ritual. As I walked by, she looked up and smiled. I waved. Children laughed and splashed in the reedy waters on the far side of the pond. A group of women made flower garlands under the thatched hut across the way. I looked up at Ma's balcony; sometimes she watched her students prepare for the ritual.

Dusk crept in. Streaks of orange and pink were being swallowed by the impending gray. Outside the temple, I set down my cushion and sat by the firepit, where the elaborate rice design dressed the fire like an evening wrap. The chanting began. Swaying back and forth to the beat, lost in the ancient mantras, we sang to The Mother. Energy coursed through me and tingled the top of my head.

As Ma was spotted walking toward the temple with her entourage, we stood. She came and sat in a wooden chair covered with bright Indian fabric and garlands. Waving her hand, she signaled for the chanting to end. A radiant light glowed around her. The air thrummed with an electric vibration. Ma's sari shimmered in the firelight.

How I loved the divine feminine; her Shakti energy flowed through me. It was an energy that empowered me, gave me strength, vibrated through me and filled me with a life force that connected me to the goddess. Shakti or kundalini is the wild, often untamed primal life force that yogis devote their lives to awakening and unite with the divine. It was the rising of energy that enabled one to have a spiritual awakening. It was the reason we meditated and practiced yoga and breathwork. Like an uncoiling serpent, this divine feminine energy rose from the base of the spine to the crown of the head. Ma taught me that as women, we were strong and powerful and each goddess in the Hindu pantheon was available to guide us; they were part of us, and we possessed the power to utilize this energy.

"Namaste, my children." Ma's voice was silky smooth. "Here we are, another year under the evening stars. Look out at this magnificent ashram."

I looked over at the pond, where tea lights flickered, illuminating the water's edge.

"Tonight is a very special night. Tonight is the night we honor my Mother Kali. Tonight, we drink her blood from the skull cup. I warn you, my children, drink from the skull only if you are truly committed to this teaching; otherwise, it could be your ruination." Ma pointed her finger toward the middle of the room at no one in particular.

I turned around to see several fearful, questioning faces. *Should I drink the blood of Kali or pass it on? What happens if I'm not committed enough? What will happen to me?*

I wasn't fearful of drinking wine from a human-skull cup,

nor was I worried about Kali's wrath. I wanted her sword to cut my attachments in my relentless pursuit of ego death. It was she who held me when I was struggling. It was she who I prayed to in my darkest moments. It was she who would guide me to my enlightenment.

"What a beautiful night to sit before the fire. We celebrate The Mother. Each one of you is moving toward liberation. All you need to do is let go of the cloud of illusion that surrounds you. Drop the layers and remove the veils of your ego. Throw what you do not need into the fire. I want this for each of you."

The stars popped out a few at a time. A sliver of moon appeared overhead. Ma nodded to the man in orange sitting at the firepit.

As he stood and walked to the temple, he began his invocation. "*Om Namah Ganesha*."

He whacked a coconut against the concrete. A whoosh of satisfaction whispered through the crowd. The coconut had smashed into tiny pieces, a sign of good things to come. He placed the remnants on a tray and sat before the fire. With legs crossed, he closed his eyes and centered himself. He dipped the ladle into a pot of ghee and poured it on the fire. The fire leaped up and danced for him as if he was charming a snake.

He chanted the first name of The Mother, calling to her like a lover. He paused and then chanted a long, drawn-out "*Swaaaa-haaa*." His voice raised an octave on the first syllable and dropped on the second syllable.

My hand dipped into the plastic cup of rice. I closed my eyes and prayed. *Mother, please free me from my unworthiness.* I tossed the rice into the fire and chanted back with everyone, "*Swaha*," so be it, it is absolute. I took another handful of rice. *Please let me be free to know God*. I set my intentions and prayed with each grain of rice I threw.

The fire captivated me, pirouetting and dancing before me, as the heat licked at my face. I wondered what our neighbors might think if they stumbled upon our gathering this night. It was one of the few occasions on which they might hear us chanting in the distance. If they walked toward us, they'd need to navigate the dark, sandy paths through the thick saw palmetto, ferns, and bushes, the sounds of our voices getting louder. They'd emerge at the opening to see a woman with long, dark hair seated on a throne-like chair, dressed in a black sari with red and white lines painted across her forehead and two hundred or more people seated at her feet in front of a raging fire, chanting in some incomprehensible language. We'd guide them to a house, offer them a cup of tea, and try to explain what we were doing.

The wood crackled. The smoke changed direction. I stifled a cough. With each ladle of ghee, the fire rose higher and higher, smoke billowing around me. I glanced at Ma every so often to make sure she didn't need anything. She, too, was lost in the ritual. Then there was silence.

"I am a devotee of Mother Kali, she who carries the sword, she who is so dark that evil has no place near her. I, your Ma, I am merely a catalyst for the great joy blossoming within you. I bow to my guru, Neem Karoli Baba, in the form of Lord Shiva. Tonight, I dance for you, my children." Her hand swept in front of her. "I share the intimacy of the dance with you while I make love to my Baba." She paused. "I am truly shy," she reminded us. "This is my gift to you."

"Begin," Ma said, waving her hand.

On cue, the chanting began, slow and seductive. Ma was escorted to the lingam, a large, phallic-shaped statue, with the face of Shiva emerging from the black stone. She stepped around the black marble shape, her hand caressing Shiva's face. Placing her thumb and index finger together in a mudra, she circled the phallic stone, moving faster and faster. She reminded me of an exotic dancer from a *National Geographic* magazine. Her arms twirled overhead with hand gestures. Her body swayed, and her hips shook. Her sari sparkled and swirled in the evening wind. She was handed a pot overflowing with yogurt. She reached into the vessel, removed a finger covered with yogurt, and licked it, her eyebrows lifted toward us. Her hips gyrated. She poured the milky ingredients over the phallic-shaped lingam. Her hands swirled up and down the stone, and her body followed. She straddled the object, bending backward, hair falling behind her in masses. The chanting rose to a feverish pitch.

A jar of honey was passed forward. Ma moved back and forth in a frenzied dance. She poured the thick, sticky substance upon the stone lingam and licked the honey from her fingers one at a time. Her fingers created a mudra. Each different configuration of the fingers meant something, Ma told us, but I had no idea what. The chanters swayed back and forth, their wide eyes watching their beloved guru dance for them. More milk, more yogurt, some rose water, and ghee. The contents of all the vessels flowed down to the base, which flattened into a wide bowl, representing a yoni, The Mother's vagina, and captured the dripping fluids.

Each person seated around the fire yearned for a glance, a look, a gesture from Ma. But then again, we always wanted Ma to "see" us. She danced in ecstasy around the firepit, yelling out, "Jai Baba, Jai Kali Ma!" Her hips twisted, her fingers undulated toward us, drawing us to her, calling us. She pleaded to her consort. She pleaded to her children. She made love to us. The chanting expanded into a full crescendo. And then it was over. The music slowed and Ma returned to her seat, her sari dripping and her hair matted and drenched. She nodded to the lead chanter. We were plunged into silence.

"My children, what you have just had the privilege of watching was your Ma becoming one with her Baba. This night is for you. I love you, my children. This ashram loves you. Your Baba loves you. I am The Mother. I am no other. Namaste." Ma rose, bowed to her Baba, and was escorted around the pond. We stood and began to chant "Mother Aarti," a Sanskrit hymn of devotion to the guru. Translated, it meant:

"You truly are my mother and you truly are my father,
You truly are my relative and you truly are my friend,
You truly are my knowledge and you truly are my wealth,
You truly are my all, my god of gods."

The aarti lamp was lit, and the little ghee wicks burned bright in the brass lamp as it was passed among the devotees. The flame was waved before the bronze and stone deities and then to our departing guru. The rest of the group swayed and chanted, their hands clasped together while their eyes remained solely on Ma.

Ma's unabashed, uninhibited dance, making love to her beloved, felt like a carnal act of pure erotica. Part of me felt like a child who'd walked in on her parents having sex. The irony was, if any of us were caught having sex on the ashram, there was no doubt we would feel Ma's wrath.

Brahmacharya[2] was our path. It was the fastest path to God in Ma's eyes. If you broke that vow, it was met with disdain. Women were touted as sluts and seductresses. Men were told they were succumbing to women and gold. Ma made an example out of anyone who broke the celibacy vow, usually in darshan. They wore a metaphorical scarlet letter until they figured out how to find their way back into Ma's good graces.

I fell off the celibate path a few times. While it was fun in the moment, living with the guilt and fear of getting caught was stressful. When I broke my vows of devotion to the guru and the teaching, dread blossomed like a black rose, the thorns needling me with the belief that I had in some way impeded my quest and chance for liberation. Ma had effectively cemented the idea that sex would somehow prevent me from finding God, being God, or attaining God.

14

They Long to Be Close to You

I ADJUSTED THE PILLOW BENEATH ME FOR evening darshan as a flurry of women in flowing clothes flitted around Ma's couch. People were getting settled in on their cushions. What we sat upon for darshan was as varied as our tribe: odd-shaped pillows, foam stadium seats, and, for the more serious meditator, the firm, round zafu was the cushion of choice.

The hum of the harmonium synchronized with the beat of the drums, and a mournful chant to The Mother radiated into the temple.

"Hey, Ma. Sri Ma. Hey, Ma Durga." Our woeful voices whined as if we were waiting for a lover we hadn't seen in months, yet we saw Ma every night.

The wooden door in the back of the room whipped open, and Ma entered the temple like a woman with her hair on fire. Her wild mane sailed like a cape behind her as she opened her arms to the room. An older male student dressed in a sherbet-colored

Indian gauze shirt and drawstring yoga pants guided Ma down the steps. A black shawl with images of the goddess Kali rested over his shoulder, and his straggly hair was tied back in a thin ponytail. He wove through us as we chanted a bit louder with Ma's arrival. The crowd shifted left and right, creating a path for Ma. It reminded me of the story of Moses parting the Red Sea I'd read when I was a young child.

Ma lowered herself onto the leopard-covered cushioned seat and folded her legs into a lotus pose. The man laid the shawl over her lap and tucked the cloth over her feet. Ma settled in, not seeming to notice the care and reverence that went into preparing her seat.

"Live in the moment. Be present. Today is here, tomorrow is gone, and the future never comes. You are all part of my garden, and each student is a petal on the lotus flower of my heart," she began.

I opened my eyes and brushed away my bangs.

"When you are completely selfless, when you serve the ashram, when you are free from attachments and put the teaching first, that's how you get closer to Ma," she explained.

The statues of Hindu deities that occupied the walls stood at attention as if they, too, were rapt with Ma's words. Paintings of gods and goddesses and childlike river scenes that Ma had painted lined the cedar walls of the large A-frame.

Tonight, there was an easel next to her couch. Ma rose from her seat. She put on her thick rhinestone glasses and picked up a Sharpie in one hand and a pointer in the other. She drew a circle in the middle of the paper on the flip chart.

"The center of the flower is your Ma and this ashram; we are one, inseparable," she explained as she tapped the center.

She continued, outlining a tight group of petals around the circle. "This group of petals represents those of you that are completely dedicated; you live only for your Ma."

She turned her head to face us, peering over the bridge of her nose, and then turned her back on us and returned to her drawing.

The pointer clicked against the easel. She pointed to each name she had written and started reciting the names of her inner circle.

"My Shody [my mother's nickname]," *click*, "my Veena [her best friend from before she became Ma]," *click*, "my Chandra [the lawyer who currently ran the ashram]," *click*, and "my Krishnapriya."

Upon hearing my name, my head rose from my notebook, and my heartbeat quickened. My breath softened, although I remained in my near-perfect meditation posture, not wanting to mess with the flow of kundalini. Ma said that moving or shifting the body while in meditation disrupted Shakti's ability to rise. Ma's gaze, my name emanating from her lips, and being mentioned with others in the inner circle was confirmation that I was one of her close ones. It didn't matter how many times Ma told you or reminded you how close you were to her; whenever she acknowledged you publicly, it was powerful and validating. It also made the rest of the satsang envious.

Ma turned her back to us, and her black marker rolled around and drew another layer of petals around the first set. "Now, these petals represent those of you who are very dedicated and devoted. You are all part of Ma's heart, but I can't have you all in my rooms now, can I?" She turned and faced us.

Several people looked as if they were about to launch themselves out of their bodies, and not in a good way. They understood that Ma was our spiritual accountant. She kept the balance of our godly selves and our lesser selves. I believed Ma was Kali incarnate and that she herself embodied the essence of the black Mother Kali. Decimation of the ego was intrinsic to our teaching, and Kali routinely swung her sword in order to free us from our attachments. If you stepped out of line, maybe appeared too attached or too familiar, or strayed too far from The Mother, the death of your ego could be swift. We called this process of ego decimation "getting killed."

Ma turned yet again to the large white paper taking on the likeness of a flower, and she drew yet another set of petals. "Those of you out here," the marker clicked, "you love Ma but are holding back. You have desires. It is those attachments that will keep you from being close to your Ma. Lust. Money. Ego. But I tend to all of you. Each of you is a petal in my heart." The Sharpie etched and squeaked across the paper while yet another layer of petals was drawn.

I looked up to review the diagram and copied each pattern in my notebook. I was one of the few permitted to take notes in class.

Ma pointed to the nether region of the paper. "Taranaga, you are out here. Because you aren't willing to walk toward this teaching and surrender."

Ouch. I winced. Taranaga had been struggling with money issues. She couldn't pay her rent. She had met with Chandra recently and asked for a reduction. It was income from the rent that kept the ashram operating. I saw a dark shadow descend over Taranaga's plump face. Her shoulders gave way.

Ma turned toward the room. Her eyes narrowed. "Taranaga knows how much I love her, but if she wants to take the next step, she needs to grow up." Ma turned away, and her eyes rested on a man seated a few rows over from me. "And you, Shyam Das. What was your other name? Gurf or something? You are a weed in my garden. You will never die."

He withered into the carpet like an ink spot in a sea of black. My body tightened. I knew this could easily be me with the tip of Ma's sword pointed at my throat. I swallowed.

"Either grow up or get pulled. I need to weed my garden, or the ashram won't grow. The weeds will strangle it," Ma said.

I put my pen and paper down carefully and sat still.

"And you, Shiva Das, you are seduced by women and gold. You are filled with lust. This is a brahmacharya teaching. That means you need to be celibate in your heart as well as in your life. You are married to Ma, but you let yourself be led around by your cock." Ma waved her writing implement at him.

My throat remained tight, as if I was the one being killed. I breathed in and out. I understood Ma was working with us, freeing us from our attachments and killing our egos. This was, after all, spiritual hardball. I wanted more than anything to evolve and be free of any attachments that stood in the way of my ultimate spiritual growth.

"Once you push the elevator button to God, there's only one way to go. You need to be able to hold the Shakti in this teaching. This teaching is real. This Ma is real. It's time to shit or get off the pot." Ma brushed her hair from her shoulder and sat back on her tucket. "Pray to Mother Kali to kill your ego and slay your attachments. Or come back next life and do it all over again."

I remembered telling my brother how much I wanted to be close to Ma. "I want God," I had told him.

"Be careful what you ask for. You may just get it," Durga Das had warned me, shrugging his shoulders. As I thought back on this moment, Ma's words interrupted my thoughts.

"Anyone in this room can have God. You write me you want to be close to Ma, which you all are, but if you really want to be close to Ma, your ego must die. Demand it, ask for it, beg for it, but remember, be careful what you ask for. Because you may just get what you ask for, and it may not come in a nice, neat package. The Mother tends to her garden. Your ego must die, you must surrender, and then and only then you will know God." Ma's hands rested in her lap, her fingers interlaced. The only sound I heard was the jangle of her bracelets.

I risked a slight turn over my right shoulder to scan the room. The woman seated behind me narrowed her eyes. She was one of Ma's girls and part of the inner circle. She lifted her chin and with no words admonished me for looking around the room. I turned back around. Some people in the room crouched behind the person in front while others leaned forward, pleading for Ma to speak to them. The man next to me clutched his pillow. His knuckles white, his mouth tight, he looked like he was scrunched into a ball.

"Close your eyes," Ma instructed us. "Breathe into your heart. Breathe in this ashram; become one with it." She guided us into the silence. "There is no difference between this Ma and the ashram." Ma paused.

A gentle hush of stillness flowed over me. I relinquished my worries, the weeds, and the petals of the lotus. I inhaled a deep breath into my heart.

One thing I knew, I wanted nothing more than to be with Ma, to be in her rooms, and to serve her. This was a coveted position in the teaching. Somehow, I thought I'd get to God faster and attain the liberation Ma promised. I wanted to live my life in an awakened state and open to higher consciousness.

In order to be liberated and live in God, Ma explained that our ego needed to die. Being killed by Ma was the only way to free ourselves from our worldly attachments or our petty selves. If your ego was in the way, Ma was there to shine the light on it or kill it dead. I was trained with an intensity that kept me highly vigilant of my actions and my words.

Don't be glib, don't be familiar, don't be cutesy, and most of all, don't be sarcastic. I remember someone once told me sarcasm was the highest form of wit, but not around Ma.

I lived in a heightened state of awareness around Ma. At times, being around her was like hurrying home alone on a dark city street later than it was safe to be out. The slightest noise conjured up stalking shadows that may or may not exist, your insides pounded, the fight-or-flight response kicked in.

There was a fine line between the fear of being killed, speaking your truth, and saying what you actually thought.

Ma circled her wagons by using her immense love for her

students. Other times, she used fear and intimidation in the name of God and our karma to wake us up and reduce our egos to ash. I was educated by her blade. She was the executioner. Her guillotine was swift and sharp.

15

Sweet Child of Mine

Being a mother was hard. Being one of Ma's girls was exhilarating. I had a newfound power and status. I was young, and the older devotees could not hide their jealousy. Everyone in the satsang wanted to be in Ma's rooms. I threw myself fully into serving the ashram.

The ashram office was a converted garage of the main house. Chandra Das was the director of the ashram. He had a tiny office in the back. The bookkeeper and treasurer shared another small room. My desk was squashed into the main room opposite the receptionist, where I had carved out a small nook to work in.

One morning, the phone on my desk rang. I rolled my chair closer and moved a pile of papers to get to it.

"Namaste, Krishnapriya. I need to speak with you about Hanuman. He's acting out. I'd like to have a parent conference with you," the principal said.

I walked across the grounds to the little red schoolhouse where the ashram children attended school. I knocked on the principal's door. She invited me to sit down.

"The teachers think maybe you aren't as present as you need to be with him. He spends too much time playing video games and reading by himself."

I leaned back into the chair. I bit the inside of my cheek. I found myself questioning a number of teachers' motives. Ma had warned me that once I got close to her, I would be surrounded by jealousy.

They always seemed to have an issue with me about one of the boys. Hanuman was a mischievous free spirit.

"I'll speak to him." I stood and walked back to the office.

Hanuman and I talked about school and keeping a low profile. It didn't help.

A few weeks later, my phone rang.

"We have a problem. Hanuman is in trouble," the principal informed me.

"What did he do?" I picked up a bronze statue and rolled it between my fingers.

"He decided he didn't like what was being served for lunch and ordered Domino's pizza."

I choked back a laugh. Hanuman had a reputation for wanting to take care of his friends, especially if they weren't, in his eyes, being treated fairly.

While the principal expounded on Hanuman's latest offense, I mentally recited the school lunch menu: tofu on Monday; pasta on Tuesday; veggie hot dogs on Wednesday; grilled cheese on Thursday; and today, Friday, was fish, dried out, overcooked, and smelly. The woman who prepared the kids' lunch was a wiry, brittle woman. She was one of those people who didn't like change, and she rarely altered the menu.

Ma had given her the job to prepare the kids' lunches. Whenever Ma bestowed a role or title to someone, it was considered a blessing, a boon, and service to the guru. When this happened, it was almost impossible to remove them from their position.

Both boys had complained about the school lunches.

"Mom, it's so disgusting. Can't you do something about it? You work in the office." Hanuman looked up from his breakfast, pleading with me to use my power to change the lunch menu.

Ganga Das chimed in. "Yeah, you should eat what we have to eat. It's gross."

The ashram kids lived on matzo, ramen noodles, and potato bread when the adults were busy meditating.

"He called Domino's to deliver pizza for everyone. And he didn't have the money to pay for it, either," the principal continued.

Okay, maybe that wasn't so funny, I thought as I sat forward.

"He'll be kept after school, and I'll be sending a letter to Ma."

I dragged my fingers through my hair. I wondered if Ma would think being kept after school was enough punishment.

Ma was the disciplinarian for all of the ashram children, yet we weren't completely forgiven from our role as parents. Ma would blame us for our inability to raise our children. Many parents were so focused on meditating or serving the guru, they didn't pay enough attention to their children. Kids ran wild without parental discipline. If children misbehaved, it was a reflection of who we were as parents.

Many of the ashram devotees adopted Ma's stern approach, strict parenting style, and open disdain for what she deemed bad parenting. It became their mission to report any perceived bad parenting to Ma. I watched when people snitched on their fellow devotees. They fed off Ma's attention. And we were encouraged to tell Ma everything. The idea was we were saving each other from any karmic missteps that might impede their enlightenment. It was as if some of Ma's students played out their own authority issues and insecurities by offering up another person. I thought that ratting on each other was disgraceful. Ma welcomed the information and was quick to deliver a swift ego killing if needed, but in the end, she had little respect for those who did the telling.

Ma used to joke, "I know how much toilet paper is on each roll. I know each and every one of you."

An hour later, I was called to Ma's rooms. She laughed as she told me about Hanuman's latest offense and asked if I knew. I nodded.

"I love your son and he is one of my favorite kids, but I need to set an example. Shody, call Rudra Das and tell him Hanuman has to work in the kitchen after school."

My mother nodded and picked up the intercom.

Ma reminded me that some of the teachers were jealous of me and that Hanuman and Ganga Das were easy targets for their envy. I sat back in my chair. My closeness to Ma gave people an opening to go after my children and question my competence as a mother. Ma knew it, I knew it, and the boys knew it.

Hanuman didn't stay out of trouble for long.

"I need to see you right away. It's about Hanuman." The principal's voice was clipped and laced with an edge of anger.

Jesus, what now, I thought to myself. I walked to the schoolhouse and knocked on the principal's door, yet again. I didn't bother to sit down.

"The fire department was just here. Hanuman called 911 from the pay phone in the dining hall," the principal informed me.

I bit the inside of my cheek. At this rate, Hanuman would be grounded for the rest of his life. What was he thinking?

"He confessed when the firemen questioned the kids at lunch. He said he didn't think anything would happen. I've sent a message to Ma."

"I'll speak to him when he gets home from school." I leaned against the red door of her office.

"This is a serious offense. It could jeopardize the ashram. Ma needs to know."

I just nodded. I realized this was out of my hands.

Back in my office, I leaned back into my chair. Hanuman had been acting out for months. What was I doing wrong? Pulling the fire alarm was a big deal. The ashram could not afford any transgressions with the outside community.

Raising two boys on my own was challenging. Having grown up a tomboy, I never felt disconnected from either son, and I'd always believed raising boys was easier than raising girls. I thought I was a great mom. I related to the boys. Yet over the years, as I got closer to Ma, my time for and attention to both boys had become challenged.

Ma called. "Come to my rooms and bring your son."

A wave of fear rose from my belly and left a nasty taste in my mouth. It was one thing to order pizza for lunch, but calling 911 had more serious implications. The public-relations angle for the ashram always needed to be considered first.

The air was thick as we walked into Ma's corral. The overpowering stench of a dead animal lodged under the deck made me gag. Ma had been complaining about it for days, but it wasn't easy to find it under the endless wooden decking.

I opened the large, red, wooden door to the small temple. Ma was waiting with my mother. This space was tiny, and the shelves of statues and photos made it feel claustrophobic. I felt like a character from *Alice in Wonderland*, large in the smallness of the space. The smell of Ma's Red perfume permeated the temple. The overpowering scent was suffocating me.

Hanuman and I sat cross-legged before her.

Ma looked down at Hanuman. She wasn't laughing today. "So, what's going on with you?"

He shrugged. "Nothing, Ma."

He would be a teenager at the end of the year. I noticed he was getting taller, but he shrunk under Ma's glare.

"You have been getting into a lot of trouble at school. The teachers have been writing me letters about you. What do you have to say for yourself?"

He stared at Ma; his hands clasped together. He wiggled at his fingers and shrugged his shoulders. "I don't know, Ma."

"You know you are my favorite kid, right? Ask your grandmother." She looked over at my mom. "Shody, haven't I always said Hanuman is my favorite?"

"Yes, Ma," my mom replied.

"So, if you are my favorite kid, the teachers can feel that. They are jealous. They are jealous of anyone they think Ma loves more than them. So, you need to be good. Do you understand?"

"Yes, Ma," he answered.

"What else?" Ma's eyes locked on my son.

Hanuman remained silent. He looked around the room and back to Ma. "Nothing, Ma."

"Why don't you and your mom give us a few minutes?" Ma told me. "And don't go too far. Matter of fact, go sit in the temple until I call you back."

When my mother and I returned, Hanuman was seated in front of Ma. He'd been crying.

Ma looked at both my mother and me. "Hanuman misses his dad. He thinks his father is wonderful and wants to see more of him."

I felt like I'd been punched in the stomach. Their father hadn't been around in years. When the boys were younger, I'd take them to their grandmother's apartment so they could visit their dad. They'd wait for him, and he'd rarely show up. I balled up my hands.

There was a shiny gleam in Ma's eyes. "I explained to your son how his father never did anything for you and never paid any support for him or his brother. I told him how he used to yell at you and beat you up."

I blanched. I had never told either of the boys about the darker side of my relationship with their father. Hanuman looked like he'd been run over by a bus.

"I want you two to take a walk and tell him everything that happened. Tell him about how his father kidnapped him when he was a baby and kept him from you. Tell him how he never gave you a dime. Tell him how he beat you up and yelled at you."

With each of Ma's directives, Hanuman's body shrank smaller. I couldn't wait to get out of there and hold him.

"Yes, Ma," I said, looking at my son.

"Namaste. Go now." She nodded toward the door.

We walked out in silence.

Hanuman spoke first. "Is it true?"

"Is what true?" I asked, considering which truth he was looking for.

"Did Dad hit you?"

"Yes."

His nose scrunched. "Why didn't you tell me?"

"Your dad had some issues. He drank a lot. That had no bearing on his love for you. I wanted you and your brother to have your own relationship with your father," I explained. "I'm sorry. I'm sorry that your dad wasn't always there for you. I just want you to be okay. I love you."

"Can I still see my dad?" he asked.

"Yes, of course, you can still see your dad."

"Am I still punished?"

"Yes, you are still punished," I told him. "And could you please stop pissing off everyone at school?"

"Okay," he said, as we meandered our way through the woods.

During this time in the teaching, I thought, along with many of the members in the satsang, that Ma knew best for our children. My parents supported this as well. Each discussion, punishment, or reprimand was karmic. There were instances when I thought Ma was prudish or old school, but if I argued in defense of my child, no doubt my ego would be challenged for being attached or not displaying enough tough love.

As the children got older, they tested the waters as preteens and teenagers do. They were routinely grounded with kitchen duty and grounds work as the penance, but there were more severe punishments, too, like being relocated to another house. I was grateful that as a parent, I never had my children relocated into Ma's house. There was a group of eight or nine children who slept in a large dorm room outside of Ma's private quarters. Each night, they rolled out their beds like a scene from *Oliver Twist*. Most of the kids had been "rescued" from their parents. Some of the parents lived in the main house with Ma, while others lived in other houses on the ashram. In Ma's house, the housemother was given full rein to act as the children's mother.

Ma's four "adopted" children shared two rooms. They were told from the time they were young that they were special. They would lead the ashram one day and help others.

One hot summer day in July, the teachers took the ashram children to the movies. I was summoned to Ma's rooms in the late afternoon. I filed in with a few other people from the inner circle. Ma was curled in a ball in her chair; her face was drawn and pale, a box of tissues rested in her lap, and the rims of her eyes were red. Chandra sat in front of Ma. My mother was next to him. Her eyes were red, too. The two girls who took care of Ma and my brother were seated nearby. The last of us to file in took seats around the room. My stomach lurched. Something very bad had happened.

"Tell them." Ma looked at Chandra.

His words were meted out as he told us a SWAT team had descended on the movie theater and taken Ma's daughter Ganga away. She was raised as Ma's child and had no idea that her biological parents had given her to Ma. Ganga was eight years old. It turned out there was never a legal adoption.

The press wrote articles about the incident. The word *cult* was in every story. Questions about Ma's other three children surfaced. The ashram spokesman, Brahma Das, attempted to shift the narrative, but it rarely worked.

The remainder of the year was spent trying to reckon with the loss. The ashram children were traumatized. Ma withdrew into her grief. My mother was the only one who saw her.

Each night, the satsang gathered to chant and meditate. My mother would come out and offer an update on Ma or relay a message.

On one such night, the back door opened and my mother approached the front of the temple. She took a deep breath. I studied her. *God, she looks worn out.*

"Ma is devastated. She doesn't know where to put this. She asks you to hold her in your hearts and be patient. She is unable to teach at this time. She loves you all."

It was many months before Ma began teaching again.

16

Tears in Heaven

DURGA DAS TURNED THE KEY, and the beige GMC Eleganza RV rumbled to life. Ma, my mother, and a group of people who ran the service arm of the ashram squeezed together on the leopard-covered seats. The van ambled down I-95 toward the County Home AIDS facility in West Palm Beach on our weekly Thursday rounds to visit the sick and dying. Ma had named the RV the Hanuman Van. Hanuman, the Hindu monkey god, embodied humility and service; his image was hand-painted across the back of the van. Next to us on the faux tiger-skin settees were trays of cookies, baseball caps, red-heart key chains stamped with "Ma Loves You," and miscellaneous paper bags labeled with the names of "special" patients.

It was the early '90s, and AIDS was rampant. Ma's gay students were losing their lovers to it. It started with a call from one of Ma's close students, who was living in Chicago with his dying lover. Then Ma's students in Los Angeles reached out to Ma for help. Before long, the focus of the teaching shifted to serving people living and dying with AIDS. The River Fund, the ashram's service organization, was created to meet this challenge. It was during this time people who came to find God and have a spiritual experience were instead sent on rounds to serve humanity.

"Service is the fastest path to God."

This would be Ma's mantra for years to come.

"Okay, Veen, what's the story?" Ma asked. Veena was Ma's close confidant and had been her best friend before Ma became a guru. She recited a list of who would be meeting us at the facility. A group of River School students rotated each week, taking turns learning how to serve. The children who grew up on the ashram and the students from the local community who went to our school were exposed to death at a young age. I think it expanded their life experience.

To this day, it has left an impression on both of my sons.

Death became real and tangible. They learned how to be with the dying.

"Ma, in addition to some of the kids, there are a few guests visiting the ashram who will be on rounds today," Veena said.

"I hope someone spoke to them about how to be around the dying. You did speak to them, didn't you?" Ma asked.

Veena nodded and returned to her list.

The van labored up to the tan building. Ma jumped out of it dressed in tight jeans and a black sweater, her gold bangles jangling as she welcomed one of the guests. The red tilak on her forehead was the only reminder she was a holy person. Trays of cookies were passed from the van to the waiting carts.

"Okay, kids, let's get going." She mussed the hair of one of the schoolkids. "Are you being good?"

He put his hands together and answered, "Yes, Ma."

I followed her to the door of the concrete building.

"Ma's here!" she shouted as she entered.

A nurse rose from her desk. Her blue scrubs wheezed against her backside. The gap between her white teeth was shocking against her cardinal-red lips.

"Ma's here, y'all!" she yelled to no one in particular, her decibels equaling Ma's. "Hey, Ma, how ya doin'?"

Other staff members began to emerge from various corners of the lobby, eyeing the sweets.

"Not too bad. Not too bad. Girl, just you look at those nails." Ma had adopted the woman's vernacular. The woman held up her two-inch curved talons, painted the same color as her lips. They were adorned with small gold beads that dangled from the tips of her nails.

How does she work with those things? I mused.

"Ma, you should get some for yourself," she squealed, waving her hands around.

"You know, girl, I grew up in the streets, don't ya? I was raised by four Black folks under the boardwalk at Coney Island."

The woman grabbed the tray of cookies from Ma. "Why, thank you, Ma."

"Now don't you go and eat them all. You best share with the others." Ma chuckled.

A towering man in khakis and a white-striped, button-down shirt entered through the set of double doors marked AUTHORIZED PERSONNEL ONLY. He waved and walked toward our motley crew.

"Ma, Ma, so good to see you."

"Hi, darling. How are you?" She extended her arms out to him. Ma turned to her guests. "This is my Lee. He's my hero. He runs this whole place. He's done more for people with AIDS in West Palm than anybody I know." She wrapped him in a tight embrace. "How's my judge doing today?" she asked.

"Not so good; he's got a bad case of pneumonia," the director told Ma.

"Okay, then let's get going." Ma walked toward the doors as we trailed behind with the goodies. The wing was long. A few rooms were dark except for the faint flickering of an overhead TV. As Ma's voice echoed down the hall, a few ambulatory patients hobbled out from their rooms. Others too sick to move waited, lying in masses of twisted bedsheets. A stale urine stench wafted by. My nose crinkled. I held my breath, desperate to ignore the churning in my belly. Glimpsing into the blackness of an open door, I spied a corpse-like face staring out at the nothingness of a blank wall.

Ma stepped in and leaned over the bed. She picked up the man's skeletal hand. "Hi, darling. It's Ma. I love you."

I thought, *How fearless she is, unafraid to touch anyone in any condition.*

We buzzed like worker bees through the halls, entering patients' rooms with cookies and presents. Some engaged with us, while others just nodded and accepted their gifts.

Later, we walked from the AIDS wing to a communal area where Alzheimer's residents gathered. A frail woman with a shadow of thin, white wisps that breezed over her mottled crown approached me. She grabbed my hand.

"When can I leave? When can I go home? I am a famous actress, you know."

I handed her cookies and smiled. "I'm sorry, I don't know."

Her clutch tightened.

The center of my chest thumped hard.

"I need to go. It's important. I have things to do at home." She squeezed tighter.

I didn't want to lie to her. She'd never be leaving.

A nurse came to rescue me. "Okay, Milly, now come along. This lady needs to go."

A slow wail emitted from Milly's throat. "No. No. I need to go. She's taking me home."

The nurse broke our bond and guided her away. I stood and watched, the bag of cookies ripping in my hand as the woman sobbed.

Our next stop was Conner's Nursery, a home that cared for

babies and children with AIDS. Many had been victim to abuses beyond the imagination. We pulled up to the ranch-style house tucked away on a side street. Young children played on the bright carpet. Babies lay in cribs on oxygen.

Ma asked the director of the home about each child. We distributed toys and clothing. A nurse handed me a limp toddler, and the baby's dull eyes looked up into mine. I smiled and cooed at her and took her for a walk in the garden. How could someone hurt one so small and innocent?

Our last stop was a home for unwed mothers. Only a handful of us were permitted in. Young teens in various stages of pregnancy looked as if they'd just come from the streets. They touched their stomachs and reached for cookies. We climbed back into the van. My brother turned back to Ma.

"Are you ready, Ma?"

"*Chalo*," Ma said, waving. He turned the key, and the Eleganza rumbled to life, homeward bound. The schedule was tight. We'd arrive home, and Ma would prepare for the evening. Everyone who had gone on rounds would need to hurry to the dining room, eat their dinner, and get to darshan on time.

The temple was darker than usual. Ma's face was drawn. It had been a long day. There was a large group of guests in darshan this evening.

"I grew up on the streets. I lived in Coney Island and spent my youth underneath the boardwalk. My first gurus were the homeless, drug addicts, prostitutes, and alcoholics who lived under the boardwalk. They shared their lives and their dreams. They shared their food. They taught me the true meaning of service. When Chews was dying of an overdose, she told me to pay back.

"Her voice rides on the winds of my beating heart. I learned one thing that day: There are no throwaway people. Each person is whole, unique, and complete. We are all God's children. This is the essence of my teaching. And this, my children, is what I do. It's what this ashram does. My kids serve and serve and never burn out. This teaching is about unconditional love. If you move a grain of sand, you change the world. You touch one person, offer a smile, or open the door for someone, your kindness can change their moment. My children, you were born to do this."

Ma leaned forward and pointed her finger at us. "You need to serve; you all need to serve. My babies are dying. My people are dying." Ma's voice cracked.

She told stories of children raped by their uncles, babies left alone without food in dirty diapers while their mothers got high, and toddlers riddled with cigarette burns. Faces in the room twisted, tears fell, and people clutched their chests.

"I have hundreds of books with photos of my people dying. The only thing that eases this Ma's heart is serving. Call my Veena if you want to come on my rounds. I invite you to serve with me."

Veena lifted her head and scowled in the corner.

"If you can't go on rounds, give a donation to my River Fund. Veena, Veena, where are you? Raise your hand. Talk to her." Ma pointed her way.

Veena forced her mouth to perform a minuscule upward turn.

"You know, kids, she's been with Ma the longest. We have been through thick and thin together. Veena serves and serves. She serves in her Ma's name."

Veena plastered a smile on her face and rose to her knees. She offered a Queen Mother wave as Ma showered her with praise, and then she withdrew into the darkness of the hall. I wondered if Veena liked anybody for real. It appeared she only cared about her gay friends, people with AIDS, or people with money who would support the River Fund.

I bit my tongue. For as long as I'd lived on the ashram, I'd watched it struggle financially. Working in the ashram office, I knew the finances or lack thereof were discussed daily.

Ma finished darshan, and I returned to the office to finish a few last-minute details. Chandra, the current director of the ashram, stared into his computer.

I propped myself up in his doorway. "Hey, what's up?"

"I'm reviewing our financials. The River Fund is sucking the ashram dry." His chair swiveled toward me, and he pressed the tips of his fingers to his lips.

"What are we going to do?" I asked him.

"I don't know. I need to talk to Ma. Veena will fight us. She thinks we're an endless piggy bank. If something doesn't change, we're going to lose the ashram. We can barely pay the bills as it is." He shook his head. "Veena doesn't care if the ashram sinks as long as the River Fund flourishes."

There was nothing to say. We both knew where Ma's allegiance lay. And we both knew Veena had Ma wrapped around her finger like a yo-yo. Veena knew just how much string to let out before reeling Ma back in. It was just one of the many battles fought for Ma's attention. The service work we did was important, but so was paying the bills.

One afternoon, Chandra asked Ma for a meeting. I sat next to him. Veena sat on the other side of the room. My mother was sitting next to Ma.

"Ma, the ashram is not in good financial shape," Chandra explained. I watched him as he chose his words carefully. I squirmed in my seat. "We need to stop bleeding money," he added. Ma and Veena's eyes connected. I knew this meeting wasn't going to end well.

"Baba will take care of us, and the money will come," Ma said. She looked at Veena. "I'll help raise money in darshan. My kids will give what they can. I need to go to California. My children are dying, and they need their Ma."

Ma's California students had begged her to come west to take care of people with AIDS. We began going to San Francisco and West Hollywood every few months.

On one such trip, we sat in a hotel room in San Francisco. It had been a difficult trip, luggage was lost, and Ma was unhappy about how she was being cared for. She pointed at me and said, "You run my ashram."

I sucked in a deep breath. Me? I wondered if I could save the ashram. Could I make a difference? Could I be the one who solved the ashram's money issues?

Chandra moved out of the office and joined a law practice in town. I was determined to effect change. The bookkeeper helped balance the finances, but it was a fragile dance. Ma needed to teach, and we needed to make money. I was twenty-nine. From this point on, I felt that if the ashram didn't succeed, I was a failure. I would come up with a plan to help the ashram make money. We started offering retreats with Ma.

During this time, I learned to be with the sick and dying. It was a truly profound experience in my life. I met, loved, and lost many people I came to know during this time. I learned to be comfortable in a room with someone in the process of dying.

Ma would remind us, "It's not about you."

Each death from the years we took care of the dying impacted me, a reminder of the fragility and impermanence of life. And while Ma taught that we would return and reincarnate to her feet, it seemed there were many rules as to how and when we'd be graced.

17

Teach Your Children

THE AIR WAS THICK, my ribbed tank top clung to my body, and my hair was damp from the humidity. Ganga Das and I drove to the corner to get some frozen yogurt. There was a haze rising over the asphalt as we walked across the Publix parking lot when he posed his unexpected question. "Mom, is Massimo my father?" He asked me as if asking about the flavor of the day.

"What made you ask that?" I stopped walking.

"I always wondered."

I hesitated. I had tucked this secret away. I didn't think it would surface after leaving New York, and I definitely didn't expect my thirteen-year-old son to be the one to unearth it.

"I don't know for sure." I tugged on my tank top.

"Is there a way to find out?"

"Yes, there is a test. I'll call Massimo. I'll talk to Ma. We'd probably need to go to New York." I put my arm around him. "Massimo has always thought of you as his son. He loves you very much."

We ate our yogurt and reminisced about our life in Queens.

Back home at the ashram, I found my mother and told her what had transpired. She said she would tell Ma. I was called into Ma's rooms immediately.

"Namaste, Ma."

She wasn't smiling. She motioned me to sit before her with a sharp flick of her wrist.

"What the fuck? How could you have kept this from me all these years? Don't you understand the karma involved here?"

I didn't move. I never imagined this would be her reaction. My stomach tightened with each question.

"And what about Ganga Das? Did you even consider him and his feelings in all of this? And Massimo, what about him?" Her accusations made me feel dirty. I felt like a slut and a whore. I loved Massimo. Ma loved Massimo. She wanted to marry us when I'd first moved to the ashram.

"I will need to do hours of prayers to correct what you have done."

I swallowed back my tears. The last thing I wanted to do now was cry in front of Ma. It would be viewed as self-indulgent and only add to the firestorm occurring.

"How long have you known that Massimo might be the real father?"

I hesitated. "I wasn't sure. When he was born, he had jet-black hair and olive skin."

"Call Massimo and get the test done. I'll pray. You should've told me this years ago. You can go. Shody, you stay."

I could only imagine what they would talk about.

I left Ma's room and called Massimo. He paused, digesting the information.

"I always wondered."

"Yes, me too. Thank you. I'll make the arrangements and let you know when we arrive."

Ganga Das and I flew to New York. We took the train into the city to take the test. Massimo and Ganga Das spent the afternoon together.

We waited for weeks until the results came back. The envelope arrived, and I opened the results. The DNA wasn't a match. Massimo wasn't Ganga Das's father. Ganga Das and Massimo were devastated. Both had hoped for different results. Chris was Ganga Das's biological father.

A few weeks later, I was called into Ma's rooms. Hanuman had been caught stealing money from one of the other kids in the boys' dorm. My mother and I sat on the itchy, faux-leopard carpet before Ma. She was dressed in black tights and a matching sports bra. A sweaty T-shirt lay crumpled nearby. Her hair was slicked back; the hair tie pulled and gathered not only her hair but her face as well. One side of her mouth appeared crooked. She peered over her rhinestone glasses. I knew this conversation would be about as pleasant as having my fingernails pulled off one by one with pliers. I massaged the carpet beneath me. Ma surrounded herself with faux fur. It covered the furniture, the instruments in the temple, and the clothes she wore. I thought everyone from Brooklyn dressed this way.

"Your son will never learn. You and your mother are constantly protecting him. And it is because of your attachment he will continue to hurt others." She tossed aside the *People* magazine she'd been perusing. "He needs tough love, which neither you nor your mother have. Idiot compassion, that's what you two have. You have ruined my child. Ruined him with your attachment."

Her words wrapped around me, choking me. I felt warm drops form. *Hold them back*, I told myself. Ma would slam me if I started to cry. *Stay open*, I willed myself. I stole a glance at my mother. Ma had already worked her over. I couldn't believe he'd stolen money from another kid. Was I really attached? I didn't think so. Kids do stupid stuff like this all the time. It's not okay to steal, but was I truly hurting him?

"Pull him out of school and the theater classes."

Take him out of school? This was going to be worse than I imagined.

She looked at me, begging me to challenge her.

"Don't even try," she said, glaring at me. "Shody, do you understand?"

"Yes, Ma." My mother nodded. Her mouth didn't even move as she choked out her answer.

"And this time, he goes to Jambavan. He works day and night. I don't care if your son sleeps in the art shed." Ma's hand slammed the arm of the chair. The gavel pounded the sentence.

My mind scrambled—this wasn't good. Jambavan, Ma's art curator, was a sacred cow, an untouchable, and not a good person. Ma had also banished her younger son to the same fate.

Later that night as we sat in darshan, the fate of my fourteen-year-old son was the first order of business.

"Do not speak to either of these boys. Not one word. And that includes his mother and his grandmother." Ma didn't bother to look at us. "These two boys are to work night and day." She turned to Jambavan.

He smiled and licked his lips. He wore his power like the fine Armani suits he wore when showing Ma's art. I scratched my arm. He was just another drain on ashram resources. Ma had given him carte blanche to do whatever he wanted with the money he and she made with sales from her art. The ashram paid for all of the supplies, trips, and incidentals, and the money funneled into a special fund that Ma controlled.

Jambavan woke the boys at dawn. Each night before darshan, he reported to Ma. He recited the long list of grueling jobs he gave the two boys. They hauled paintings, cleaned the studio, and did whatever errands arose. They worked until late into the night. I worried about Hanuman. I knew Jambavan was not a kind person. I felt powerless to help my son. I was mad. Mad at Ma, and definitely mad at Jambavan.

I thought the sentence for the kid's crime was cruel punishment.

I went to speak with my mother. "I don't trust Jambavan, and now I'm not even allowed to speak to Hanuman."

"You need to trust Ma. She's trying to help Hanuman," she said as she prepared Ma's supplements for the night.

Later that evening, I turned on the television and flipped through channels, coming across the show *Scared Straight*. It portrayed teenagers on the road to juvenile delinquency. Young people were taken to prison and met with inmates in an attempt to demonstrate what could happen if you chose the wrong path. I wondered if this would help.

The next day, I proposed the idea to Ma. She loved it. I made arrangements with a prison about an hour from the ashram, and two weeks later, the high school students were loaded onto the school bus along with Kali, one of the teachers in the school. We arrived at the prison dragging fifteen unwilling, cynical teenagers behind us.

Kali was beautiful. She had toffee skin and a smattering of freckles, the product of her African American mother and white Jewish father. She pushed a mass of curly black ringlets out of her large brown eyes as we entered the prison.

The teens assembled in the main room, and a prison guard sauntered in. He was big. His gray, button-down shirt gaped around his midsection. The buttons hung on for dear life. His cropped military haircut made him look as menacing as any prisoner. He explained his job and what life in prison was like. The teens slouched in sand-colored plastic chairs, rolling their eyes at each other.

We stepped into the main area of prisoners. The room, a beige jungle, came alive.

"Yo, yo baby, hey, hey, come here, come over here and gimme some sugar," a row of prisoners yelped from their cells. They whistled and catcalled and whooped at us. They rattled the bars of the cells and jumped up and down. "Come on, ladies, now come on, come to Daddy." Tongues flickered and lolled. Hands grabbed between their legs. Straightening myself to full height, I walked slowly and stared back, all five-foot-four of me. What had I been thinking wearing a skirt today?

The teenagers awakened from their jaded facades, and their faces paled. They stepped closer behind us. Kali and I were scared. Shaken by the end of our tour, we retreated to the safety of the bus.

The impact on the kids was short-lived, though. Hanuman was caught stealing from some visiting guests. I was at a loss as to why Hanuman was acting out. He never talked about what was actually happening and why he kept getting in trouble. We called a family meeting. My mother, my brother, and I discussed our options.

"I have no idea what to do with Hanuman," I sobbed.

"I am going to be more hands-on. I'll see if I can have him work on the grounds with me," Durga Das offered.

"I think that's a good idea. Ma is fed up with him," my mother added.

I was in the office when I received a call from the local authorities. The woman on the other end of the phone explained I was under investigation for child abuse. I hung up the phone and put my head on my desk. How could this happen? The authorities said they'd be sending someone to investigate the claims. Who had reported this?

Ma was out of town. Hysterical, I called my mother and left a message.

My mother returned the call within minutes. I could hear Ma in the background. But Ma didn't get on the phone; instead, she relayed her message through my mother.

"It's time for Hanuman to go. Call his father and have him

come pick him up immediately. He doesn't want to be here. He has put Ma and this ashram in jeopardy. I wash my hands. This is the ultimate betrayal. After everything I did for that child. He has betrayed Ma. He has betrayed this ashram. Hanuman must grow up. He doesn't want to be here."

My mother paused every so often so she could catch Ma's words. I could tell Ma was angry. Her tone was clipped and sharp. She yelled that Hanuman needed to learn and tough love was the only way. She yelled at my mother and me.

"Neither of you are able to give Hanuman what he needs," she spat out. Once again, I had failed as a mother. There would be no punishment or discussion. Ma's edict stood. Hanuman would need to go. My mother hung up.

I dropped to the sandy driveway. Tears fell in torrents from my eyes, blurring everything around me. Heaving and trying to breathe between sobs, I thought, *Why would Ma send my son away?* I was devastated and heartbroken.

I waited with Hanuman on the curb for his father to pick him up. Hanuman would go live with Chris and his girlfriend in Orlando.

I sobbed and kicked the pile of crumpled tissues strewn on the coquina. "I don't understand."

"I didn't call anyone. I told my friend that I was having a hard time at home. Maybe her mother called," Hanuman said.

"You understand what all this means? You've not only jeopardized Ma and the ashram. They are coming to investigate me for child abuse."

"I didn't mean for this to happen." He looked off into the darkness, as if searching for something only he knew about.

"Did you want to go live with your father?"

"Somewhere, yes. I don't want to be here anymore. I'm always in trouble."

A beat-up blue Chrysler pulled into the sandy circular drive.

"Hey there, buddy." Chris sauntered over and hugged Hanuman.

"So, KP, what's this all about?" He lifted his chest like a mating peacock, ready to take on his challenger.

My teeth clenched as they always did when I had to interact with Chris. I wiped my nose. "I think I explained it on the phone to you." Damn him and his accusing bullshit.

"Is this all you have?" Chris asked Hanuman as he lifted his suitcase. What remained were two rumpled garbage bags, five banker boxes of comic books, and his collection of video games.

"Yes." Hanuman moved to collect his things.

"I'll get it. You say goodbye to your mother," Chris said.

"I love you. I'll miss you. I'm not supposed to talk to you for a while. Your dad will take care of you," I said. Choking back the salty, bitter tears burning the back of my throat, I grabbed my son and held on tight.

"I love you too, Mom," he said as he crawled into the front seat. The beat-up, nondescript, faded blue box pulled away with one red taillight staring back at me. I waited until they turned onto the main road and ran to my room—our room—and curled up in a ball. I questioned myself. Was it my attachments that had caused this? I doubted myself time and time again. Was I a bad mother? Was I too attached? What could I have done differently?

There were times I'd felt like a failure as a parent, when I'd yelled and screamed and lost my temper or when I'd allowed Ma to be the disciplinarian to my children. But I was unable to save my son from himself.

The authorities never came to the ashram. There was no formal inquiry. My mother and I were told we were forbidden to have any further contact with Hanuman.

I remember the letter Hanuman wrote to me shortly after his departure. My son's signature scratchy handwriting squashed onto the top third of a piece of crumpled lined paper, folded into messy quarters. It opened like one of those Chinese origami fortunes.

Dear Mom,

It's only now after I've left that I can finally tell you that I'm happy things happened this way. I never asked for this life. I think that all of you are being lied to and judged. I wanted to leave, and you never let me. I'm sick of being judged. It's only now that I can see how miserable I was while living there. Ma is not my guru. I don't believe in her. I think you, Grandmom, and Uncle Durga Das are cowards for siding with her over me. What kind of person gives his or her kids over to someone else to raise? Dad was right about the ashram all along. He was smart, leaving when he did. He saw the ashram for what it really was. I hope I never go back.

Love Hanuman

I slid down from the edge of the bed. I couldn't believe this was how he felt. I wondered, *Did his dad help write this?* Surely Hanuman would never say these things about Ma.

It would be a year before I snuck away to see my son.

18

Losing My Religion

OVER THE NEXT FEW YEARS, the ashram began to change. The Parliament of the World's Religions opened new doors for the ashram. It was during this time we started to shift our image. Waco and Ruby Ridge had created bad press and haunted us. The locals deemed us a cult. We shifted from our mostly Hindu leanings to become an interfaith community.

The Chicago event in 1993 drew ten thousand participants and religious leaders from around the world. Ma reconnected with other spiritual teachers and gurus she had met in the '70s when she had begun her journey as a spiritual teacher. Swami Satchidananda clearly remembered her. She was, in fact, hard to forget. Loud, brash, outspoken, and uncontained, Ma said what was on her mind, often to her own detriment.

"I never use two people against each other unless both go to God," she reminded us.

She spoke on a panel with the Dalai Lama, and soon the ashram championed the Free Tibet movement. It was during this time she met Yogi Bhajan, also known as Yogiji. He was the creator of the Kundalini yoga movement and founder of Sikh Dharma in the West. Yogiji was a force to be reckoned with, and he and Ma became friends of sorts.

This catapulted me into another role as a liaison between a myriad of spiritual masters, teachers, and yogis. After meeting Ma, Yogiji sent two of his students to visit to see if our ashram could be the host for the 3HO Sikh community's winter solstice.

I waited in the kitchen for his two representatives to arrive. A couple arrived at the glass sliding doors. Sampuran, a thin man outfitted in a silky white dress and tights with epaulets on his uniform that broadened his shoulders and a turban on his head, offered a distinct air of authority as he nodded and said, "*Satnam*." [1]

He had a youthful manner about him, even with the long, auburn beard streaked with gray and mustache that covered his face. His wife, dressed in flowing white, was beautiful and slight with a sweet smile. Veena and I greeted them with hugs and welcomed them to the ashram. I guided them into the temple, while Veena rang Ma on the intercom to let her know the guests had arrived.

"Ma will see you now," Veena nodded without a smile.

We led them through the corral to the Lion Kuti, the temple where Ma met privately with people. Ma was already seated on her oversize, leopard-print chair waiting for us. I watched them look around the temple. I wondered what they thought of the hundreds of photos, the statues, the faux fur carpeting the walls—all remnants of the rampage era. Brass statues of Hindu gods rested on shelves lined with faux cheetah fur.

The couple greeted Ma, placing their hands in prayer position. "*Satnam,* Ma."

I noticed how they were not new to meeting holy people. They took a seat on the floor in a yogic posture before Ma.

"Namaste, my children. I am The Mother of thousands of gays

and lesbians. My children are dying of AIDS. My life is only about service," Ma explained.

Ma was on her good behavior. "Take them for a tour of the ashram," she said, looking at Veena and me. Veena's eyes flashed dark, and I smiled.

"I'll see you in darshan," Ma said.

We escorted the couple out to the kitchen for lunch and a tour. Veena talked about Ma's service work. I liked them. After lunch, I showed them around the ashram.

"This is the Hanuman Temple. Hanuman is the god of service. Ma's favorite quote of Hanuman is 'Save me, save me, from the tentacles of egoism.' We hold fire pujas here," I explained, pointing out the smoking *dhuni*. [2]

We entered the temple, and the screen door whined as I opened the door to the meditation room. They each bowed. I guided them around the pond, visiting each of the temples, and walked out to the thirty-five acres of the undeveloped ashram to explore the site for their winter event.

A dark shadow and a storm brewed in Veena's eyes. She was suffering through our assignment. She hated anything to do with the ashram that wasn't about service. I, on the other hand, was curious. I wanted to know about them, what they believed, and who they were.

A few weeks later, I was called to Ma's rooms. It was early in the morning, and I was wary as to why I was being summoned so early.

"Namaste, Ma," I said when I found her in her dressing room.

"Call the Yogiji, tell him I feel Guru Hargobind here with me," she whispered.

My heart pounded. I felt like I was privy to the secrets of the universe between these two great spiritual beings and their ethereal antics.

"Tell him Guru Hargobind has been with me and won't leave me alone; he wants Ma to pick up the sword and fight."

I wrote down the message carefully, trying to capture every word Ma uttered.

"Tell him I'll meet him in the ethers." Ma's eyes fluttered.

I walked into her living room and dialed the number to Yogiji's ranch.

"*Satnam.*" His voice yielded a quiet strength.

I wondered if I'd woken him. "*Satnam,* sir, it's Krishnapriya. How are you?" I asked in my best loving business tone.

"Hello, daughter. I am fine by the grace of the guru," he murmured.

"Ma asked me to call you. She wants you to know she feels the essence of Guru Hargobind in her rooms and all around her right this second." I relayed the message exactly as Ma had instructed.

"Tell Ma she is the Mother Teresa of the West." His voice boomed in my ear. His thick Punjabi accent melted me. He said Ma was blessed by Guru Ram Das. He spoke of Ma's service work and how good it was she was taking care of the babies dying of AIDS. My pen moved rapidly across the paper. His thick accent made it harder to catch everything he said. I flipped the pages on my notebook over and over, trying to capture each word.

"Ma said she'll meet you in the ethers." I repeated her words.

"Yes, yes, we will." His voice began to fade. "Tell Ma she is good."

"Yes sir, I will. Thank you." I put my pen down.

"Love you. *Satnam,*" he whispered.

"*Satnam*. I love you, too," I whispered back. There was a click and then a dial tone.

My body hummed. It was alive with energy. There was a circle of warmth embedded in my chest. I felt blessed by the mere phone presence of this spiritual teacher. He was unlike my guru in almost every way. I was intrigued by him.

I packed up my notebook and returned to Ma's living room. "Ma?" I looked around for her. She raced out of the bathroom.

"What did he say?" She was wide-eyed and half naked.

I repeated the conversation verbatim. I even included the fact that I thought I'd woken him.

"He never sleeps." She waved her hand, brushing away my comment. "Call him back. Tell him I am going to build a gurdwara[3] in the ashram in his honor."

"Right now?" My mouth opened.

"Right this minute."

I departed back into the other room to make the call. My jaw tightened as I stared at the phone. I picked up the receiver and put it down. I waited. I sat for a minute, procrastinating. I'd just called him. I couldn't believe she wanted me to call him back. I didn't want to be a pest. He might be resting. And there was no way I could go back in and tell her I didn't want to bother him.

I bit my lip, picked up the phone, and dialed.

He answered on the first ring.

"Sir, sorry to bother you."

He seemed unfazed by my call and the round of messages. I returned once again to find Ma.

"Call Sampuran. Tell him about the call with Yogiji. Tell him to come to see his Ma. We need to talk," she said.

"Yes, Ma." At least this call was a fun assignment.

Sampuran, one of the directors of Yogi Bhajan's ashram, started to visit our ashram regularly. We became good friends and kindred spirits on the spiritual path. We found common understanding of the spiritual journey, devotion to a teacher, and all that came with these choices.

Sampuran was enamored with Ma. As Yogiji's ambassador, he had visited many ashrams and met many gurus and spiritual teachers. Ma, he said, was like no teacher he had ever met. She was love incarnate. He loved her wildness. He thirsted for the deep space of stillness he felt with her.

When I met Sampuran, my world expanded beyond my ashram beliefs and conditioning. We shared the similarities and differences in our ashram worlds. I learned about his masculine teaching and he learned from mine, a feminine, goddess-driven teaching. They were different yet very much alike. We shared our lives and our challenges on the spiritual path.

19

Take Me to the River

THE PILOT ANNOUNCED OUR FINAL DESCENT into Albuquerque. The landscape below was brown, dry, dead. It was 1993. I was flying in to support my father after Luanne, his second wife, committed suicide while on the phone with him. They had separated, and she was desperate to reconcile.

As I entered their home, there were no signs of the incident.

My dad was seated at the kitchen table writing something on a pad of paper. I hugged him.

"Dad, oh my God. How are you?"

The rims of his eyes were red and swollen. "I can't believe she's gone. I don't understand. Why?" My father shook his head. He pulled a handkerchief out of his pocket and blew his nose.

I noticed how thin he'd become.

"I need to go to the funeral home. I need to make arrangements for her," he said.

As we drove to the funeral home, my father kept going over the details of his wife's death. I pulled in and parked. My father's friend Parvati met us.

We were guided into a nondescript, beige room by the funeral director. A lifeless body lay on the gurney, covered with a blanket. My dad, Parvati, and I knelt in front of it.

After a long time, my dad spoke. "I'd like to read something from *The Tibetan Book of the Dead.*"

I watched him. His grief bled into the room. In a helpless reality, he wanted to help his wife.

He handed Parvati the book, which I hadn't realized he'd brought with him.

The Tibetan Book of the Dead explains the journey one takes after they die. It's recited to ease the consciousness of the dead through death and assist the soul into a favorable rebirth. Each chapter guides the soul's experiences through the different bardos—the intervals between death and the next rebirth.

Parvati began to read.

She read what occurs in the first step on the journey of death. It sounded positive, I thought. Initially, there was radiance and light on the journey. For the first three days, the soul doesn't even realize it is dead.

Parvati handed the book to my dad.

"The soul encounters the Lord of Death, a fearsome demonic deity who appears in the smoke and fire and subjects the soul to a judgment. If the dead person protests that he has done no evil, the Lord of Death holds up before him the Mirror of Karma; this is where every good and evil act is vividly reflected. Now the demons approach and begin to inflict torments and punishments upon the soul for his evil deeds," he read.

Dad sobbed between words and held the feet of his wife.

Each word took me deeper into the realm of darkness. *What? Demons, judgment, fire, brimstone? This was nothing like what Ma taught us about the dying process.* I flinched at the words. Fierce hell creatures coming toward you, testing you. In my mind's eye, I visualized demons and vicious creatures tormenting Luanne.

Ma taught us that Yama, the Hindu god of death, was kind and compassionate. She spoke of the beauty of death and how Yama helped people cross the threshold of impermanence into the beyond. When Ma painted Yama, he was handsome, with flowing black hair. Shirtless and barefoot, he wandered the cremation grounds, guiding souls through the journey of death.

We finished the reading, and Parvati guided my father to the car while I remained to discuss arrangements with the funeral director.

"Do you want Luanne's personal effects?" he asked.

"Yes, I guess so."

He handed me a large plastic garbage bag. It was heavy. I opened it to take stock of the contents. The odor hit me—unbearable, metallic, and sharp. I recoiled from the stench of death. It was unmistakable: death, violent, raw, and final. I gagged and handed the bag back to him. "Maybe you should dispose of this."

He nodded and took the blood-soaked contents from my hands.

I breathed in. Not even the stale air of the funeral home could alleviate the scent in my nostrils. It lingered as I walked toward the car. I looked in my bag for oil, perfume, a mint, anything.

"Everything okay?" my dad asked.

"Yes, everything is set for the cremation."

My next undertaking was to help organize the memorial service. The renowned spiritual teacher Baba Ram Dass would officiate. My father loved and respected him dearly. He had interviewed him for his New Age radio show several times. I'd yet to meet him, but I knew of Ram Dass and Ma's falling out. It happened before my parents met Ma. Ram Dass wrote an exposé in the *New York Times* and a book about his experience with Ma. On more than one occasion, Ma would tell her side of the story in darshan.

She'd laugh and say, "If I fucked Ram Dass, he would have stayed fucked."

Their breakup was legendary in the spiritual world. I believed Ma's side of the story.

Ram Dass arrived at the house, and he and my dad embraced.

"Hey, Dass, I'd like you to meet my daughter, Krishnapriya."

Ram Dass's brow arched at the mention of my name. We shook hands. My dad explained I was a student of Ma's, and Ram Dass's expression remained even, although he unconsciously took a step back.

Standing next to him was Jai Laxman, whom I hadn't seen since I was a young teenager. He had lived in Ma's houses early in the teaching and left after a few years.

"I remember you well," he said with a laugh. "You were a wild teenager—raised hell everywhere you went."

Ram Dass and I found a quiet place to organize the memorial.

The phone rang. It was my mom calling from Rome. She asked about my dad.

"When is the memorial?"

"Tomorrow. Ram Dass is officiating the ceremony."

"Send your father my love. I love you. Miss you tons. Ma sends you all of her love. She's proud of you."

We hung up.

I lay down in my bed and fell asleep. Much later, I heard a phone ringing. Was I dreaming? I picked up the phone—it was my mother.

"Krishnapriya, I'm here with Ma."

I looked at my watch. It was 4:30 a.m.

"Hello," I mumbled.

"Ma wants to speak with you."

I sat up and gathered myself.

"Namaste, my daughter. How are you? How's my Rudra Ram?"

"Okay. He's okay." I wiped the sleep from my eyes and yawned.

"And Ram Dass?"

I told her about meeting him and seeing Jai Laxman.

"Did you send them Ma's love?"

"Yes, of course." I didn't tell her their reaction. *Tepid* was kind.

"Do you have a pen and paper nearby?"

She had told me years ago to always carry a pen and paper and be ready. "Yes, yes, I do."

"I want you to write down something from Ma for the service for you to read. Are you ready?"

"Yes."

She recited her River Poem.

"Children play by my river,
Old men stay by my river,
Sadhus pray by my river . . ."

Her thick Brooklyn accent disappeared as the poem went on and on.

Focusing, attempting to keep up, I scratched her words out. My handwriting splayed across the paper. *God, I hope I'll be able to read it when I'm done.*

"Do you have it all?" she asked.

"Yes. I got it, Ma." I looked at the pages of poetry, probably illegible to anyone else.

"Read it back to me."

What? Oh my God. I looked down at the multitude of pages. I put the pen to my mouth for a moment before reading the poem back to her.

"Perfect. Okay. You read it. It's my gift to Luanne. Bring The Mother to the memorial. Make sure you look at Ram Dass when you read it." A tight knot formed in my stomach.

Shit. How was I going to manage this? I knew in my heart that this would be met with contempt by Ram Dass and his followers.

"Okay," I eked out.

"Don't let me down. I love you. Bring The Mother. Luanne needs my words to help her cross over. Namaste, my daughter."

"Namaste, Ma." I looked at my watch. 6:00 a.m.

I pulled out a few sheets of paper and rewrote the piece, then contemplated the message. Ma's poetry was rhythmic and beautiful. It conjured up images of India, where I yearned to go and visit the temples.

I swallowed. I knew Ram Dass and his students would see right through this.

20

If You Go into the Woods Tonight

Ma returned from Europe, and I returned from New Mexico.

AIDS was ravaging Ma's gay students. Death was ever present. Someone was always dying. Ma's teachings were a constant reminder that in each moment we were moving toward our own eventual deaths and we needed to learn how to die well.

"I teach those living how to die while alive and those dying how to live fully until they die." For those of us living, our death meant the swift killing of our egos.

And like a Girl Scout, I wanted to be prepared.

Randy and his lover, Danny, had met Ma at an AIDS benefit in West Palm Beach. They both had AIDS and found a place of love and acceptance with Ma. The ashram community embraced them. Randy was the first to die. We had watched him slowly wither away. His ruddy complexion paled, his once full frame thinned, and his exhaustion was evident with each breath he took. He was a fighter, and even while he was dying, he joined Ma on rounds, raised money for AIDS, and came to the evening darshan.

It was a warm, balmy night as we prepared for Randy's memorial. I walked across the ashram grounds into the woods. Chanting echoed in the distance. A lone whippoorwill joined in. Tea candles in brown paper bags illuminated the dirt path that led to an RV parked under a thick patch of oaks. Spanish moss hung from their branches, caressing the roof of the vehicle. The woods were alive with night sounds. Crickets chirped. A barn owl hooted. Something buzzed in my ear. I smacked a mosquito on my upper arm, and a smear of blood streaked across my flesh.

I climbed up the rickety steps of the RV parked in the woods. Inside, the cold temperature puckered my skin as the generator hummed. Randy was laid out on the RV's fold-out bed. A few of the satsang women had begun the ashram ritual for the dead. They washed his body with rose water. Red and white carnations were placed around his body. One woman tucked a holy shawl sprayed with Ma's Red perfume gently over his lower torso and legs.

Ma sat vigil by the body. She held Danny in her arms. His swollen eyes remained glued on his partner's lifeless body.

I approached the bed. Randy no longer looked like himself. His cheeks were sunken and his complexion waxy. Leaning down, I kissed his cold forehead and touched his stiff feet. My white carnation joined the others upon his heart. I gave Ma a hug, and then Danny.

"Move the shawl a bit, so it's not bunched up like that," Ma told one of the women.

My mother held a box of tissues in her lap. A group of Randy and Danny's close ashram friends squeezed in on the settee of the makeshift funeral home converted into a Hindu temple.

"Okay, my son, are you ready?" Ma asked Danny.

He nodded.

The door to the RV creaked open. A line of people wove its way out, down the metal steps to the dirt path, and into the night. A mournful Sanskrit chant keened into the darkness. I excused myself and went out to check on things. The metal stairs screeched and rattled as I stepped down.

A frantic man pulled me aside. "We have a problem."

"What's wrong?" I scanned the path.

"The sheriff and his deputy are here. They want to speak to someone in charge. They received a call about a disturbance in the woods."

Shit. Shit. Shit. I quickly surveyed the scene. A hundred and fifty people chanting in a foreign tongue deep in the woods, with a dead body in a van ensconced by candles and incense, and holding the hand of the dead was an eccentric woman with wild, long, ebony hair, dressed head to toe in black with a large splotch of red between her brows.

"Go back and tell him I'll be right with him. Stall him." I hopped back into the van and caught Ma's eye.

"Namaste, Ma. I just want to let you know the sheriff is here. There was a noise complaint. I'm going to speak to him."

Ma assessed the gravity of our situation. "Well, this should be rich. Make sure you tell him who I am and that we take care of people with AIDS. I'll do the puja."

As I made my way to the uniformed men with flashlights, I was grateful we were all wearing street clothes tonight. "Good evening, Officer," I said, smiling and extending my hand.

"Good evening, ma'am." He tipped his hat. "We received a report of noise in the woods. I'm here to check it out."

"Well, Officer, we are holding a ceremony for a friend who just passed away. The singing is part of the ceremony."

His deputy paled. He looked as if he'd seen a ghost. His hand held tight to his holster.

The sheriff tried to listen, but his eyes were glued on the RV beyond me. "What's in there?" he nodded toward the van.

I hesitated. "It's an RV," I said.

"I need to go in there." His voice was gruff and authoritative.

Shit, shit, shit. I couldn't talk my way out of this. "Sure, follow me." I led the way, walking extra slowly and taking care not to trip. Leaves and sticks crackled underfoot as I pushed Spanish moss out of the way. They were no longer the graceful vines hanging from the trees but eerie cobwebs. Smoke rose from the luminaries, shrouding the van in a haze.

The sheriff's forehead glistened. His deputy was close behind; his hand remained poised on his hip. I told the sheriff that they would be meeting Ma, the spiritual director of the community.

"Ma is world-renowned for her work with death and dying. She is an interfaith spiritual teacher. One of Ma's close students passed away this evening. In our tradition, we sing and say goodbye to him." I was mindful not to use the words *guru* or *ashram* or *AIDS*. The van shook as we stepped up the ladder. I knocked.

"Hi, Ma. I'm here with the sheriff," I practically yelled as I opened the door and stepped over the threshold.

"Hello, Officer, I'm Ma." Ma extended her hand. "Did my daughter tell you about me?"

"Uh, uh, yes, ma'am." Both officers' eyes bulged as they stared at Randy's lifeless body. The sheriff wiped his forehead. "Do you all have a permit?"

Ma chuckled.

I cringed.

"I didn't know we needed a permit." Ma fluttered her eyelids. "We are almost finished. The cremation home is on its way here to pick up Randy. Do you know them?" Ma looked at Veena. "Veena?"

"Donna and Rich of Goodrich Cremations," Veena answered on cue.

"Oh, they're very nice people. They take care of all of our dead." Ma waved her hand toward Randy as she met the sheriff's gaze.

The officers shifted back on their heels.

The hanging shawl, the burning scent of jasmine, the roses, and the carnations made it look more like a bordello than a wake. My body was as stiff as Randy's at this point. I wanted Ma and Veena to end their banter with the sheriff and allow me to escort the officers out of the van.

"The funeral home will be here any moment," Veena added.

"Okay. Well then," the sheriff said. "Umm, maybe you all could lower the singing a bit." He tipped his hat and nodded to Ma.

I led the men out and walked them back to their patrol car.

When I returned to the van, everyone was laughing.

"Did you see their faces?" Ma looked at me with a sly grin.

I was still shaking.

Danny died a year later. Ma promised she would take care of him too. He instructed his caregivers that he wanted to be with Ma when his time came. They hadn't counted on him dying in his home in West Palm Beach. The caregivers carried Danny out of his house, loaded his body into the RV, and pulled out of the driveway. A neighbor watching from the window called the police.

My mother, Veena, and I met in Ma's private rooms to prepare for Danny's memorial. Veena paced across the leopard carpet. Ma was seated at her desk.

"Ma, we just received a call from Danny's caregiver," Veena said.

"They put out an APB on the RV and it got stopped heading north on I-95. The body was confiscated."

"What do you mean? What about my Danny? I promised him I would take care of him." Ma's eyes shot back and forth.

"They won't release the body until they do an autopsy."

"How long will that be?"

"At least a day, maybe two."

The next day, Danny's body was released to his caregivers and he was laid on the same bed as his lover previously had been. A group of women washed and prepared his body.

I stepped into the van. "Namaste, Ma," I said, placing my hands together.

"Look at this," she said, touching the top of Danny's head.

At first, I thought she was doing something spiritual. Her fingertips circled his head like she was about to open a jar. She wiggled the top of his head back and forth.

"When they autopsied him, they sewed the flap of his crown back on, but it wiggles." She chuckled as she moved the toupee-like part of his head up and down.

I stared at her and shook my head. My mother paled.

"Veena, you need to tell people not to kiss his forehead and just touch his feet." Ma wiggled his head again and chuckled. "Ah, how I love death."

The image of Danny's flaccid scalp was forever imprinted in my mind.

In Swami Rudrananda's book *Spiritual Cannibalism,* he wrote, "Consume life whole and eat it like an apple."

Ma would repeat the teaching and tell us to consume life or life would consume you. I believe that there is truth to living life fully, letting go of things that no longer serve you, and living a life of kindness and compassion. I still think that being open, vulnerable, and in touch with one's feelings and humanness is equally important for growth and transformation.

When Ma told us not to be self-indulgent, though, there was an unspoken message that we should not dwell on our personal feelings, emotions, or experiences. Somehow, it would not help us on our path to enlightenment.

21

Wake Up Dead

THE TEMPLE WAS DARKER THAN USUAL. I could tell Ma was in a mood. I took a deep breath and settled into my cushion.

"Die! Die! Die!" Ma chanted. I stole a glance at the statue of Kali. She looked fiercer and blacker than usual. She seemed to come alive as Ma chanted. White plaster skulls lay scattered at her feet; their hollow stares reminded me of my own impermanence. There was never a day or night that went by that death wasn't present in the teaching or my consciousness.

"Wake up. Wake up, dead." Ma's voice was sharp.

Oh yeah, it's going to be a good night. I adjusted my meditation cushion, remembering the moonless puja night around the fire when Ma had first spoken those words. Arlo Guthrie, who'd been in attendance, took the words and wrote a song about it.

Ma turned slowly, her eyes searching. Ma, like the Mother Kali, wore a long strand of skull malas[1] carved from yak bone around her neck. Her long, black mass of hair exploded around her. Her gaze landed on the man seated next to me.

"Kailash, you are slimy and insincere. Get real," Ma told him.

My throat tightened. *Ouch.* I liked Kailash. His shoulders slumped.

Ma leaned forward. "Get it together and die already. Do you understand?"

When Ma killed us, or we were admonished for our indiscretions, the rest of satsang retreated from the person whose ego was being disemboweled. They became the proverbial runt of the ashram litter. Having the ego sliced away publicly was a bit like having the headlights of a car shine on you while you were going to the bathroom on the side of a road.

He nodded. "Yes, Ma."

I cringed at his response, a bit oily and wimpy. I was hyperaware of the tone of voice any of us used to speak to Ma. Too familiar—expect to be killed. Too cocky—expect to be killed. Too self-indulgent—expect to be killed. Try to be funny with her, well, that was a crapshoot. Some days it was okay, and other days, not so much.

And then there was the saccharin-infused, singsong voice, "Ohhhhh Maaaa, thank you soooo very much."

This would be accompanied by a gesture like a gentle clasp of the hands at the heart and a glassy, wide-eyed gaze with a slight tilt of the head. This was clearly sucking up.

"I asked Baba to send me the worst of the lot. And here you are. I will free you of your unworthiness. I will free you of your attachments. I will slay your ego so you can be free from your small selves."

I remained upright, not moving a muscle. The air around me was thick as Ma sat ever so still on her couch. The three lines of white painted across her forehead became stark against her ever-darkening skin. Her black top and pants mimicked Kali's skin. Her eyes stared out like the fleshless skulls in the back of the room.

The labels of your lesser personality traits often stuck, and even when you found yourself back in the good graces of the guru, they were hard to shake. It was like when you say something about someone that is harsh or mean, it is often difficult to take those words back. And so it was with each of our ego deaths. I used to joke about the number of times I'd been killed by Ma. The closer you were to her, the hotter it got.

"Death is nothing but an interruption, a hesitation. My children, you need to be prepared for your death. There are many choices during the process of dying." Ma paused.

The beating in my heart pulsed in my ears. Playful Ma was not in the temple tonight. The itch on my foot would have to wait. When Ma taught, she demanded our stillness.

"You don't want to disrupt the flow of Mother Kundalini." Ma was serious about our liberation, and any movement in darshan might be followed by a swift sword to the throat. And yet we wore our ego-death killings like badges of honor.

"The flames of Mother Kali's tongue will burn away what you do not need." Ma's teeth gleamed. She hadn't moved an inch for almost a half hour now. "There are choices in death. It's a vast journey we are on, wild, and filled with love and, yes, my children, so much power. And riding along with you on this journey is the mind. If you don't work through your samskaras[2] this life and reconcile the habits you repeat lifetime after lifetime, you'll just have to come back and do it all over again next lifetime."

Shit, my foot had fallen asleep. The burning sensation increased. I wiggled my toes under my shawl, peeked at Ma, and then eyed my notebook. I knew attempting any notes tonight would be instant death. I'd need to find someone to transcribe the tape to recall these pearls this night.

I thought about all of my conditioning and bad habits that had become ingrained and been repeated over and over like the grooves on a record. My need to thoroughly transcend my samskaras in this life had resulted in a desire for perfection in my spiritual development and in everything I did.

"If you get quiet, you can smell the scent of your own body burning on the funeral pyre. Light your own fire and let the flames burn your egos."

I took a deep breath in. The earthy smoke of Nag Champa incense thickened in my nose and filled my throat, accompanied by the image of my body burning in the cremation grounds. Ah, how I loved this death stuff.

Ma promised me we would go to India together and visit the cremation grounds. We would meditate on death with Mother Kali herself. I longed for the day I'd travel to India.

"You don't need to worry, my children. Close your eyes, my children, and let me show you what death will feel like." Ma's voice dropped.

Thank God, she was going to take us into a deep state of meditation. I closed my eyes. My shoulders rolled back and down, my chin tucked a bit, and my breathing slowed.

"Focus way over the head; breathe in the breath. Feel the spirit, like smoke rising."

"Let go, my children. This is what you live for."

My body vibrated. The top of my head tingled. Heat rose from the base of my spine and up my back. My insides were on fire, and my skin was hot. I felt lost in the space. My body was light and floaty. I barely heard her words any longer. Yet I was aware; my breath guided to where it needed to be. The long pauses between Ma's words led me into a delicious silence. The essence in the room thickened around me, and I sank deeper and deeper into the space.

Ma whispered, "*Samadhi* means uniting with everything that is, everything that will be, and becoming total bliss. Remember, death is only an interruption of life."

The room remained exceptionally quiet.

"Death, I call you to me. In this space of love, you must be acknowledged. In this space of love, the fear of death disappears."

Her words were poetry leaking into my soul. Why would anyone fear death if this was what death felt like?

Ma clapped her hands and whipped us back into the present space. I resigned myself and opened my eyes. Ma's face looked distorted, like a Picasso painting. There was a haze all around her, she was fading in and out, and looked as if she was about to disappear into the abyss of nothingness. I felt like I was tripping on acid.

I closed my eyes again, feeling like my whole being was rearranged. My cells were charged by a thousand volts of electrical current.

When I opened my eyes again, Ma was looking at me. Love and fear existed in the space around Ma most of the time. She had a great capacity to draw us to her and love us with what I thought was her unconditional love. If she saw something in us that needed to change, she was a ferocious mother bear clawing it out of us. Very few were excused from being publicly eviscerated by Ma. Did I grow from these experiences? I think so.

Ma acknowledged and praised my strengths, which elevated and lifted me. But my individuality, my own fiery independent spirit, was often targeted by my "deaths" at her hand.

If Ma threw a fit about something, it would be excused away with, "Remember, Ma is like a child," or "We aren't holding Ma," or "Ma is working with our karma," or "We just aren't willing to die and live in our higher selves."

One evening darshan while Ma was teaching, I saw movement on the other side of the tall picture window. I watched as a rat ran up the drain spout outside. I clutched my pillow. I wasn't the only person in the satsang who noticed, either. Another rat scurried up behind the first. This wasn't going to be good. Ma hated rodents. Ma, unaware, continued teaching the class. A third rat followed. A scene from *The Pied Piper* eclipsed my mind. Someone in the back of the room gasped. *Damn*. Ma looked around and noticed many of us were no longer present. Our gaze was fixed on a point beyond her.

"What's wrong? What's going on?" Ma turned her head to see what we were all captivated by. She turned back to us. "If this is how you take care of the guru, you all better take a good hard look at yourselves." Then she stood up and stormed out of the room.

Most of us sat stunned. Part of me felt totally responsible for our lack of caring for the guru and the other part of me felt utterly confused. I am not a fan of rats, but they were, after all, outside, and Ma wasn't in any danger from them.

A few minutes later, someone came out from Ma's rooms and explained how we had let Ma down. We were not taking care of the guru. And so, we learned that somehow, if Ma felt like she wasn't being cared for, we were responsible.

22

Sympathy for the Devil

Sampuran had requested Ma see a parent of one of the students living at his ashram.

"Namaste. *Satnam*. I'm Krishnapriya, and I'll be taking you to see Ma." The parent was a marshmallow of a woman, white, pasty, and a bit squishy. Her turban was wrapped around her head so tightly, it pulled her face up and pushed her cheeks out.

"*Satnam*, thank you, yes, okay." She bowed her head and rose.

I escorted her out the back door and through the wooden gate into Ma's inner sanctum. The gate creaked as it swung open. I needed to tell someone to fix that. The woman tugged at her white tunic. Her eyes darted from side to side.

"Ma will see you in the Lion Kuti. This is where she sees guests," I explained, as we walked from the relative safety of the temple into a junglelike garden area surrounded by a six-foot wooden fence. The narrow path was lit with little pagoda lamps peeking up from the ground every few feet. I opened the screen door and entered the screened-in deck. Ghostly skulls painted across the wooden structure might make one a bit hesitant, so I delivered the Kali 101 speed tutorial as we approached the door.

"The skulls represent the death of our ego," I said, as she glanced above the entryway, where a spectral-gray clay image of Kali's head with her tongue lolling stood guard like a gargoyle sentry atop an ancient building. I knocked on the wooden door and entered the small black and red room. My mother, Veena, and a few of the other girls were seated around the temple.

"Namaste, Ma. This is Mohinder." I guided the woman to a spot on the floor.

Mohinder's head swung from wall to ceiling to Ma. Whenever anyone entered this space for the first time, it took them a moment to adjust to the chaos of the room.

"How do you like my ashram?" Ma asked.

"It's quite beautiful. A paradise. The temples are astounding. And peaceful."

Mohinder didn't appear too wacky.

Ma smiled and leaned forward. "Tell me about yourself."

"Thank you for taking care of my daughter," Mohinder said. Her moon face was the color of silly putty.

"I love your daughter. Now, what about you? Who hurt you?"

"I am not well. I don't know what is happening to me. I have been sick for a long time. I can't get better." Her shoulders slumped.

"What do you mean?"

"I feel darkness inside. It's eating at me. My skin crawls. I feel ill. I have a rash all over my body." Mohinder's body trembled, and she shook as she spoke. Her eyes became empty and dull.

A cool shiver rose up my spine.

"Okay, let's help free you of this. I want you to look in my eyes. I will take some of the pain and darkness from you." Ma explained about her power to take people's pain.

A dark aura passed overhead and through the room. *Did I just imagine that?*

Ma grabbed the phurba, a Tibetan dagger of protection, that was tucked in the seat cushion, and then she leaned back.

Uh-oh. We have a problem. Any time Ma grabbed the phurba, it was a sign that there was something dark and nefarious at play and the need for additional protection was necessary.

Ma stared into Mohinder's lifeless, protruding eyes.

Mohinder fidgeted. She broke eye contact within seconds.

"Don't back away; keep your eyes open." Ma's tone was a bit sharp.

They tried again. Mohinder leaned back and pulled away, her eyes averted. She wouldn't look at Ma and put her head down, offering an odd stare at the floor. Her shoulders hunched forward.

The room closed in around me, and I felt like I was being squashed into the back of a crowded elevator. My breath caught. I inhaled to capture it back.

Mohinder's head shook back and forth. It picked up speed. She wanted no part of whatever Ma was doing.

"Relax, darling," Ma said, sitting up erect. "I am going to talk to what's in you." She placed her hand on Mohinder's forehead. "Press into my hand."

Mohinder leaned forward. A low, guttural growl released from her.

Holy shit, she's really not okay. I took a long, deep breath, held it, and then exhaled. My hands balled up. I sat up. My ears pricked. My skin crawled. It sounded like there was a wolf in the room.

"All of you, sit up." I was already there. Ma's half-closed eyes resembled a lizard. It looked like lightning bolts were about to burst forth from those black orbs and reduce anything that moved to ash.

"Breathe in the light and exhale it out into the room." Ma wasn't speaking to the woman any longer. She was speaking to us. I did as instructed.

"Get out of my child. Get. Out. Of my child!" Ma shouted, pointing her finger.

Mohinder sat back and hissed.

I leaned back.

The woman just hissed. Foam formed at the corners of her mouth. She was rabid.

Whoa, no way. My nails gouged into the flesh of my knees. My legs and feet were numb from sitting in half lotus for so long, but I didn't dare move. A slithery sensation ran up my back.

"I command you to leave. The light is too powerful in this place. You are nothing here!" Ma's voice thundered.

Mohinder's head thrashed from side to side. Her body flailed. The words from her mouth were unintelligible. Her tongue lolled. She started to roll on the floor, and she barked. She sounded like an animal with its hind leg caught in a trap.

"Sit up. I command you to sit up," Ma said.

Mohinder sat up.

Ma pointed the phurba at her. "In the name of my guru, leave this child." Ma's voice shattered the tiny room and ricocheted off the ceiling.

Mohinder stilled. Her chest heaved, rising and falling. Her body no longer undulated.

I unclenched my fists and opened my hands. There was a row of indents in the middle of my palms that glowed a deep purple.

Ma began to talk to Mohinder in a soft, melodic tone. She told her it was okay to let go. "Allow the light in."

Mohinder glared at Ma. She growled and started to shake again.

"Whatever is in you has a strong hold, but you can do this. You can. You have the power in you to get rid of this darkness."

Mohinder rocked her head back and forth. She stopped and hunched over. She reminded me of a hyena.

I wondered if she'd lunge. Her eyes pleaded. She wanted Ma to heal her. She wanted to be freed.

I readjusted my body, so I was able to jump up if need be. An hour had passed. My body was coiled tightly from the tension in the space. Drops of sweat tickled the back of my neck, but I didn't dare wipe them away.

Mohinder's breath shifted, a loud, wheezing sound rattling in the small space, reminding me of my own childhood asthma attacks.

"Good. Good. This is good," Ma said to her. "Relax and slow your breath down."

Mohinder's head dropped. The wheeze was like a hyena or coyote keening in the night.

Ma sat without speaking.

Mohinder's breath slowed and then stopped. It was over. She collapsed and folded onto the floor, headfirst.

No one in the room moved.

Finally, Mohinder lifted her head. Her eyes were vacant, her face ashen.

"Are you okay, child?" Ma asked.

"I think so." Her color was returning.

"I love you. Everything is going to be okay."

"Thank you."

Ma touched Mohinder's forehead but didn't hug her, which was unusual. Ma hugged everyone.

I didn't take my eyes off Mohinder. She appeared lighter. I brushed my damp hair out of my face, wiped my forehead with my sleeve, and took some long, deep breaths to relax the tension in my body. I felt like I was a supporting actress in the latest Wes Craven movie, and I had a strong dislike of horror flicks.

"I'll see you in darshan," Ma said to Mohinder.

Mohinder mustered a numb, robotic response. "Thank you, Ma."

I stood and escorted her back to the temple. Funny, I never thought twice about being alone with her in the dark.

When I returned, Ma was still seated. She lifted her arms. Her shirt was drenched with large, wet rings. "That, my children, was pure evil. You just saw Ma perform a full-on exorcism. It's been many years, right, Veena?"

Veena nodded and offered a wicked smirk as if she'd just eaten the most delicious two-hour scene for dinner.

Ma licked her lips and smiled a twisted smile. "I used to do them all the time in the early days, remember?"

"Yes."

"That woman had enormous darkness in her. I got it out, but she needs to do the rest. She allowed it to take over. She is attached to it."

"Ma, how does someone get attached to the darkness inside of them?" my mother asked.

"Well, Shody, it's almost as if she enjoys it. It has become part of her. It's hard to get rid of something you have grown comfortable or familiar with. You guys just need to remember if someone comes at you with darkness, all you need to do is point at them and say, 'In the name of Christ, who are you?' Or call out the name of whomever you believe strongly in: Mother Kali, Baba, or Ma. Just make sure you say it with conviction. The darkness will back down from the light."

Ma extended her arm and pointed her index finger to demonstrate. "Go wash your hands in cold water. Whenever you come in contact with negativity, it's important to wash it away. Water is healing and grounding. And there will be less puja for Ma to do for each of you. This way, you can help Ma absorb some of the darkness without letting it stick to you."

We washed our hands and waited for Ma in silence, each deep in our own thoughts. I shook off the images in my head. I hoped I'd never meet that kind of darkness again, but at least I'd know what to do.

23

Who Hurt You?

I FINISHED THE ANNOUNCEMENTS and returned to my seat. The temple was packed with people for Saturday darshan. Once Ma settled in, kids came up and received their lollipops and hugs. Then I shuffled up a few guests to greet Ma. The last one was a student of Amrit Desai, a sweet spiritual teacher who had recently fallen from grace. I loved Amrit Desai. He was a wise teacher. He had made the unfortunate mistake of sleeping with one of his students. It was his downfall. Kripalu, the organization he'd founded, kicked him out and refused to give his body of teachings. He relocated to North Florida and came to visit Ma.

I guided the man up the steps to Ma's couch, leaned over, and whispered in Ma's ear.

"Ma, this is Joseph. He's a student of Amrit Desai." I had briefed her earlier that Joseph, a rotund, portly gentleman, had made his fortune in construction. He was a devoted and loyal student to Amrit Desai and was visiting the ashram on his guru's behalf to see about using it for an upcoming yoga workshop.

Joseph bowed his head and looked into Ma's eyes. "Hi there, Ma, nice to meet you. How are you doing today?" He handed her a bouquet of flowers.

My eye twitched, and I stood at attention. I had expected him to be versed in guru protocol. I went over to him, ready to help him up, when Ma raised her hand. I sat back down.

"Who hurt you?" Ma asked.

He looked confused. "I'm sorry, ma'am?"

"Who hurt you? You are in pain," Ma repeated.

"Aren't we all hurt by someone?" he answered.

I felt myself recoil. This wasn't going well. The awkward interaction was playing out in slow motion.

"Would you like to get rid of some of this pain?" Ma asked.

He laughed just a bit too loudly. "Yes, ma'am."

Ma perched on the edge of her seat, licked her lips, and took a sip of Perrier. She leaned forward. "I was given a gift on the banks of the Ganges, a gift to take the pain of others, a gift from Mother Kali herself."

Good, this is good. Ma is going to take care of him.

"Do you know anything about my Mother?" Ma asked.

He shook his head.

"Turn around and look at her."

He gazed toward the back beyond the hundreds of people sitting in the room. The Kali statue stared back, shining black, red blood dripping from her fangs and bone-white skulls hanging from her neck.

"Isn't she beautiful?"

He swallowed and sort of nodded before looking back at Ma.

She grabbed his hands. "Look into my eyes."

He followed her instructions.

"Do you feel this?"

He nodded his head up and down.

"What do you feel?"

"Energy."

"This is Shakti. This is The Mother. Now, give me your pain, let it go, let me devour it."

He didn't move a muscle.

"Your guru loves you very much," she continued. "You are devoted to him. He's lucky to have you."

The interaction was completed in minutes, although I felt like it had taken an eternity.

"Come stay with me. Send Amrit my *pranams*[1] and tell him my ashram is his. I love you, son. Now give me a hug." She opened her arms and wrapped them around his bulk.

I helped him up.

"Namaste, my children." Evening darshan commenced.

"When I go nuts, the Shakti goes wild. You are all allowed a certain amount of wildness in your life. Go wild with me. No matter how I react. I'm reacting that way not because I need to react that way but because you need me to. It's all for you." She gazed into the darkened room.

I looked around and saw a few nods of perceived understanding.

"Everything that occurs, any reaction I have, it's all for you. The Shakti is alive, she is in you, she is around you, she calls to you. Drink it, suckle it."

The air was thick. Everyone was still.

"We are all karma yogis. We practice selfless service. We serve and serve and never burn out. My kids take care of the dying. Those who work in my office and on this sacred ashram never draw lines. They take care of The Mother." Her eyes came to rest on me. "My daughter works day and night. Ask her what you can do to serve this ashram and take care of this sacred place."

I felt the heat in my body as she looked at me again.

"You need more volume and texture." She gazed at me, and my eyes met hers.

My body went stiff.

"My daughter loves the Shakti. Sometimes it makes her crazy,"

Ma explained, as if I wasn't there. She looked back at me. "If you want to hold the Shakti, you need to become more solid and grounded in yourself."

I sank into my seat. This was big. I needed to get this. She was giving me a key to having more Shakti. "What do you mean? What do I need to do?" I asked, almost pleading.

"I mean just what I said; you need more texture and more volume." She stared at me. "It comes with time and learning. I want you to be the best you can be. I want you to have it all." She was not yelling, nor was she smiling.

Shifting in my seat, I nodded and put my hands together.

"You'll get it eventually. Namaste. I love you, my children." Ma put her hands together, rose to her feet, and left the room.

I stood and wondered—had I failed? Had I done something wrong? Was I not good enough? I tried to make sense out of the message.

I was pulled out of my suffering when I found myself face-to-face with Joseph.

"That was amazing," he said. "I feel like I had surgery on my heart. I feel lighter and more alive than ever." His belly wobbled as he told me about his experience.

I guided him to one of the elders, who would sit with him, and I excused myself and walked back to my mother's office. She was in the hallway doling out Ma's supplements.

Tears welled in my eyes. "What was that about? Is there something I need to do better? Why do I feel so bad about what Ma said? Is she mad at me?"

"No, you're fine. Ma is just fine-tuning you. You are important to her. She wants you to be the best," my mother explained.

"I feel like shit. I feel bad. I feel like I just got creamed."

"Ma only has your best interest at heart."

"I don't get it. Texture, volume. What is she talking about?" I bit my lip.

My mother had to get back to Ma. "Maybe you should sit with it, absorb what Ma is saying. You are trying to overthink it; get out of your head and into your heart. It's okay. Ma adores you." She kissed my cheek and gave me a hug.

I watched her walk with her tray through the door into the inner sanctum.

24

Black Magic Woman

"MA'S ALIVE?" A FARAWAY MALE VOICE ASKED on the other end of the phone.

I leaned my elbows onto my desk. "Um, yes, very much so." The connection crackled.

"I heard she died of a brain tumor."

"She had a temporal lobe seizure but didn't die."

"I need to come and see her."

Phoenix had met Ma in the early days of the teaching. He was living in Thailand now and had read an article about Ma. He was overcome with joy to learn of her resurrection.

He came to see Ma soon after our call and fell in love with her all over again. During the next few years, he commissioned a number of life-size statues for Ma. The first was of Ma's guru, Neem Karoli Baba, and another was of Swami Nithyananda, the Hindu saint who taught detachment. His greatest gift was a five-foot bronze statue of Smashan Kali, the fiercest aspect of the goddess.

The Smashan Kali was installed in a converted shed in Ma's private corral. The shed's interior walls were painted black, and white plaster skulls hung on the walls. It was a small, cave-like temple.

"This Mother is going to change everything," Ma said. "The ashram will grow, and so will our prosperity because of this Mother. My children will learn at her feet. And they better not fuck around with her, either. I want each of my kids to spend the night with Mother in my private temple. Veena, you will stay with The Mother first. This is my gift to you. Shody, make a list of residents to stay in the temple."

Oh, for God's sake, I thought, *another list to maintain.* We had dog-walking lists, phone lists, temple lists, babysitting lists, kitchen-duty lists, monk lists, and now a sleep-with-The-Mother-in-the-temple list.

"There is a ritual one needs to do to spend the night with her." Ma rattled off ten more names. I waited to hear my name mentioned. I wanted to sit with the new Mother.

"She is the Smashan Kali, an aspect of the goddess that dances on your corpse in the cremation grounds."

My heart thumped with excitement. I was already the *pujari*[1] of the Mother Kali that resided in a small temple in Ma's bedroom. Ma said it was one of the most powerful places on the ashram. It was one of the many boons and responsibilities I was given over the years. I picked up my book and made notes about the new Mother's unique attributes.

"Call Sampuran and tell him about Mother. Tell him Ma wants him to spend the night with her. And tell him he is the only nonresident I am allowing to be with her. Because he's my spiritual son."

"Okay, Ma." I talked to Sampuran all the time, but this would be official duty. He often teased me when I called with my business voice.

"She is very powerful. Her Shakti energy is going to make this ashram go through the roof." Ma looked out over her balcony. "You all better not get crazy on me. You all better hold the Shakti. You are all a bunch of Shakti junkies, feeding off the energy. If I give you any more Shakti, you'll be even crazier than you already are." She looked at me. "You, especially."

My grin widened. "I love Shakti. I can handle it. The more, the better."

"You better use it to take care of the ashram."

I nodded. "Of course, Ma." The top of my head vibrated.

"I'll tell my kids about this tonight in darshan. Be back here at five p.m. I'm calling you in early tonight. Only those who want God in the deepest part of their being should sit before her. When you pray to this Mother, she will grant you an experience beyond your wildest imagination. My *chelas* need to know there is a price. The Mother doesn't do cheap. My *chelas* need to be ready to pay up. But my kids have nothing to fear. You have been waiting for this all your lives." Ma's eyes sparkled and darkened at the same time.

I wanted this. I lived for this. I couldn't believe she hadn't put me on the list. *Detach, Krishnapriya*, I told myself. *It's not about you*.

"When my residents spend the night with her, they will be transformed. You will meditate on your own death. And I want you to write down what happens. You are all spiritual warriors. Each of you will feel the power of the Mother Smashan. Her power will protect us."

Eventually, I got the call, and I practiced the rituals necessary leading up to my evening with The Mother. They were precise directions.

I jumped in the shower for the third time. I chanted, "Om Ganesha, Om Shiva, Om Kali," eleven times. I dressed entirely in black. (Ma wanted us to wear only tantric colors—either black or red.) I gathered the things I'd need for the ritual. Into a duffel bag, I stuffed an extra-large, fuzzy white sheepskin, a blanket, my favorite incense, a thermos of rose water, a washcloth, water to drink, candles, and a flashlight. The bag burst at the seams. I lugged it to the car and went back for the vases of flowers I'd bought as my offering.

At Ma's house, I unloaded the contents of my car in preparation for my evening. I dragged the duffel bag to the gate and set it by the door. It reminded me of a dead body waiting to be dumped in the East River.

I disappeared into the house to find my mother and then stood in her doorway in my ninja-like outfit. "Hi, Mom. I'm getting ready to spend the night with Mother."

"Hi, pumpkin."

"I'm heading to the temple—want to walk over with me?" I bent over to pick up the bag.

"What's all that?" she asked.

"It's my stuff for spending the night with Mother. I have already made two trips to the temple with my flower offerings."

She shook her head. "You look like you're planning to stay for a month. Don't forget to be out by five-thirty. Ma will be in the corral early to begin her puja."

The corral was still. The moon was full. The heady scent of night-blooming jasmine was intoxicating. I opened the screen door of the small temple, bowed to bronze Mother, and placed the flowers on the altar at her feet. Then I arranged myself cross-legged on the sheepskin, lit the candles, and relaxed across from the statue of Smashan Kali.

The deity stared back at me. Her black marble eyes drilled into me. I lit a stick of incense and waved it before her. "Om Namah Ganesha, Om Namah Ganesha, Om Namah Ganesha," I chanted.

I reread the instructions Ma had dictated. "First, chant the names of each Mother." I chanted the ten names of the goddess.

The instructions fluttered in my hand. "Three signs of goodness will come to you. Write them down. Wait for the striking hour. This occurs around ten-thirty or eleven-thirty p.m."

I checked my watch.

"Keep a journal, and write down whatever The Mother says. Ask her to speak to you. Ask her how to take care of Ma. And write to Ma and tell her what Mother said to you."

Okay, no problem. I finished reading the last paragraph. "It is okay to sleep, but the Shakti may do either one of two things: knock you out or keep you awake. Pour rose water on your hands as purification and then see if The Mother speaks to you again. You don't need to write this time. Remember to be grateful."

I crossed my legs and directed my attention to the breath—in and out, my chest rising and falling, I followed my breath. It did not take long before I was enveloped in the silence. I noted how quiet it was. My mind hopped around a bit. I lassoed it in and brought my awareness back to the breath. My mind stilled. My body became motionless.

I opened my eyes and stared at The Mother. She hadn't taken her eyes off me. It was as if she was delving deep into my soul. Her chest was moving. Was she breathing? My mind stepped in. *Is this really happening? I can see her breathing. I see her seeing me.* I could not feel my body. I was somewhere else. *Get out of your head*, I reminded myself. *Get back into the moment, or you will lose what is occurring.* I refocused my breath.

I felt myself expand and the walls expanded and breathed with me. The Smashan Mother breathed in synchronized harmony with both the walls and me. I felt one with everything around me. This moment was it. I was having the ultimate spiritual experience with the Mother Kali herself. I watched, seeing it, feeling it, witnessing it. My body trembled with excitement. I was experiencing what every seeker yearned for. I was aware of every moment of the experience. *Go back to the breath*, I reminded myself. An overwhelming understanding of "I am" filled me, along with a complete sense of being-ness. The moment was so clear.

The alarm went off, and I jumped. *Shit*, it was 5:00 a.m.

I bowed down to the black Mother. "Thank you," I whispered.

I looked at my journal. It was blank. What about my three signs of goodness? I picked up my pen and jotted down a few paragraphs. None of it even came close to articulating the depth or essence of what I had felt. I collected my belongings and left the corral.

The images of my full-moon night were fresh in my head, and I was excited to tell Ma about my experience. "Namaste, Ma," I said, grinning as I entered her rooms.

"Namaste, daughter," she replied, peering over her glasses.

"I had an amazing night with Mother last night. It was awesome. She came alive." My enthusiasm leaked into the room. I relayed the details of my experience.

"What did you write? I didn't get an email."

I explained that I'd meditated all night. "I wrote a few paragraphs in the morning," I added.

"That was not the instructions."

I smiled. "I was having an experience unlike anything I'd ever experienced."

"You didn't get it. You didn't follow the instructions." Her pointy chin led as she pulled off her glasses. She wasn't smiling.

This isn't going to be good.

"You didn't do what you were supposed to do. Instead, you allowed yourself to go into the depth of the space."

"But Ma, it was amazing. The Mother was breathing. The space was expansive," I protested.

She glared. "You were supposed to write down what was happening as it happened. You didn't do it right."

I felt like a bean in a pressure cooker with a lid that wasn't on properly. I'd just had one of the most mind-blowing spiritual experiences of my entire life, and I'd done it wrong? I fussed with the pile of papers in front of me. I didn't really understand why I was being killed for having a spiritual experience. After all, wasn't that the point of the spiritual path?

That night in darshan, Ma launched into a teaching about

sitting with Mother. "When I ask you to write down your experience, there is a reason that I do this. There is a reason you dress in the tantric colors, there is a reason you light the candles and offer the flowers." She glared at me with her mouth tight.

No one else in the room was aware of my offense. They sat blissfully, adoring their guru.

I felt that I'd experienced something so real and so profound that staying present with it was the right choice. After all, the entire teaching was about being present.

When I got back to my room, I called Sampuran to tell him the story.

"She was mad because you challenged her authority."

"Maybe. She was definitely mad."

"Here, let me read you an awesome poem. It's by the Persian poet Hafiz. It's called 'Something Invisible.'"

Once I asked my Master,
"What is the difference
Between you and me?"
And he replied
"Hafiz, only this:
If a herd of wild buffalo
Broke into our house
And knocked over
Our empty begging bowls,
Not a drop would spill from yours.
But there is Something Invisible
That God has placed in mine.
If that spilled from my bowl,
It could drown this whole world."

"Wow, that's awesome. What's in the bowl?" I asked.

"It's exactly what you experienced last night," he said.

25

Nothing Else Matters

The summer of 1997 was a transformational time for me. Sampuran and I shared poetry, discussed spirituality, and spoke on the phone on a regular basis. He and his wife had separated a few years earlier and our friendship grew.

Ma left for her summer retreat, and Sampuran and I made plans to hang out.

"You free tomorrow night?" he asked.

I pressed the phone to my ear and grinned.

"I was thinking of coming down."

"That sounds like fun."

"See you around four or five."

"Okay, looking forward to it."

When he arrived, we sat by the river on the benches at the end of the memorial boardwalk, where the names of the dead were etched in the planks. The rattle of the cicadas trembled above the tree canopy in the steamy heat of this particular evening in August. The crescendo of chirping swelled, shaking the inside of my skull, and then the moment surrendered to a silent stillness that impregnated the dense air. The ashram was deserted. A mullet jumped. We talked about God, gurus, and spiritual growth.

"I don't understand why gurus make up the rules they do," I said, as I tossed a stone in the river. "And they surround themselves with awful 'yes' people."

"I love when they send you on ridiculous errands that need to be done immediately," Sampuran added.

"They use the karma card to get us to do what they want or get what they need," I said.

"Or they pressure people to give them money," Sampuran added.

"And then make us grovel when we make a mistake. We have to write an apology letter," I said.

We made lists of the things our respective teachers did to their students and joked that there must be a guru handbook.

"We should compile all the crazy things gurus do to keep their students in line," Sampuran said.

The night quieted as we sat on the bench. I stood to stretch. He leaned over and brushed against me. He stood up. It was so quiet in the woods. He wrapped his arms around me and pulled me in close to him. My senses came alive. Neither of us said a word for a few minutes.

"I've wanted to do this for a long time," he whispered.

My breath stopped. I hiccupped in some air. "What took you so long?" I whispered back. I sank deeper into his embrace.

The mosquitoes arrived, and we walked back to my house, somewhat quieter than usual. I led the way up the stairs to my room. A silky, red Indian scarf draped over the lampshade illuminated the room in a smooth red hue. We sat at the base of my bed on the faux Persian rug. He wrapped his strong swimmer's arms around me. *God, he felt really good. Really good. What was he waiting for? Kiss me already.* I felt the rise and fall of his breath in my ear and found myself breathing in synchronicity with him. For God's sake, what was he waiting for? I rolled toward him. Our lips were a breath away from each other.

He placed his lips on mine. His beard tickled my face as his tongue explored mine. My heart pounded. My body was on fire. *Holy shit, this feels amazing.* We kissed. It was gentle, then harder, then needful, almost desperate. It was dawn before he slipped into the guest room next door. It had been a long time since I'd kissed someone.

I crept down the hall to the bathroom. The image looking back at me in the mirror was quite different than the one I'd seen earlier. My pixie hair was sticking out in all directions. My eyes were darker than I remembered—big, almost black. My cheeks were flushed, and a red rash had formed on my chin.

That morning, we drove to the beach. Saying goodbye was different this day. I'd crossed the line with someone with just a kiss.

During the weeks that followed, my life cracked open. Sampuran and I spoke on the phone almost every night. My heart was full.

We made plans to rendezvous in Melbourne, Florida, at a hotel on the beach. I was nervous and had no idea what to expect of our meeting. I went to the store and picked up a bottle of B&B, brie cheese, crackers, roasted red peppers, and dark chocolate.

I pulled into the hotel parking lot and texted Sampuran to let him know I'd arrived.

There was a ding, and I flipped open the phone. "I'm in room 524."

I knocked on the door. Sampuran opened it, smiling, and I fell into his embrace.

The room was immense. Walking to the sliders, I took in the view of the ocean. I noted the king-size bed.

"I have something with me," he said. "I wonder if you'd like to try?"

"What is it?"

"Ecstasy."

"What does it do?"

"It opens you. Creates a space of expansion." He handed me one of the pills.

I held it up and examined it. I had done lots of drugs. LSD had opened the doors of perception so much when I was a young girl that I'd had to stop when I started reading my friend's mind.

The white curtains flapped in the breeze, and crashing waves roared beneath us. I was always ready to embark on a new experience.

"May the night take us into a place of love and openness," he said, setting an intention for our evening. We smiled and swallowed the pills.

We moved chairs to the window to see the waves lapping at the shore as the sun lowered in the sky to meet the horizon. The scent of the sea surrounded me. If someone could bottle this smell, they could make a fortune. I curled up in the chair.

I became aware of a lightheadedness at first. That feeling shifted as I became enveloped by a fuzzy, woozy sensation and lost in a dreamlike space. My heart began to race. I had experimented with numerous substances growing up, but none had ever felt like this.

"Wow, this is wild. I feel like I'm drifting and floating." I moved closer to him. Like a magnet, I was being pulled toward him. I wanted to kiss him.

He reached out and touched my arm. Tiny filaments of energy coursed through me, entering my veins and surging in my cells. He pulled me into him.

Oh my God, what is going on? I am no longer in control. "God, this feels so right, so perfect," I whispered.

"Yes, it does." He kissed me, a long, gentle kiss. His lips were soft and urgent against mine. His mustache and wiry gray beard caressed my face. My head spun. I lost my balance. I tried to catch my breath, but it was far away. Still entwined in each other's arms, neither of us willing to break the kiss, he guided us toward the massive bed. My body shook from the energy surging through me like the waves below. He kissed me. Slow, easy, and tender. The tempo increased, and the energy increased. It had been so long since I'd felt this intense passion.

As I lay on my back, he was perched above me. I looked up at him looking down at me. His mane of hair fell around his face. He looked like a strong, beautiful lion. His lean torso hovered over me as he held himself in a cobra pose.

"God, you are beautiful. Did I just say that?" I said.

He held himself up by his arms, his biceps strained and bulging from his own weight. "Look who's talking."

"Oh my God, what is happening? I feel . . . so strange. I don't know . . ." I was unable to articulate the sensation I was experiencing. "My body is shaking."

"It's love. That's all. It's just love. Love that is present in the space."

I relaxed. His body lowered over me, and his lips met mine. I felt my body respond in a symphony of sensory overload. "Take them off," I urged, tugging at his underwear.

His head snapped up. "I'm not sure that's a good idea." Sweat beaded on his forehead.

"Please, I just want to feel you against me. I don't want anything between us," I pleaded.

"I'm not sure that's a good idea." He pulled back. His eyes searched mine. I tugged on his underwear. He wiggled out of them. He pulled off my tank top. He helped me slip off my black bikini underwear. His body was soft against mine.

"Oh my God, this feels so good," I moaned. Our hands explored our bare flesh. "Oh my God. You feel so good. I want you inside of me."

I heard a primal growl emerge.

Had I just blurted that out? Wow, this stuff really did make you uninhibited.

His body stiffened. He didn't move. He shook his head.

I begged.

"You know I didn't bring you here for this?" he said.

My body writhed with need. "Please."

"Are you sure?" I watched him search my face for an answer.

"I've never been more sure of anything." I pulled him to me. He waited as if he wanted me to take a moment to consider the implications. I didn't want to consider anything. I didn't even feel any guilt in this moment. He closed his eyes and let go.

He was measured and gentle at first. It had been a long time for me. I couldn't believe this was happening. And then, like two people who'd been famished and starved for years, we feasted. Our bodies slid against each other. We were unrestrained in our love, unreserved with appetites. Time no longer existed. He lowered himself into me. Our bodies trembled and shook. My head banged into the headboard. Fast and slow, gentle and sweet, he pulled out and released himself on my stomach.

He lifted his head and smiled at me. "Are you okay?" He wrapped his arms around me.

My body was still shaking. "Oh my God. I am wonderful. That was amazing."

"I didn't think we would go that far. In my mind, I just thought we'd hang out and kiss a bit." There was a tinge of apology in his voice.

"Please don't apologize. It was amazing. And perfect in every way."

"Thank you." He pulled me closer. "Thank you. It was more than I ever expected. A beautiful gift." His tear dropped on my cheek.

I buried my head in his neck. "Thank you. I've never experienced love like that, ever." My whole being was alive. I was alive.

It was during this time I decided it was time to reconnect with Hanuman. I couldn't tell anyone. I called Sampuran and asked him if he would help me.

We found a park to meet. I saw Hanuman first. I jumped out of the car and ran to him.

I held him tight. "I am so sorry."

"It's okay, Mom."

"No, it's not," I cried.

We agreed to pick up the pieces of our fractured relationship. It was the first time I realized I was mad at myself and angry with Ma. How could I have let Ma get between us?

Fall arrived quicker than I had wished, and Ma returned home. I was swallowed back up into my world, but Sampuran and I talked on the phone every night. We stole away whenever possible. And when I went to Orlando, I made sure to visit Hanuman. I was grateful to have my son back in my life, and I was in love.

26

Doctor, Doctor, Give Me the News

It was October, and I ran down the stairs to wake Ganga Das for school. If he was late again, the teachers would tell Ma, and he would definitely get punished. I ran through the long hall and passed the warren of rooms that was once a garage.

Rapping on the door, I gently opened it. "Ganga Das, get up. You're going to be late," I whispered. "Hey, it's time to get up." I lowered myself onto the mattress on the floor and nudged him. At fifteen, he was lanky and long. His feet touched the end of the bed.

He rolled over and pulled up the covers. Like me, he wasn't a morning person. It was probably all those years I'd worked late and woken the kids up when I got home. We'd cozy up on the sectional and watch David Letterman and sleep until late in the morning.

"Mom, my throat hurts," he moaned.

I put my hand on his forehead. "You feel a bit warm. Stay home today and rest." His head fell back onto the pillow. "I'll check on you at lunch. Go up to my room if you want." I pulled up the comforter and kissed the top of his head. Ganga Das stayed home the following day as well. He camped out in my bed with soup, TV, tinctures, and supplements.

When I came home from work that evening, I brought a dinner tray up with me. "Hi, sweetheart, how are you?"

"Mom, something isn't right." His voice cracked.

"What do you mean?"

"Look at my neck." He pulled down his T-shirt. His throat and neck were swollen like a goiter. It reminded me of our pet boa constrictor after his weekly meal lodged in his neck undigested.

I touched Ganga Das's neck. It was hard.

He flinched and pulled back. "It hurts to swallow."

A lump formed in my own throat. "I'm not sure what this is. Maybe it's swollen glands. Let's go over to Grandmom and see what she thinks. We can have the nurse take a look." I gathered my keys and led him to my Honda. We drove across the ashram to see my mother.

Ganga Das and I entered the living room. My mother was seated on the couch talking to a woman.

"Hi, Mom. I need to speak with you. I need you to look at something." We moved across the room away from the group of people watching TV.

"Show Grandmom your neck."

Ganga Das lifted his shirt, and my mother examined his swollen neck.

"Can Janaki Ma look at this?" I asked.

My mother walked across the room and whispered into the ear of the heavyset woman laughing at the show on the screen.

Janaki Ma had been a nurse for as long as she'd lived on the ashram. She worked at the local hospital. She pressed and prodded Ganga Das's neck. "Maybe it's a virus. Let's get Chandra Devi to look at it," she advised.

My mother called Chandra Devi and asked her to come over. She arrived within minutes and repeated the same examination. "I don't know what this is, but I don't think it's a virus. Let's have him see Dr. Pierone." Dr. Pierone was the local infectious-disease doctor she worked for, who was renowned for his work with people with AIDS.

We got up early the next morning and then waited in a sterile white room. A young, freckled man in a white lab coat tapped on the door and slipped into the room. "Hi, I am Dr. Pierone." He smiled.

I shook his hand.

"Ganga Das, why don't you hop up here and let me examine you."

Ganga Das sat on the table, and the waxy paper crinkled beneath his body. The doctor examined my son's body, his hands working methodically.

"Do you mind lying down?" he asked in a gentle manner and continued his exploration. "Okay, you can sit up now." He offered Ganga Das a hand.

I stood in the corner, feeling useless.

The doctor turned to me. "I'm going to send you guys over to the hospital to get some X-rays. I'll take a look at the results and see if we can determine what is going on."

"When do we do that?" I asked.

"Right now, after you leave here."

I nodded my head and looked at my son.

The hospital was across the street. We checked in and were directed to the second floor. A television rattled overhead. Magazines lay strewn across the table. Fluorescent lights flickered, emitting an unnatural yellowish light. We crunched down on the matted, beige pleather chairs. The smell of chemicals and disinfectants made me gag. A woman with a cast on her leg and a young couple with a child looked as if they were waiting for sentencing.

"Welch?" a nurse with a clipboard called out. She didn't even bother trying to pronounce Ganga Das's first name. It was such a small town, she knew where we were from. We followed her down a long, long hallway. The light faded. The fluorescents flickered above us.

"You can wait here." The nurse pointed to a brown pleather bench outside the radiation room.

"Okay, thank you." I sat as she led Ganga Das away. I picked up a *People* magazine and flipped through it. I tossed it aside, leaned my head back, and closed my eyes. A half hour later, Ganga Das was standing over me.

"I'm done. Can we get something to eat? I'm starving."

We meandered back through the catacomb of hallways and entered the elevator. As the doors to the elevator slid closed, the nurse appeared from nowhere and placed her foot in the doors, forcing them open.

"The doctor would like you to return to his office." She was breathing heavily. A set of X-rays flapped in her hands.

"Are you sure?" I questioned her.

Her face appeared guarded. She was short with wiry, gray hair. The back of my neck tingled. Her foot persisted.

"The doc just called," she assured me.

I stepped toward her. "He's seen the X-rays already?"

"Yes." She looked away, the films behind her back.

"What's going on?" I pressed her.

"I am not at liberty to discuss any results of an X-ray. That is the doctor's job. Please, just go back to Dr. Pierone's office. He'll discuss the results with you." She knew exactly the secret of those films. She removed her foot. Her eyes watered. I watched her until the heavy metal doors merged. The buttons lit up as we descended to the first floor.

Ganga Das held his stomach. "I'm starving."

"Hopefully, this won't take long."

We were back in the doctor's office five minutes later. The receptionist excused herself from the window with a knowing look. Dr. Pierone returned in her place.

"Come on back, guys." He opened the door and escorted us back to the same room we'd started in. "Please have a seat." His hands gestured to two chairs, and he sat in a rolling stool across from us. "I have some concerns. It appears that there is a growth."

I clutched the chair.

"I'd like to schedule a biopsy."

"A biopsy?" My mouth was dry.

"There is some indication that leads me to believe that Ganga Das may have cancer." He was careful, meticulous, and gentle in his delivery.

Don't panic. Don't panic. Don't panic. I took a deep breath and straightened my back against the metal of the chair.

"I have made arrangements for the biopsy tomorrow morning."

"Tomorrow morning?" I squeaked out.

"Once we have the biopsy, we will know more. They are going to remove some of the lymph nodes in his neck. If they are cancerous, then we will need to take the next step," he explained.

Ganga Das listened, his face unflinching.

"It's an outpatient procedure. They administer general anesthesia, extract some of his lymph tissues, and he can leave once he's out of recovery." The doc's voice was even as he walked us through an overview of what the procedure entailed. We received a short lesson about the lymphatic system. He'd call us as soon as he had results.

I stood slowly and shook his hand, offering a weak smile. "Thank you." *Don't cry. Don't cry. Don't cry.* Ganga Das was already at the door. I knew that I needed to be strong and calm. *Be the warrior that you are*, I told myself.

"You okay?" I asked back in the car.

"Yes." His face was pale, and his neck was still swollen. An eerie blue hue accentuated the bulbous thing nested in his throat.

"Let's pick up some food and go home." I looked over my shoulder and backed the car into reverse.

Back home, I settled him into my bed. "I'm going over to talk to Grandmom. Call me if you need anything."

He nodded, chewing his bagel, and aimed the remote at the TV. I closed the door to my room and drove to my mother's house.

"Hey, Mom."

She was hanging up the phone. "Oh, there you are. You're back. How was your visit with Dr. Pierone? Did you send him Ma's love?"

I nodded.

"What did he have to say?"

I choked out the words. "Dr. Pierone thinks Ganga Das may have cancer."

"What? Oh my God. No, no." She put her hands to her mouth, closing off her gasp.

I explained what the doctor had told us. When I was done, she grabbed the blue intercom on her desk and pressed the red button on the wall. "Ma, it's Yashoda." She used her business voice. She only called in when it was very important; otherwise, it was Ma who called out.

I heard Ma on the other end. "What's up, Shody?"

"Krishnapriya and Ganga Das just got back from Dr. Pierone's."

"What happened?"

"Dr. Pierone is concerned, Ma." My mom was cautious and deliberate as she spoke. She picked and chose her words. She was skilled at delivering bad news to Ma. "He scheduled a biopsy for Ganga Das in the morning. They are going to remove some of his lymph nodes." Her voice quivered.

"What are you saying, Shody? What are you saying?" Ma's voice pitched through the pale-blue princess receiver. By this time, I had slid down to the floor, my mind racing, calculating all the possibilities of what was happening.

"Dr. Pierone thinks Ganga Das may have cancer," my mom choked out.

There was a momentary pause and then . . . wailing. "Not my child! Not my child!" She screamed so loudly, the receiver vibrated in my mom's hand. "What the fuck? How did this happen? When is this test?"

My mother answered the easy questions.

My knees were tucked into my chest. I drove my front teeth into my kneecap. I wanted to cry, but I didn't dare.

My mother hung up. "Ma wants us to come in right away."

I stood and we embraced, holding tightly to each other.

"We better go to Ma," my mother said, grabbing the set of keys on her desk.

"Come in, Shody. Is your daughter there?" Ma said as she heard the key turn in the door. She did have owl-like precision hearing at times.

"Yes, Ma. Krishnapriya is here."

"Both of you come in here." She was crumpled in her chair. It made her look smaller than usual. "Okay, tell me everything from the beginning."

I sat on my heels next to her and repeated the morning's events.

"What did Dr. Pierone say? Exactly," she asked. "Did he say 'cancer'? Did he know what kind?" She began flapping her body with every question she fired. "I need to know, so I know what to start praying for." Her nostrils flared.

"Ma, we won't know anything until we get the results of his biopsy," I repeated for the third time.

After we left Ma, my mom and I didn't waste any time. We sucked up our fears and went into battle mode. My mom called a local oncologist, Kabir, also known in town as Dr. Geffen, a longtime friend of the family and a former student of Ma's. He could help us navigate the waters of the world of biopsies, testing, and cancer. Then she called Ma's chiropractic healer from

Martha's Vineyard and discussed supplementation. I surfed the internet until my eyes were bleary, and I called Sampuran to tell him and see what the folks in his ashram did about cancer therapy.

27

Killing Me Softly

"How are you?" I entered my bedroom. Ganga Das was propped up in my double bed as the TV illuminated my room with a bluish hue.

"I'm okay." He sipped on a glass of orange juice.

"Are you nervous?" I sank onto the bed and touched his forehead.

"A little bit," he admitted.

"That makes sense. It's going to be okay." I put my arms around him and held him. "You hungry? You won't be able to eat after midnight."

"Yeah, I am kind of hungry."

"Okay, how about I cook up some penne pasta, fresh sauce, and broccoli?"

"Sounds good."

The next morning, the alarm blared and shook me upright. Light-gray clouds laden with dark, charcoal underbellies puffed across the sky like wisps of cotton candy. A tinge of orange lay low on the horizon in an attempt to shake off the darkness of night.

As I drove, I chewed on a hangnail and reviewed the morning's procedure with my son. We entered the outpatient building and sat in the brown fabric chairs in the waiting room. An old man with a cane sat across from us. He nodded. A woman with a multicolored silk scarf wrapped around her head looked up at Ganga Das and smiled a sad smile.

"Ganga Das Welch," the nurse called out. We followed her to a room with a metal gurney and a thin mattress. "Here's a gown and a bag for your clothes." She handed him a folded, blue cotton outfit. Ganga Das went to the bathroom to change and then handed the nurse the plastic bag with his clothes.

Next the anesthesiologist entered. A thin, reedy fellow, he leaned over and shook Ganga Das's hand. "This will take no time. Before you know it, you'll be floating and never feel a thing."

Ganga Das nodded. The nurse puttered around, preparing the IV. I stood next to Ganga Das, watching each step of the process. "Okay, Ganga, here it goes. Just relax," the anesthesiologist said as he injected the needle into my son's arm and the clear liquid dripped into the line.

Ganga Das began a jabberwocky of incoherent sentences and laughed at his own wit as if he was a witness to an inside joke between him and his drunken mind. I held his hand, more for myself than for him. He faded, lying on the gurney.

It unsettled me. *Please let him be okay. Please.*

He was wheeled away. A nurse pointed me to the waiting room, where I prayed. First, I called on the deity Ganesh, and then I turned to Mother Kali. If any goddess was able to help, it was the black Mother. Her ferocity could eat anything in the way. I stood up. I sat down. I picked up something to read. I tossed it aside.

A nurse in blue-flowered scrubs appeared. "Everything went well. Your son is in recovery. You can go back and see him now."

"Thank you." She led the way through the labyrinth of halls. The recovery room was almost dark with the minimal light accentuating the stainless steel surrounding the bed. Machines hummed in the background. Ganga Das was lying under a thin beige blanket. He stirred, then stilled again. I stood nearby and waited. He roused again and found me through dull, confused eyes.

"Hey there, how are you doing?" I whispered and rubbed his shoulder.

"All right," he mumbled.

"The nurse said everything went well. They removed what they needed for the biopsy. I can take you home soon."

He didn't respond. He'd fallen back asleep.

He woke up again.

The nurse came over, fussing at the table nearby. "Can you sit up, Ganga Das?"

"Ahh. Yeah, I think so." He leaned up on his elbows.

"Do you need help?" I asked.

"No, I got it." He sat up, and I handed him some water. He sipped through the straw.

The nurse came over and handed him his clothes. "I'll help you to the bathroom to change."

Once he was dressed, the nurse put Ganga Das in a wheelchair and wheeled him to the front door. I got the car and reclined the passenger seat, and Ganga Das got in, put his head back, and closed his eyes. He looked terrible. He needed to drink water to flush the drugs from his system. At home, I settled him in bed, and he dozed off.

Now it was a waiting game. I had no idea how long it would take for the doctor to call us with the results. Ganga Das slept. I paced. My mother wept.

The next day, the phone rang.

"Krishnapriya. Hi, it's Dr. Pierone."

"Hi, Doc. How are you?" I asked, not really wanting to know. *Just tell me what the biopsy results show.*

"I've looked over the test results. The lymph nodes read positive for cancer."

I placed my head in my hands.

"Krishnapriya, are you there?"

"Yes, Doc. I'm here. So, what's next?"

He told me it was time to find an oncologist.

"Dr. Geffen is who we will see," I muttered.

"Okay, that's good. I'll call him."

"Thank you."

Ganga Das was sleeping. I placed the phone down and sat on the floor at the end of my bed. I would tell him in a bit.

I called my mother. "The results are positive. Ganga Das has cancer."

"Oh my God," my mother said on the other end of the phone.

"We need to call Kabir. We need to figure out what type of cancer it is. Once we know what type of cancer, we can treat it."

I went over to my mother's to call Kabir.

"We'll need to admit Ganga Das into the hospital. We'll run more tests," he told us.

"When?" I asked.

"I'd like to admit him in the morning."

"Tomorrow?" My voice hiccupped.

Kabir suggested a family meeting at the hospital to answer any questions we might have. I called Sampuran and filled him in on the results.

"Do you need anything?" he asked.

"Can you bring Hanuman to see his brother?"

Ma had suggested that he come. She hadn't seen him since he'd been banished from the ashram and had no idea I'd been stealing away to Orlando to see him.

"Yes, of course. I'll see you tomorrow."

"Thank you. I am glad you'll be here." It would be good to have Sampuran's calm presence.

Ganga Das packed a bag for his hospital stay. Kabir wasn't sure how long we'd be there.

Walking into the main entrance, I trembled. “Okay, here we go.”

We were directed to the third floor, where we both looked around and investigated our surroundings.

A nurse came in. “Hi, Ganga Das, how are you doing? I’ll be your nurse today. And you are?”

“Hi, I’m his mom, Krishnapriya.” I extended my hand.

“I need to ask you both some questions.” She tapped her clipboard.

She went through another series of papers and release forms, checking off our answers. “No, there’s no history of cancer in the family. No heart disease. Oh, well, my grandmother had a heart attack years ago, does that count? Allergies? No.” Her voice dulled as I answered, “No. No. No,” to each question.

After she left, I arranged a small altar on one of the shelves with a photo of Ma and Baba and a small statue of Ganesh.

An older nurse grinned at Ganga Das. “Oh, you sure are cute.”

“And look at those dimples,” the younger one cooed.

Ganga Das flashed them a grin.

“Your brother is coming down with Sampuran,” I told him. “He’ll hang out with you while we meet with Kabir.”

“Who’s coming to the meeting?”

“Ma, Grandmom, Sampuran, and your uncle. I’m not sure who else will be with Ma.”

Kabir popped in to say hello. His frame was wiry, and his ’fro-like salt-and-pepper hair was cropped tight to his head. “How are you, Ganga Das?”

“I’m okay.”

Kabir clasped his shoulder. “I’m good at what I do.”

“That’s good.” Ganga Das smiled back at him.

Kabir sat down next to the bed. “I’ll be with you every step of this journey.” He turned to me. “How are you?”

“I’m okay.”

“Ma will be here at seven. We can go over any questions

you might have, and I'll walk you through the next few days."

"Sure," I muttered.

Hanuman and Sampuran arrived first. I stood up and hugged Hanuman. It was good to hold my son.

"Hey there; you look like shit," Hanuman said to his brother as he approached the bed.

"Thanks. You always look like shit," Ganga Das shot back.

My shoulders relaxed. I looked at Sampuran. Thank God he was here. Just his presence helped release a bit of the bundled tension. "Thank you for coming. Thank you for bringing Hanuman." We hugged. "Ma will be here at any moment."

Hanuman heard me. He was on edge.

"It will be okay," I said to him.

Ma arrived on the floor wearing a tight, low-cut leopard top, her ample cleavage peeking out over the plunging neckline, revealing her chest, leathered from years of sun. Her tight, black, clingy pants were complemented by a gold chain belt. Gold bangles and tattoos adorned both arms, and her long, jet-black hair swayed as she moved. You would never guess her to be a spiritual teacher except for the small, painted, red Revlon dot. If not for the tattoos and dot on her forehead, you might have thought she was old-school Miami Beach.

She seemed more subdued today. No yelling, no shrieking, no pronouncements of arrival. Her face was drawn.

My mom and brother followed behind Ma. A few other students also followed. Ma walked straight to Hanuman, who stood like a soldier. She pulled him into her embrace. "All is forgiven, what is past is past; we start fresh from here." She placed her hands on his shoulders.

"Yes, Ma." He bowed his head and sighed as he stepped back. I wiped a tear with haste. If I let any more flow, it would be a torrent.

Ma hugged Sampuran. "Thank you for coming, my son."

Then she turned to Ganga Das at his bedside. "You are going to be fine. I am doing heavy puja for you."

A nurse directed us to the meeting room. Sampuran, my mother, and I walked alongside Ma. The rest of the group followed behind us. I noted the people in the hall passing us. Eyes locked onto Ma first. No matter what she wore, she commanded attention. Eyebrows rose as they looked at Sampuran. His full, white, flowing outfit and turban were definitely out of place in our small-town hospital. Strangers passed us and held a questioning look as they tried to figure out who the important person was.

We were ushered into a small room, where Kabir and Ma embraced.

"I am trusting you to take care of my child." She finished hugging him and looked at him. It was both a plea and a warning. Kabir sat on the edge of a table like he was about to give a college lecture. The others sat on the beige couches. I sat alone in a chair.

"Ganga Das has a form of cancer called Hodgkin's lymphoma. He has an eight-inch mass in his chest. Some of the lymph nodes in his neck and below his diaphragm are also affected. Hodgkin's is normally a very treatable form of cancer. Ganga Das has a stage-three diagnosis." Kabir's voice was calm, matter-of-fact, and doctor-like. The crevices on the sides of his face deepened. They weren't quite dimples but more like long, deep fissures embedded into his face. His brows were black and bushy, almost a unibrow, and they rose as he explained about the type of cancer my son had.

"What kind of tumor? What kind of treatment? How long will he be in the hospital? How did he get it?" Ma belted out question after question.

He answered the barrage of questions one at a time. "There is no way to tell how he got the disease," Kabir explained. He was unwilling to speculate. "Hodgkin's usually affects boys fourteen to twenty-five, though—"

Ma interrupted his flow. "Will he need chemotherapy? How long will he need it for? How will it affect him?" She fired off the questions in her machine-gun fashion.

God, please just stop asking so many damn questions. Just let him speak. Adjusting my position in the chair, I cringed and looked up from my notebook, willing her to be quiet. My throat shut. My body felt like jelly, but the questions kept coming.

Ma cast her eyes over me. "You know, after she married Chris and had Hanuman, I warned her not to leave me. I told her that her life would be a disaster."

I sat up. How had the conversation turned to me?

"And then she started sleeping with Massimo, his best friend, but the truth is he actually was her true love. God, he was gorgeous. I tried to marry them."

I stuck the pen in my mouth and bit down. *What the fuck?*

"She was sleeping with both of them." Ma's shoulders rose, and she tilted her head. I shrank. Ma postured herself as if giving darshan, sitting cross-legged on the couch. "Then she ended up pregnant and had no idea who was the father was." She lifted both her hands in the air, with an "oy vey" gesture.

I pulled my knees to my chest.

"I prayed for her every day while she was away from me." She jutted her chin toward my mom. "Her poor mother was down here for years worrying about her."

My mother's face was frozen. She looked as if she about to crack, but I knew she wouldn't dare interrupt Ma's diatribe, especially because it was me Ma was addressing.

I closed my eyes, wishing Ma would shut up. *Please stop telling everyone about my past.* My mind flipped through all the stories I had trusted her with. A deluge of tears dammed up just behind my lids. My mouth felt like it was filled with dry crackers. I felt like I was going to throw up. I felt like a five-year-old.

I looked up. Sampuran was the only one whose eyes met mine. I met his gaze and looked away. *Oh God. I can't believe he's hearing this.* I pulled my shirt tighter.

Ma continued her rambling. "Chris was abusive to my daughter.

I tried to help him. I gave him a life, but he couldn't take my love." She lifted her head to the sky.

Please, please stop. My youngest son has just been diagnosed with cancer.

And then it stopped. The silence was met with an even greater silence. No one said a word.

Kabir cleared his throat. "I want to begin treatment as soon as possible. Ganga Das will require at least six months of chemotherapy, followed by six months of radiation."

I remained with Ganga Das in the hospital for a week, calling my mother daily to report on what was happening. She relayed the information to Ma, who solicited worldwide prayer for Ganga Das. Letters and emails poured into my computer screen. I received calls from spiritual teachers and religious leaders.

The phone next to the hospital bed rang.

"Krishnapriya. It is Yogiji. Your son is sick?" His powerful voice boomed into my ear.

"Yes, sir."

"I will pray for him."

"Thank you, sir."

"I love you."

"I love you, too."

Within days, everyone in our world knew. I was grateful that people were praying for Ganga Das. I was terrified something bad would happen. I knew the power of pray would save him. The swamis were given special mantras that they chanted. I, too, was given a special ritual to practice by my son's bedside. A fund was started to help defray the cost of care. We settled into the dull hum of the medical equipment that surrounded us. I slept on a pullout chair. Nurses rolled in a cart and attached several IV lines with chemo drugs. Drip, drip, drip. I swallowed hard as the neon colors entered his veins. Each day, we were wheeled in and out of rooms for tests.

I kept a record of every procedure and conversation that occurred and every medicine given. I read about the side effects from the drugs. I watched toxic yellow laxatives be administered. I held my son's head as he threw up. They'd give him something for nausea. He'd throw that up, too. It was a vicious cycle of meds to counter other meds to counter each symptom he experienced. I refused to cry. I refused to break. Each day, each test, and each injection, I prayed for my son to get well.

Tufts of hair fell from Ganga Das's head and lay strewn across his pillow. It reminded me of my childhood German shepherd's relentless shedding. We shaved his head.

Ganga Das turned sixteen two days before he was sent home from his first week in the hospital. I was scheduled to facilitate a retreat and would speak on the night of our return home. The thought of hundreds of people feeling sorry for me and offering their sympathies overwhelmed me. I packed the bags of cards and well-wishes from the hospital room and returned home to the ashram.

Happy to be back in his room, Ganga Das settled in at home. He dozed in his bed. He was thinner, dark circles formed under his eyes, and his lack of hair made him appear taller. I kissed him good night and went to my room.

A cellular exhaustion hummed through my body. I curled into my bed and fell into a deep sleep.

I woke with a start, the sheets strangling me. The upcoming weekend loomed, haunting my mind. The clock illuminated the time in bright red; it was midnight. I tossed and turned. Time was messing with me again. Red numbers flipped one at a time, *click, click, click*. Sleep became a futile endeavor. I got up and meditated.

Breathing in and breathing out. All I heard was the clicking, the shifting of time, invading my head. Across the room, a large photo of Ramana Maharshi loomed. His dark marble eyes met mine. They penetrated deep into me. Was he breathing? *Please help me*, I asked. *Please guide me this weekend. Please be with me when I speak tomorrow night.* I closed my eyes and finally drifted.

I was not quite awake and definitely not fully asleep when I heard Ramana speak to me.

Be who you are. There is no need to worry. Keep it simple. Follow your heart. Be who you are. Whatever you say will be perfect.

The sound of alligators grunting and the deep-throated squawking of sandhill cranes overhead roused me. Sun radiated into my eastern window through the wooden slats. I slid out of bed.

28

Say a Little Prayer

"You both better listen to what the doctor tells you. None of this natural shit, do you hear me?"

Ahh, Ma knew my mother and me so well. We had already implemented a natural diet. No processed foods, no sugar, and no white flour—only organic foods.

"We are doing everything Kabir tells us, Ma," I said. "And he's fine with us supporting Ganga Das with supplements."

"Make sure you tell him every single vitamin you give my child." Her lips pursed with disdain.

"Yes. I'll let him know." I won that battle.

"You two need to get flu shots, too," she added, baiting me just because she was willing to roll up her sleeve. She knew how I felt about flu shots. I rarely took pain relievers, let alone allowed myself to be injected with some concoction of viruses.

Ganga Das took drugs to help him sleep and shots to keep his blood count up. I fussed with recipes to coax him into eating. My mother bought a juicer and made fresh organic juice each morning.

Two weeks into his treatment, Ma spoke to me in her room after we had finished with morning messages. Sweaty from weight lifting, she placed the dumbbells at her feet and looked at me. "I want Ganga Das to move here, under my roof, where my prayers are most powerful."

I felt a low, guttural growl within me. Ganga Das would freak out. "Ma, I'm not sure that—"

"I don't want to hear it. You want your son to live?" she asked.

I choked back my words. *Dirty pool. How does one challenge that?*

"Tell him it's a matter of life and death. Baba agrees. And don't look at me like that. Oh, you're a little pissed off at Ma. I am doing everything to save your son's life. Do you understand? I don't care if he doesn't want to be here. I am doing it to save him." Ma's eyes narrowed, taunting me—testing me—to see if I'd challenge her.

"I'll speak to him tonight." Ma dismissed me.

I found my mother in the hallway. "I hate this. What is she thinking about taking him out of his room and moving him? His whole life is already in turmoil. Why not just push him all the way over the edge?"

"I will be here at night to check on him, and the office is steps away, so you can check on him during the day."

"This sucks. He's going to hate this." I stormed off into the night. How would I tell him about Ma's edict? He wasn't happy about the move.

I came by every day to give him his supplements. "Mom. How many of these damn pills am I taking?" Ganga Das groaned, popping them down by the handful.

"I know it's a lot, but each one is important."

He was taking almost fifty supplements a day. I brewed some essiac tea. "Okay, we're going to try this tea; it's good for cancer patients and has regenerative properties." I handed him the jar.

"Uukkkk." He spit out the murky fluid. "That sucks." He wiped his mouth.

"Just drink some of it, please."

He guzzled half of it and pushed the rest at me.

The ashram saw its share of healers and supplements and a revolving door of the latest wellness crazes.

Ganga Das was subjected to light therapy and aromatherapy. He was covered with crystals, rubbed by numerous massage therapists, and fawned over by wanton energy healers and Reiki masters. He endured each modality.

A plump healer in a colorless smock top held her hands a few inches over his body. "Now, Ganga Das, feel the energy move through your body. Direct the energy toward your cancer. Ask it to kindly leave your body and return to whence it came." She had a big crystal hanging from her neck that looked like it was going to take out one of Ganga Das's eyes every time she passed her hands over his body.

Ganga Das shot me a look and rolled his eyes. We thanked the smiling woman and took our leave.

He kicked the dirt as we walked home. "Really, Mom. Was she for real?"

"Okay, well, we tried. We don't have to go back to anyone you don't feel comfortable with."

"Thank God. She was weird."

Mostly he was patient with all of our healing attempts, though.

"I made an appointment for you with Ma's chiropractor. He'll do an adjustment and maybe recommend different supplements."

He shrugged his shoulders. "Yeah, okay."

Dr. Versandahl was a chiropractor and proponent of a well-known supplement company. He and Ma had hit it off right away. He promised her good health and well-being and offered her special weight-loss supplements.

Ma encouraged the satsang to make an appointment with the new chiropractor. Ma always joked with us that we were the biggest hypochondriacs on the planet.

The following day was our appointment with the chiropractor. We waited in the kitchen until we were called in.

"Hello, my boy. How are you today?" The doctor whomped Ganga Das between his bony shoulder blades.

I glared. He was just a bit too enthusiastic for me.

"Here, here," he said, "now just lie on the table and let me take a look at you."

I took a seat in the chair nearby, perched with a pen and paper in hand. He cracked and popped Ganga Das's skeletal frame like he was tenderizing a side of beef with a ten-pound mallet.

"Darling, I have something that will help this young man heal his cancer." He lifted his head from his adjustment and met my eyes.

I perked up. Maybe he had a new supplement that would help Ganga Das's healing process.

"Oils. It's all about oils. What he needs is to have his internal body lubricated."

He had my full attention. I reviewed my memory bank for good oils: flaxseed, omega-3s, cod liver oil, cold-pressed oils. "What type of oils do you recommend?"

"Almond Roca. What he needs is Almond Roca." The doctor clasped his hands.

"I'm not sure I understand."

"Almond Roca. Give him as much as he wants. The oils will lubricate his insides and help cure him of cancer."

Ganga Das sat up, and the doctor patted his back. "Yes, this here young man will be as good as new in no time."

Did he just prescribe a toffee and almond candy dipped in chocolate and rolled in a ground almond coating? My teeth hurt.

The doctor rambled on about oils, and Ganga Das moved to escape his clutches.

"Are you ready to go?" I motioned my head toward the door.

Ganga Das was on my heels. "What's wrong, Mom?"

"Almond Roca? Really? That's insane. I can't believe this

guy just prescribed candy to you. What an asshole thing to do."

I tracked down my mother and found her sitting at her desk.

"Hi, babe. How'd it go?"

I stood in her doorway with my hands on my hips. "He wants Ganga Das to eat Almond Roca. The oils will cure him."

"He prescribed Almond Roca to Ma as well. He told her she would lose weight, eat chocolate, and get her essential oils."

"What bullshit." I threw my hands up in the air.

"We'll be called into Ma's room early tonight. Just be on time. She's made mention of your being late."

"Right, because I have nothing better going on." I tossed my arms up. "I need to take Ganga Das to the doc for his shots. I'll be back in time."

When I arrived at Ma's rooms, the doctor had told her his prescription for Ganga Das.

"Have you given Ganga Das his oils?" Ma asked with a mouthful of chocolate leaking out the corner of her mouth.

"No, Ma." I watched the chocolate fall out onto her lap.

"You know, Dr. Versandahl is very important. He takes care of your Ma." Her eyes locked on me. "You need to do what he tells you to do."

I bit the inside of my mouth. "Ganga Das isn't doing any sugar right now, Ma." I knew I was treading on thin ice.

"Are you saying you know more than the doctor?" She stopped chewing and looked up at me. "Go out, buy the damn Almond Roca, and give it to him immediately." Her lips were pressed together so tightly, every wrinkle in her face popped. "This is an eminent doctor, and if he thinks that this will help Ganga Das, you need to look at it. Maybe there is something more to it."

"Ma. It's candy, processed sugar—"

I was met with her palm and cut off mid-sentence. "This is karmic. It's all karmic. Everything I do is karmic. You have no idea what I am doing. Do you understand I am working through this doctor? So end it now."

I swallowed hard.

"I want you to stop being negative this second. Your negativity will stop me from healing your son. Do you hear me?"

Without waiting for me to acknowledge her question, she looked across the room at my mother. "Do you?" she asked.

My mother nodded. "Of course, Ma."

"I will cover it," Ma added to make me feel better. "Krishna Bai, send someone to get me more Almond Roca today. And make sure she gets a box to give to her son."

I stormed home, tears blinding me as I trudged through the woods. Almond Roca for oils. I knew this was bullshit. Karmic or not, I didn't care.

The following day, I knocked on Ganga Das's door. "Hi, it's me."

"Come in." Ganga Das was lying on his bed.

"I need to give you one of these to say we did it, okay?" I handed him the pink-and-gold-wrapped candy.

He unwrapped the confection. It had been months since he'd had anything processed. "Wow, this is nasty." His nose wrinkled. He leaned over the garbage can and spit it out.

"Great, well, now I can say you had it."

He smirked. "I guess I won't be going back to Dr. Whosy-whatsy."

"Nice, Ganga Das." I pushed his shoulder. It was bony. "You need to eat; you've lost more weight."

"I know, Mom. I'm trying. I'm just not hungry."

"I know, sweetheart, but it's important. It will help you get strong." I kissed his forehead and swept my hand across his shiny, hairless crown. "I need to go. I'm going to get called into Ma's rooms soon. I'll check in with you later."

I raced over to Ma's rooms.

"Namaste, Ma." I walked into her rooms. There was a rim of chocolate around the corners of her mouth. Almond pieces rested on her chin.

"Did you give Ganga Das the Almond Roca?"

"Yes, Ma."

"If you need more, let me know. Here, have some. *Prasad*."[1] She handed me a piece of candy. There was no way to avoid accepting *prasad*. *Prasad* from the guru was a gift, a blessing from her lotus hands. Ma watched as I popped it into my mouth. The toffee stuck to my teeth. It was so sweet that my mouth revolted. I chewed with long, deliberate movements. I did not want to be offered another.

Devotees ran out to buy Almond Roca for Ma, but it soon was impossible to find any in the entire county. Through the grapevine, students were told about the new method for lubricating your internal organs with oils. Boxes and cans of Almond Roca arrived from around the country.

I knew that this fad would pass, as did many of the healing remedies and cure-alls that came and went in our teaching. Some had validity, while others like this lacked any standing or reality. They were, in my opinion, about as genuine as snake oil.

Dr. Versandahl eventually faded from our lives. Ma never did anything in moderation, and the doc hadn't counted on that. She gained twenty pounds using his protocol.

While Ganga Das was sick, Ma became singularly focused on his illness. Each night, she spoke about his fight to survive night and day. She told us how hard she was praying for him. She told everyone to pray for him. She made anyone who was visiting the ashram pray for him. And I was grateful that she raised money for his medical bills. Part of me was also thankful for her interceding with God on our behalf. I wanted nothing more than for Ganga Das to be healed. Ma claimed she and she alone would work day and night to barter with the gods and goddesses for his life.

But part of me wanted to hide from all of the attention we received.

It was as if Ma gained energy from his illness. It was about her pain, her anguish, and my son's illness. I took care of him physically, but Ma held him up on display like a pet. She owned him and his disease. At times, I was driven mad by her blatant appropriation. But I was willing to do anything for him to be well.

29

Paint It Black

GANGA DAS RETURNED TO SCHOOL, and I returned my focus to ashram business. Ma was about to launch a new chapter in our teaching.

The alarm went off for morning darshan. I rubbed my eyes awake. I was never a morning person.

Once we were gathered, Ma said, "Namaste, my children. Swami Muktananda had a peacock feather, Sai Baba manifested *vibhuti*[1] out of thin air, and there's that woman who hugs everyone. What's her name? Every holy person has a shtick." She was leaning toward us as she ticked off a list of yogic masters and their special powers, called *siddhis*.

"I paint. That's how I take on karma," she explained. "I am going to change the face of the ashram. Each of my *chelas* will have a chance to sit before their Ma while I paint them a painting and take their pain."

Thursday nights became the designated night for Painted Kali Reading darshan. People sat before Ma, and she looked deeply into the eyes of the person before her. We asked questions that burned our souls. We revealed our deepest fears and freed ourselves from karma, as she painted a personalized aspect of the goddess Kali before us.

One such night, a few people who'd been given specific jobs to assist Ma in her new endeavor prepared the area for Ma to paint. Brushes and paints were laid out, Ma's couch was covered to protect it, and canvases were set nearby.

Ma arrived dressed in her paint clothes: black leggings and a black, long-sleeved T-shirt. "Namaste, my *chelas*," Ma screeched as she entered the room.

A middle-aged woman stood up to tie Ma's apron around her back. This was her particular boon. Another student was responsible for handing Ma a canvas and the correct size paintbrushes at Ma's request. Another member of the art team offered her a squirt of hand cream before the next set of rubber gloves was slipped on. This member would also catalog and write down everything that transpired between Ma and the person receiving the painting.

Boons came in many forms. Each was taken very seriously as a means of being closer to the guru and serving her personally.

"Well, kids, another night in this temple of ours. So many years, so many pujas."

I adjusted my pillow. It was going to be a long night.

"Each paint stroke is karma in action. Each word uttered is a prayer for you to heal. Each painting is a meditation tool. It is time my kids have more of their Ma. Order your paintings from the office and get on the list."

People sat and waited in the temple for their name to be called. Some had a list of questions; others would wing it.

"All of my residents need to order a Painted Kali Reading." The $250 price tag didn't deter all of her students.

"Okay, who's first?" she asked, tapping her red nails on the varnished wood of her chair. Hands shot up in the air. She pointed to a tall man seated in the middle of the room. He crept up toward Ma in an almost crawl to the front of the room and sat before her.

"Well, now, aren't you brave?" Ma said to her longtime *chela*. He grinned back at her. She put the brush to the canvas and began to speak to him. "When are you going to give up your attachments and stop hiding?"

"I don't know, Ma. Now?"

"Good answer." She chuckled. Her hands moved the brush around, swishing reds and blacks across the canvas. This guy had not come prepared.

I made a note in my book. I had stacks of moleskin leather books with teachings and reminders. Someday I planned to go through them.

"You need to get your act together. You need to serve this ashram." Ma looked up from painting for half a second, and her eyes darkened. Then she went back to work. The man's back and shoulders slumped. Ma added a few final swipes to take any residual karma and held up the painting. The small, square canvas oozed with red and black paint, the excess dripping into a pan that was held by yet another person whose boon it was to catch the left-over paint.

I stared at the dancing goddess with fangs dripping blood from her mouth, and a golden halo around her head was illuminated for the satsang to see. There was a collective murmur of "ooohs" and "ahhhs" that filled the room.

"What do you think, Shody?" Ma asked, turning the canvas toward her.

My mother smiled from the corner of the room and murmured, "It's lovely, Ma. Very beautiful."

Ma nodded with a broad grin. Five more people were called to the front, one by one. Some *chelas* were given meditations. Others were loved up, and some were given new ashram jobs or boons.

I heard my name called, and I scrambled up. I was a bit nervous.

Ma grabbed a brush. "What do you want?" She pointed her brush at me.

"God," I said without hesitation.

"You were born to be at my feet." Her eyes remained locked on mine as her brush swirled, scraped, spun, and dug into the canvas. She wasn't even looking at the painting.

Have you ever played the staring game with a dog? You lock eyes with the dog and see who'll break away from the stare first. I remember as kids we were told the dog could always outstare you. It was like that with Ma this moment. I was unable to look away.

"All you need to do is hold on to the feet, serve the ashram." My head swirled like the brush. "You are Kali's daughter, you are my daughter, and your heart is so big."

Ma's words danced in my head, spinning and twirling. The top of my head tingled, and heat coursed through my pores. Ma held her brush up in the air, like a conductor drawing the final notes to a close. She lifted the goddess up and held it in front of me. "Look into her eyes, watch the paint drip, and let go. This Mother will give you the strength to run this ashram. Meditate on her and feel her in you."

I focused as all of my fears dripped into the pan under the painting. A golden goddess, a beautiful golden goddess, danced on my canvas. Her ferocity was mine. I was protected by her.

"I love you, my daughter." Ma opened her arms, and I bounded into them.

"Thank you, Ma."

She laughed. "Okay, next."

Another person raced forward. They bowed with their hands in prayer.

Painted Kali Readings lasted for many years. I remember one intensive retreat, Ma left a roomful of people to sit and chant until she finished her paintings. It took hours. Another time, she had Sampuran teach an impromptu Kundalini yoga class while she painted. I became exceedingly frustrated with Ma and the time it took her to paint while people sat in the temple. I suggested we designate time in the intensive schedule for Ma to do her readings. People loved being in Ma's presence. They'd order a second and third painting, just so they could sit in front of her.

Ma used to joke about it. "You don't even care about the paintings. You just want to be with your Ma."

On one occasion, Ma asked me, "How many people do I have to do out there?"

"Ma, we have twenty-five people on the list. You average five paintings per darshan."

"Who's on the list?"

I read off names.

"I don't want to do her tonight," Ma said.

"Ma, you have to do some of the new people."

She crossed her arms. "I don't want to."

I shook my head.

In the end, I would negotiate a deal. We'd do some of the Atlanta satsang, and then tomorrow I'd slip in some new folks once they had a chance to see how it worked, so there would be no mistakes of unconscious or bad behavior. Some of the newer students to Ma's teaching didn't understand how to be with a guru. Everyone needed to be trained how to address and respect the guru.

Before darshan, I explained to the group that because there were so many people on the list, not everyone would be able to sit before Ma this weekend.

I called the first person up to Ma.

"What is it you would like to ask?" Ma said.

"Ma, I want to know how I can serve you."

Ma's brush hit the canvas. She looked at the handsome man. "Who hurt you?" she asked. Her glasses slid down her nose.

"I . . . I don't know."

"Think. I want to take this deep pain."

"My father. He did things."

"You know I love you." Ma smiled at him. "Look into The Mother's eyes and let me take your pain." She held up the painting. The eyes of the goddess dripped blood-red paint, cascading like a waterfall and pooling in the pan beneath the canvas.

The woman next to me raised her hand. "Oh, Ma, that's beautiful. I have never seen this Mother and yet her fierceness is so utterly present and evident." She put her palms together and tilted her head.

"Ahhh yes, the qualities of this goddess will enable my child here to do his work in the world. The fierceness will protect him from pain." Ma looked down at the man in front of her.

He jumped into her arms.

"Okay, that was a great day. You all should meet at the Baba Temple tomorrow for fire puja." She looked over at me. "What time?"

I quickly calculated our schedule. "Six a.m." That was the latest I could push it.

"Make it five. Namaste, my children."

Right, five it is. I grumbled and made a note. Tomorrow would be a long day.

For many people in the era of Painted Kali Readings, to sit with Ma and have her dig up their gunk was a transformative experience. She pulled out their insecurities, neuroses, issues, and dark crap. People lined up and paid good money to sit before Ma.

I, on the other hand, grew to detest it.

Over the years, Ma sold all manner of items to raise money for the ashram. On more than one occasion, Ma convinced me to participate in some type of multilevel marketing scheme. We sold beverages and supplements like Calorad, Thinyu, blue green algae, and aromatherapy.

"I want you to sign up. We can make money," she said with enthusiasm.

Whatever product we undertook to sell eventually lost steam and fizzled. The person who signed up early might make a few dollars, but mostly it ended without any significant money.

Each time this happened, I felt like a snake oil salesman, hawking wares I didn't believe in. I began to loathe any type of sales, whether it was the latest multilevel marketing scheme or newest diet craze. Ma even tried to tap her way to weight loss with Emotional Freedom Technique.

The energy in Ma's rooms felt frenetic when I arrived to give her messages.

"Namaste, my daughter."

"Namaste, Ma." I sat next to her and opened my notebook.

"I've been studying this all night." She waved a booklet at me.

"We are all starting this new diet. It's called the Weigh Down Diet. It's a Christian-based weight-loss program." She brandished her wrist with the letters *WWJD* stamped on a yellow rubber bracelet. I had no idea what the letters signified.

"What would Jesus do?" Ma explained. "We are going to pray ourselves thin."

I shook my head. *Here we go again.*

30

I Need a Dollar

MA SETTLED IN TO HER CHAIR and surveyed the darshan room. "Namaste, my children." Her greeting was louder than usual and grated on me. I looked up from my notebook. I could tell she was in a mood. The room was packed. It was Saturday night, and we had opened our doors to the public.

"Who the hell are all of you? Where did you come from? Did she warn you about me?" Ma turned to me. I nodded and smiled, but as she turned away, my smile melted. *Shit, shit. I forgot to mention the muffins.* I panicked and my throat closed. Oh God, it was too late now. I tried to relax, but it was impossible. I pawed at my meditation cushion and crushed it with my hands. If no one raised their hands and purchased muffins, Ma would freak out.

Only a few weeks ago, that had occurred, and she'd screamed at us for ten minutes. "It is inappropriate to leave the guru sitting around like a mamaluke,"[1] Ma hissed at us that night after no one bought a muffin. "You need to take care of the guru. If no one raises their hands, my children need to." She got up and stormed out.

Pulled back from reliving the last muffin debacle, I continued to fret about forgetting the muffins in announcements. Ma was warming up.

"So, first things first. As you know, we are an ashram of service. We give and give and never burn out. We take care of people with AIDS. We take care of the poor. We live to serve. And Ma gives away all our money." Ma chuckled.

I cringed.

"I am The Mother of thousands . . ." Ma looked at the curly-haired lesbian seated next to her and cued her with a look.

The woman sat up and belted out the rest of the sentence, "Of thousands of gay and lesbian children around the world." She batted her eyes at Ma.

Oh God, I wished we could put that one to rest, too. I tugged on a lock of my hair. This routine was old. I bit my finger. Shit, all I could think was, *I hope some people raise their hands tonight*.

"We need to raise money to help do the work we do. My Rudra Das spends all day baking muffins." Her eyes darted about to find the muffin maker. He ducked into the room, breathless, and slipped in behind Ma.

"Ah, there you are. What flavor muffins do we have tonight?" Ma asked.

"Chocolate chip, Ma."

"Ahhhh, they're still warm." She placed the muffin to her nose and inhaled and tossed one back and forth in her hands. "These muffins are blessed by Ma and filled with Shakti. The money raised from the muffins takes care of our ashram, our people with AIDS, the children, and all the work we do. Who wants to buy a muffin?"

The guests were confused, but the residents were ready.

"Come on now, raise your hands."

A few hands rose into the air. Projectile muffins were tossed at high velocity toward extended arms. Ma screamed out names as muffins hurled through the air. My office colleague Usha sat nearby and wrote with ferocity, attempting to capture each name Ma yelled. Feeling like I had been transported into the midst of a cattle auction, I rubbed my temples and dipped my head toward my own notebook. So much for her earlier promise to me to immerse us in the silence. The recipients of the muffins held their prizes to their chests. All the muffins sold. I offered a silent *thank God*, grateful that a potential muffin disaster had been averted.

I had seen my fair share of things sold to make money for the ashram: Painted rocks, crystals, remedies, and brews were all sold at one time or another. We existed in a constant state of poverty consciousness. An insatiable black hole of neediness. We were always selling something.

Eventually, Ma stopped hurling freshly baked muffins. At least the paintings offered people an opportunity to sit in front of Ma and potentially have a spiritual experience or some type of personal transformation.

31

A Whiter Shade of Pale

GANGA DAS'S HEALTH WAS STABLE, AND HE WAS IN REMISSION.

It was two days before the New Year of 1999, and I was deep in planning the ashram's New Year's Eve celebration.

The phone rang.

"Dr. Geffen would like to speak with you," a nurse from his office explained. Music blared through the earpiece while I waited for Kabir and the results from Ganga Das's last round of tests.

"Krishnapriya, Kabir here. The results from the PET scan are in."

"And?"

"The scan revealed a spot in his chest. The cancer is active," he said with an even voice. My stomach tightened. A sour taste formed in the back of my mouth. "What? What are you saying? I thought this type of cancer was easy to treat." My voice cracked as I recalled Kabir's "I'll eat my hat" comment when we'd initially discussed Ganga Das's Hodgkin's lymphoma diagnosis.

"It's never a hundred percent with cancer. I spoke to your mother earlier. I'd like to come over and discuss the next steps that will need to be taken. It won't be as easy this time. The treatment is more difficult. This is much more serious."

I pushed the papers across my desk. "How serious? How difficult?"

"We can't treat it the same way. I'll be over tonight to see you guys."

I slammed the cell phone shut. *Fuck me.*

I found my mother sitting at her desk, the rims of her eyes pink and swollen.

"Mom." I fell into her arms. "Does Ma know yet?"

"Yes, she wants to see Ganga Das before Kabir comes over. She says it's important for him to hear about it from her. She doesn't want him to lose hope."

I was pissed that Kabir had called my mother first but attempted to push away the feelings. This was my small self, my ego creating my anger. I wrestled with the fact that Ma wanted to be the one to tell him about his reoccurrence. I was his mother.

"Okay, I'll let him know to stick around." I bit my lip and tamped down my anger.

The intercom rang. "You and your daughter come in right away," I heard Ma tell my mom.

When we arrived in her bedroom, Ma was curled in her chair. The scent of lavender filled her rooms. My mother and I sat in silence.

"What did Kabir say? What is the next step? What stage is this? Thank God for the PET scan."

I was always amazed by Ma's inability to contain her pain. Years of teaching us detached compassion, working with the dying, and dealing with disease, you'd think she could be more of a pillar of strength. I sat back and watched her.

"Call Acharya Durga Das in New York. Get him on the phone," Ma said to my mom.

Ma had given the name Durga Das to both my brother and the head of our New York ashram. I rolled my eyes. My mom dialed the number and handed the phone to Ma. She never seemed to care how ridiculous Ma got. My mother was the mother in this relationship. She took care of Ma like a child. It was as if she was immune to Ma's uncontained leaking of emotional outbursts. Or she'd excuse it away.

"Ma's like a child. She's simple."

"Ma has a hard time in her body."

"Ma's working with karma."

Ma never moved from her chair, and yet the energy in the room spun around me. "Call Kabir in," she ordered.

"Oh, Durga Das, my Durga Das, my Ganga Das, his cancer is back," she wailed into the phone.

I heard Durga Das's muffled voice, and I leaned my head back and closed my eyes.

Ma hung up. "My Durga Das is in so much pain. When I told him Ganga Das was sick again, he screamed a scream like I've never heard. I'll never forget that sound as long as I live."

I couldn't have cared less about what they had discussed or how they had processed their pain around my son.

"My NY Durga Das loves Ganga Das like his own son," Ma added. "He loves all of the ashram children so much. He knows how to hold his Ma in times of pain."

Jesus Christ. What bullshit. This guy couldn't give a shit about my son. If only I could slap some tape across everyone's mouths right about now, I thought. I felt like I was going to throw up. How much longer would I need to endure Ma's inane banter?

Ganga Das slipped into the room. He leaned down and gave Ma a kiss.

"I need you to know that we received the results of your tests . . ." she started.

He looked at her, and before she could say anything else, he blurted out the reality of his illness. "It's back."

Her mouth dropped wide open. "How did you know?"

"I just did. I could tell."

"We'll fight this. I'm not going to let anything happen to you. Do you understand?" She put her hands on his shoulders.

"It will be okay, Ma," he assured her.

"He will need a stem cell transplant," Kabir explained.

My body went erect.

"What does that mean?" my mom asked.

"First, we'll remove Ganga Das's stem cells. The next step will be to administer high doses of chemotherapy and then reintroduce the stem cells back into his blood."

"When?" I asked.

"We'll admit him to the hospital here for a few rounds of chemotherapy, and then you will need to take him to Shands Hospital in Gainesville for treatments." Kabir paused, letting the information sink in.

"Who oversees this if we're in Gainesville?" I asked.

"I have connected with the Bone Marrow Transplant Unit there and have a doctor who will work with you. He comes highly recommended."

I looked at Ma and then at my mother.

"You and Ganga Das could be there for a while, three months at least," Kabir said as he turned to me.

Ma sat up. I hadn't been away for any significant amount of time since moving back to the ashram twelve years ago.

Kabir looked at me. "This is serious. You might want to consider a sperm bank. This treatment will most likely render Ganga Das sterile."

A lump formed in my throat, but I nodded and made a note in my journal. I closed my eyes and prayed. *Please, God, please let him be okay. Please help him get through this. Please allow him to be healed.* I negotiated with the gods and goddesses for my son's well-being. I prayed to Mother Kali. *Please, Mother, take his cancer.* My nails dug deeply into my thighs.

"Ganga Das, do you have any questions?" Kabir asked.

"No. I think I understand," he said evenly.

"Anyone else?"

"Not at this point. I'm sure I'll have tons after you leave," I mumbled.

"It will be okay," Ma reassured Ganga Das. "I want his friends here now. I want to tell them. Get Chun and Mae, Jaya Ma, Durgaya . . ." Ma ticked off a list of teenagers' names.

Ganga Das shot me a look. I shrugged helplessly. The last thing Ganga Das wanted was a roomful of his peers feeling sorry for him. Interminable meetings in Ma's rooms were always painful, but this was turning into a nightmare.

The teens gathered around Ma as she explained what was happening. When the meeting ended, the kids kissed Ma good night. I gathered my stuff and followed them out. I kissed Ganga Das and watched him walk off with his friends, then I took the long way home through the woods.

Once in the safety of my space, I called Sampuran. "Hi." I held my pillow close to my chest.

"Hey, how's it going?" he asked.

"We've hit a little bump in the road. Ganga Das's PET scan came back positive. His cancer has returned," I said, rubbing the lump in my throat. I explained the next steps to deal with Ganga Das's treatment.

"I'd like to help. Is there anything you need?"

"I'm not sure at this point. I'm trying to figure out all the details. I need to make arrangements for a place to stay and get ready to go up there."

"I can come up and help you get settled."

"Thank you. I'll let you know. That might be helpful." I was grateful to have Sampuran in my life. He was steady, practical, and safe. When he showed up, he wasn't looking for anything from me. He had been a refuge from the insanity of my life for several years now.

Over the upcoming weeks, I packed and organized the things I thought I'd need for the next few months. I made arrangements for a hotel suite with a kitchen near the hospital. It was mostly for cooking meals, not staying there, since I'd stay in the hospital room with Ganga Das.

I packed the Honda. My mom and a few of the office staff were on hand to send us off. My mom stood in the driveway waving goodbye, her eyes puffy and swollen.

"Let's go," Ganga Das said as we folded ourselves into the car stuffed with boxes and suitcases. I could barely see out the back window as I put the car in reverse.

"What is all this shit?" Ganga Das asked.

"The juicer, the blender, two boxes of organic fruits and vegetables, dry goods, my homeopathic books, and Grandmom packed a box full of supplements and herbs," I explained.

Ganga Das rolled his eyes. "You really think we'll use all this? It looks like we're going away for a year."

I smiled as we drove the length of the dusty driveway. A few hours later, we arrived at the Residence Inn, our new home away from home. Sampuran was waiting in the driveway.

"I'm hungry," Ganga Das said.

"Let's unload, and we can go eat." Sampuran grabbed some bags and found a Mexican restaurant nearby. We ordered food. Ganga Das and I stirred our rice and beans together, adding a little guacamole and salsa to our mixture. Sampuran's meal remained separated and divided.

I poked my fork at him. "Do you always eat your food like that?"

"I do. Otherwise, it confuses me." He scooped another mouthful of beans into his mouth. After dinner, he dropped us back at the hotel.

"I'll call you tomorrow and be back in a few days," he said.

"Thank you," I whispered. Part of me wished he wasn't leaving, but I knew I needed to navigate the coming days with my son alone.

The following morning, Ganga Das and I went to the first of many meetings before the actual transplant.

"Ganga Das will need to meet with a hospital psychologist and social worker," the woman who was our liaison for the process said.

The night before Ganga Das was admitted to the hospital, Sampuran returned. The three of us went for pizza. Afterward, Ganga Das was tired. I put him to bed downstairs, and Sampuran and I went to the bedroom upstairs.

"I'm glad you are here," I whispered. I leaned in and kissed him.

"Me too."

We slipped out of our clothes.

"God, you feel good," I murmured.

"You okay with this?" he asked.

"Yes," I whispered. I hoped Ganga Das was finally sound asleep.

We made love. Quietly. I fell asleep wrapped in Sampuran's arms.

Ganga Das was admitted into the Bone Marrow Transplant Unit of Shands Hospital the next day.

The first procedure was a bone marrow test. A man with salt-and-pepper hair and a white lab coat entered the room. "Hi, Ganga Das. I'm Dr. Winegard. Today we are going to administer a bone marrow test. You'll be given a local anesthetic, and then we will use a tool to drill into your back and extract some of the bone from your spine to biopsy."

Ganga Das nodded.

"Are you ready?"

"Um, sure." Ganga Das was instructed to lie down on his stomach on the table. My knees wobbled as the doctor injected a long needle into his back.

"This may pinch a little," he said as he drove in the needle. Ganga Das barely flinched. The doctor drew out the needle. I unfurled my nails from my fists.

"Okay, Ganga, that was good. Now I'm going to drill into your spine next." He held up the menacing silver instrument. Absolutely medieval. I bit my lip. This looked like a tool the Marquis de Sade might have enjoyed. The doctor drove the metal implement into Ganga Das's back, grunting as he applied a considerable amount of pressure. I watched his hairy hand turn the handle of the contraption, winding the handle as the drill bit went deeper into Ganga Das's back. My hands balled up again, and I took a breath in as a woozy feeling filled my head. I did not want to pass out.

Ganga Das's body stiffened. He closed his eyes. His hands clutched the side of the table, bunching up the sterile white paper. I flinched at the sound of it crunching under the weight of his long fingers. A sharp pain stabbed the center of my chest.

"You may feel this a bit," the doctor said as he rewound the tool back out of Ganga Das's spine. Blood drained from Ganga Das's face. He was as white as an eggshell.

The doctor left the room for a moment.

My hand touched Ganga Das's forehead. "Are you okay?"

"I feel sick."

"I'll get you some water." I walked over to the sink and extracted a paper cup from the cold metal sleeve.

Ganga Das sat up. "That really hurt."

"It looked like it hurt."

A week later, it was finally time to harvest Ganga Das's stem cells. We entered the small room on the second floor of the hospital unit.

"Have a seat right here, young man." The nurse smiled and pointed to the green pleather chair that rested amid black hoses attached to a large machine with a washing machine–type cylinder. I sat in a folding chair next to Ganga Das, whose arms were then attached to the hoses, which would suck the blood from his veins and return it.

His blood spinning around, the machine whirled, removing his cells, after which the blood flowed back into another long tube and reentered his body. Hooked to the machine, Ganga Das reminded me of the Marvel comic character Doctor Octopus. All of the attached hoses merged into my son, giving him the appearance of some half-human/half-machine entity.

He would undergo chemotherapy treatments in a few days. That round of drugs would kill everything in his body. Once this step was done, the doctors and medical team would inject his stem cells back into his blood. In the meantime, we spent our days shuffling between tests, injections, and more tests. Build him up and break him down, extract his life force, and pump him up with drugs to strengthen him for the next step.

Each day, Ganga Das's frame thinned a bit more. I ran back to the hotel every morning and made fresh organic juice and cooked foods I hoped he might eat. Soon he would be quarantined and no longer permitted to eat raw foods.

After five days of chemo, Ganga Das lay listless on the metal hospital bed. The chemotherapy had taken its toll. His flesh was gray. His face was sunken and gaunt. Pain meds were pumped into his emaciated body to keep him comfortable. I barely remembered what he looked like with hair. It had been years since he'd had any. He would be eighteen soon.

The night after his final chemo treatment before his transplant, I settled in for the evening, curled up in the convertible chair-bed, and began reading. Unable to concentrate, I noticed the hairs on my skin flicker. An uneasy feeling crept into me. It filled the room. It was a familiar feeling and not a comfortable one. My heart pounded. The only sound in the room was the beating of my heart between my temples. It was so loud, it drowned out the machines my son was attached to.

I recognized the feeling. Death was in the room with me. It hovered near Ganga Das. It wasn't the gentle, peaceful, and tranquil death I'd experienced at the bedside of others dying. This felt thick and heavy, weighty and terrifying.

I sensed it so profoundly, I rose from the chair and moved to the bed to put my hand under Ganga Das's nose. He was barely breathing. Fear choked me, rising from the pit of my belly and reaching around my throat. My fear mingled with death in the room. My heartbeat was out of control, pounding so hard that my head hurt.

"Ganga Das?" I whispered.

No response. His breath was ever so slight but there. I put my hand on his heart. My tears stained the sheets.

I dug for my phone. "Mom?"

"What's wrong?" The deep connection between mother and child filled the space between our cell phones. She knew me so well.

"Mom, he doesn't look good. I feel death in the room. He's gray and unresponsive. He's breathing. But I can feel death around him over the bed. Call Ma. Tell her. Ask her to do something."

"I'll call her right away." The phone clicked.

My phone rang minutes later.

"Namaste, my daughter, it's your Ma."

"Namaste, Ma."

"Put the phone by his ear. I want to speak to him."

"Okay." I walked over, placed the phone by his ear, and poked at him. "Ganga Das, Ma wants to speak with you."

He moaned as I held the phone by his ear. "Namaste, Ganga Das, it's your Ma. It's not time for you to go. You need to want to live. I know it's been hard. You have too much to do in this life. You need to fight." She spoke in a gentle but firm voice.

I watched helplessly as she tried to coax my son back to life. Then I pulled the phone back to my ear.

"Sit now and see the light all around him. I am going into my temple and will do the same. I am going to spend the rest of the night doing puja. I love you, my daughter."

"Thank you, Ma." The phone went dead.

I sat in the chair and meditated for the rest of the night, only opening my eyes to check on him and make sure he was breathing. I noticed the room become lighter. A tinge of color came back to his face. I sat back in the chair and resumed my meditation. I eventually fell asleep in the chair.

The doctors arrived on their rounds, and Ganga Das woke up.

"Good morning, Ganga Das, how are you feeling?"

"Not so good," he answered. He rarely complained, so I knew he was hurting.

"It will take a few days for the cells to graft. You probably won't feel good for a bit." The doctor reviewed Ganga Das's chart. "Everything looks good and is moving ahead accordingly. Ganga Das is responding as should be," he assured me. "You'll be going home before you know it," he added with a smile at Ganga Das.

I wondered what he would say if I told him about death's visit last night. I believed Ma had saved my son.

32

Make You Feel My Love

Easter arrived, and Hanuman came to visit his brother. Sampuran came to visit me. Hanuman spent the night in the hospital with Ganga Das. Sampuran and I spent the night at the hotel.

Ganga Das and I returned back to the ashram at the end of April. His journey to recovery took time. There were still doctors to see and tests to take, but both of us tried to ground ourselves and find some semblance of normalcy in our lives. He returned to school, and I returned to work.

I stood over my desk in the office. *Where do I begin?* I had no clue where to start after months of being away. I felt disconnected. The office had run just fine in my absence, for the most part. However, most of our ashram activities had come to a grinding halt, and all travel plans had been canceled while I was away. I even missed the late-night visit of then-superstar Ricky Martin to the ashram. He was greeted by a group of pajama-clad yogis, who told him Ma was unavailable to meet with him. Usha caught hell for that one.

My desk was as blank as I felt. Clean. Neat. Not how I usually worked. There were no stacks of files resting on the top left side of the desk, no pads of paper with lists of to-do notes, no pink message memos piled in the order I'd attempt to return the calls. No masses of yellow Post-it notes strewn across the bottom of my computer screen. There was only one pink Post-it affixed to the bottom of the monitor that read "Don't be a salmon," written in my handwriting in block print with a black marker. It was my reminder not to swim upstream and fight against the current. A vase of red and pink carnations and delicate white baby's breath was the only thing on my desk. A note from Ma was tucked under the vase. It read:

"Welcome home, daughter. Love, Ma."

I lowered myself into the executive chair. The pleather whined as my hips sunk into the cushion.

The upcoming trip to South Africa in December to attend the Parliament of the World's Religions was as good as any place to start after I checked Ma's emails. I reached under the desk and pushed the button, and the computer whirred to life.

The phone rang. "Can you come out and play tomorrow?"

A warm heat filled my head, hearing his voice on the other end of the phone.

"And what did you have in mind?" I curled the cord around my fingers.

"How about we meet at the beach?"

"Well, it just so happens Ma isn't teaching tomorrow."

"Good then. I'll call you after work, and we can make a time to meet."

"I'll bring the B&B." I closed my eyes and visualized us on the sandy beach sipping the warm amber liquid. A rush of energy rippled up between my legs. Damn, I was horny.

"Always thinking ahead."

How is it you can feel someone smiling on the other end of the phone? "I'm excited. I can't wait to see you," I whispered.

"Good. Me too. Okay then, till tomorrow."

Later that day, I stretched out on my bed. The bottle of almond oil near the nightstand beckoned me. I put some on my fingertips and slid my hands between my legs.

The next day, I could barely concentrate, and the day was endless. I swished papers from one end of my wooden desk to the other. Finally, I went next door.

"Ush, I'm going to head home. I'm not getting anything done," I told my colleague, good friend, and right-hand woman.

"Oh, okay. I'll see you later."

"Umm, yeah, sure." My car would be long gone before she got home.

My bare feet calloused from years of not wearing shoes, I ran through the woods back to my house. Inside, I leaped up the stairs, retrieved my backpack from the corner of the closet, extracted the B&B, and tucked it into my bag with my swimsuit, towel, and blanket. I thought I'd go to the store to buy cheese and crackers for our night. Although I wasn't sure we'd eat. I had other things on my mind.

I looked at my watch. There was an hour before I needed to meet. I drove to our designated meeting spot, which was always the same, and I hopped into his Explorer.

"Hi there." His face brightened to a light shade of pink.

I kissed him. "Hi there yourself." I laughed.

He turned on the ignition and headed the car east. We parked near the shipyard, where the cruise ships were getting ready for their evening departures.

"Shall we take a walk?" Sampuran asked. We skipped across the rocky jetty.

"Do you hear that?" he asked.

"Yes, where's it coming from?"

"Look over there."

As we walked, we saw dozens of feral cats mewing and darting in and among the rocks. Their fur gnarled and tatty, they searched us over to see if we had any offerings.

"I've never seen so many cats in one place." I slipped off the jetty. Screeching wails rose from different spots in the rocks. Some were longing wails, while others were vicious and predatory. We sat and watched the Carnival Cruise ship depart for its sunset booze cruise, and then we walked to shore. I ran to the water and stuck my toes in, a ritual I performed whenever I came in contact with a body of water. We settled into the sand and watched the sun fade into the sea.

"Shall we go back to the car?" Sampuran asked. He reached his hands out and pulled me from the sand, and we walked arm in arm. I dug my bag out of the back seat and poured us each a brandy snifter.

"Cheers." I smiled and clinked his glass.

He took a sip and wheezed. "God, this stuff is intense."

"Like us." I met his eyes.

We finished the first drink, and I poured another. Sampuran took a small sip and said he was done. He wasn't accustomed to drinking alcohol. It was highly illegal in his ashram.

I turned my head toward him. "I love the way this makes me feel."

He leaned over and placed his lips gently on mine. "Mmmm, I like the way it makes you feel, too." He smiled as he moved closer.

"Let's move into the back," he said, and he guided me over the front seats. He'd already laid out a blanket. Our bodies slid comfortably together. I was no longer shy. I reached for him. He met me. Our clothes came off clumsily as we tore off what little we had on. I lowered down, kissing his chest, gently circling his nipples with my tongue. His head shook side to side. I moved down his body, caressing it with my lips, nipping at parts of him with my teeth.

"Oh my God," he whispered. I could hear the sound of cats off in the distance as the SUV rocked back and forth.

There was a blaring sound, getting louder and louder.

Sampuran jumped up. "What the hell?" He gasped, scrambling himself over the seat. "Where are my fucking keys?" Our car horn blared louder. I grabbed a towel and covered my exposed breasts. I didn't know who looked crazier. My hair was a wild, tangled nest, my face flushed. Sampuran was frantically shaking out his pants, searching wildly for his set of keys. The windows were so fogged, I couldn't see if anyone was walking toward the car. Sampuran plunged the key into the ignition. And then there was nothing but the sound of cats.

I laughed. "Oh my God."

Sampuran clutched the wheel. This was what a caveman might have looked like after hunting down dinner. "Holy shit, that was crazy." He crawled back to me, and we laughed until our sides hurt.

"How did that happen?" I asked.

"I blame you. All that wild energy. You set it off."

"Hmm, it takes one to know one."

He touched my face, and I fell into his arms. He lowered me down onto my back and kissed my neck. Now it was his turn to move down my body. My body shook as his tongue found its way between my thighs.

"Oh my God. You feel so amazing." Waves of energy pulsed through me. "Oh my God," I whispered.

Sampuran rose and slowly lowered into me. The car vibrated to the rhythm of our bodies. My nails sank into his back. Sirens. I heard sirens. Blaring. Getting closer.

"What the hell?" he muttered. We both lifted our heads. Red flashing lights pulled up to the lot we were parked in. Sampuran slid out of me. I wiped the window.

"It looks as if the fire brigade has arrived." I chuckled.

"What is going on tonight?" He pulled on his shirt.

I was already searching for my underwear. We climbed into the front seats, both breathing heavily. I looked at him and burst into a fit of laughter, grateful we weren't arrested for indecent exposure.

33

Rolling in the Deep

My assistant Radhe and I flew to Cape Town, South Africa, for the Parliament of the World's Religions. Ma would arrive a few days later. Over the last few years, we had worked hard to establish ourselves as an interfaith community to give us more credibility in the world, and this event was pivotal.

The main hall of the hotel was a cacophony of chaos. Buddhist monks swathed in red; Hindu swamis wrapped in orange; priests in their tight collars; Western Sikhs in white, flowing outfits and turbans; Indian Sikhs in Western clothes; and Native Americans adorned with turquoise and feathers wandered the grand hall as academics in suits scurried by, looking important. I stood in the sea of religious humanity. A group of people who looked as if they had just floated down the Nile walked by. Two male attendants each carried large, white feathers on a pole. Their female leader, a Western woman, resplendent in an Egyptian headdress, a white tunic, and jeweled sandals, glided by with an entourage of followers.

Radhe and I were in charge of two hundred members of the ashram and a handful of dignitaries on the trip. Ma's red-and-black sari swished as she walked. Brahma Das and I walked by her side and introduced her to dignitaries.

"I want a meeting arranged with the Dalai Lama," Ma told Brahma Das. He glared at Ma.

"I'll try," he said as he leaned against his staff.

"Make it happen. Both of you work on it." Ma carried on.

"Getting an audience with the Dalai Lama is not going to be easy," he said to me.

"Do you have any interviews set up?" I asked.

"I am working on some ideas, focusing on the AIDS and service work. Ma can't expect that the international press will necessarily write a story about her and her work. She isn't that well known." His troll-like body turned toward me, his face gnarled as he spit out his words. He reminded me of Gollum. Over the last year, he had cultivated a relationship with the Tibetans. I took a deeper look. *He's hiding something, and I bet he doesn't want to jeopardize his reputation.*

I waved the file in my hand. "That's your job. You are the PR person." I walked away and rejoined Ma as we escorted her to her hotel room. I laid out my notes and began to prep Ma.

"You are speaking at the opening event and five different sessions. We are in charge of the opening ceremony, and—"

"I want Yogiji honored and to meet the Dalai Lama. And make sure I am next to him during the closing ceremony."

"Ma, you're speaking on the Mutual Irradiation panel after the ceremony."

"What the fuck is that? I can't even say it." She looked ahead while NY Durga Das teased her hair.

God, I hope he doesn't create some weird hairdo.

"It's a Quaker concept, where in understanding another truth, one's own beliefs might be illuminated and reveal a glimpse of a hidden, shared truth with another faith or belief," I said. Ma stared at me as if I was speaking in an alien language.

"What a stupid thing. I don't want to do it."

"You are doing it. You've already accepted." I tugged at my hair. *How is she going to pull off this talk?* What was I thinking when I'd accepted the invitation on her behalf?

"You'll be fine. Just speak about kindness being your religion."

The following day, we gathered for the opening event. We placed Ma in the front row, Yogiji beside her and Arlo Guthrie behind her. My Punjabi dress was soaked. I watched from around the edges of the main seating area, one eye on Ma and another on everything else. A commotion brewed on the field a few yards away.

Someone whispered in my ear, "They think it's a bomb."

I choked. Jesus Christ, was this really happening? I looked at Ma and all of the dignitaries seated. I summoned the closest person I could find and sent them to investigate.

I turned my attention to the sound of loud music approaching. Hundreds of Asians from a religious sect I couldn't identify were heading toward us. An attractive Asian woman in a flowing yellow outfit and a large, floppy, yellow hat led the group. Instruments clanged, bells chimed, and their chanting drowned out the people speaking.

Ma caught my eye and motioned for me. I crouched down.

"Who the fuck is that and what the fuck is going on?"

"I have no idea, but we sent a few guys to redirect them."

"Make them stop; it's disrupting the ceremony."

"I'm working on it."

The bag with the possible bomb was removed from the area without incident. And the religious group disappeared toward the buildings across the lawn.

The next ten days were a blur. We weren't the only group seeking validation. Everyone was jockeying for their religion, teacher, or cause. We had one more event to get through: the closing ceremony.

Rudra Das and Brahma Das were on stage to capture a photo of Ma and the Dalai Lama. Each dignitary was instructed to walk across the stage and take their place. The ashram photographers scurried around the stage creating a spectacle. I watched from the audience as Ma marched across the stage toward the Dalai Lama. She slowed and bowed to him. She stayed put before him. I cringed. Oh my God, she's not moving. She's trying to speak with him. Bile rose from the pit of my stomach. I placed my head in my hands. I couldn't watch the scene unfolding before me. I turned my head and glanced at the thousands of people seated behind me. Did anyone else notice her desperate attempt to capture the Dalai Lama's attention?

Ma took her place and stared out at us with a defiant smile. *Could I just be swallowed whole and disappear from this moment?*

A group of us met Ma after the closing. "What the fuck is wrong with you both? I asked for one thing, the most important thing, and you fuck it up. You created a spectacle up there," she said.

I felt for both men. We followed Ma to her rooms. I went for a drink.

We returned to Florida. Brahma Das left the teaching. The trip, coupled with a substantial inheritance and his desire to become important with the Tibetan cause and get closer to the Dalai Lama, all factored into his exit.

A few weeks later, I left for the West Hollywood ashram ahead of Ma to prepare for our next intensive retreat. Retreats, we decided, conjured up images of spa and rejuvenation, often misleading participants. That's not what you got when you came to a weekend with Ma.

Ma, my mother, my brother, Rudra Das, and Ma's girls arrived a few days later. Ma went on rounds to feed the homeless. The girls set up Ma's rooms, and the rest of us prepared food and the darshan space for the weekend.

I was called into Ma's rooms early in the day on Saturday. Something was up.

Ma was seated on a big, puffy chair. Behind her hung one of

her large canvas paintings of a ferocious black goddess. Red paint dripped from between the image's legs; her fangs were bared, dripping blood. The image's wild eyes stared into the room. I looked around at the group of people assembled.

The people who ran the LA ashram and NY Durga Das, who was considered one of Ma's close ones and ran the New York ashram, were already seated in the room. There was a flurry of activity around Ma. She was frowning and staring at my mother, who was on the phone.

"I see," my mother said. "How long? Okay, call me back when you know anything else."

"Chun has been released. Ganga Das is still in jail," my mother told Ma.

What the fuck?

"Your son and Chun have been arrested for possession of pot," Ma sneered at me.

I didn't move and remained silent.

"How could those fucking assholes jeopardize my ashram? I gave them everything. This is how they pay me back?" A white, foamy substance pooled at the corners of her mouth. I handed her a tissue. She grabbed it and wiped her nose. I pointed to the corners of her mouth. She scowled at me, removed the gunk, and threw the tissue to the floor.

The phone rang again, and my mother picked up. Ma extracted the details of the crime and status of both my son and Ma's adopted son Chun as my mother played intermediary. Veena and Chandra on the other end explained the situation.

"Call Durga Das and Rudra Das in immediately." We sat squished around Ma in the tiny living room.

My mother relayed the information. "The boys were in the car. They were pulled over because of expired tags. The cops smelled the marijuana and found a roach in the ashtray. After a further search, they found an ounce of marijuana in the car. Ganga Das admitted it was his. Anything over an ounce is a felony in Florida. Because he was eighteen, he was taken to jail. Chun was underage and released."

"Let him spend the night in jail. That will teach him. Chunny, too. He should spend the night as well." Ma tossed her glasses aside.

Oh God, this is terrible. Hundreds of questions spun through my mind. Whose car? Whose weed? What had they been thinking?

I knew to be careful. I could not reveal myself or how I felt or she'd accuse me of being attached or worse in this moment. She was in a fury, while I was three thousand miles away, helpless as my son sat in a Vero Beach jail.

She turned toward me. "I saved your son's life, and this is what he does. He will be lucky if his cancer doesn't return."

I tightened and held back any facial expression. *Oh, great. She's using the damn cancer card, again.*

Ma ranted and shrieked. My palms were on the verge of bleeding. My mom stepped into the hall so she could hear on the phone. Ma continued to yell.

My mother returned and explained the plan. Chandra Das would bail Ganga Das out of jail in the morning and then figure out the next steps. Ganga Das would need to appear before a judge. Because it was his first offense, they might let him off with probation and he'd be eligible for a special program for first-time offenders.

"Chandra Das said that the judges in Vero are renowned for their no drug tolerance. They have a reputation for setting examples with first-time offenders," my mother said. You'd never know she was speaking about her grandson.

My stomach knotted, and my mind wouldn't shut up. *Ganga Das was in possession of an ounce of pot? Where did he get the money to buy that amount?* It didn't make sense.

We sat in the room for hours, Ma beating the story into the ground without taking a breath the entire time. She not only exhausted herself but also everyone else around her. I wished she'd leave and go lock up in her room. I needed to call Chandra myself. Veena would take care of Chun; he was her nephew. But who would take care of Ganga Das?

Ma pointed her finger into the middle of the room. "I want them both grounded."

We slogged through the rest of the weekend. In the morning, we got up and taught yoga; Ma gave darshan and answered questions about enlightenment.

I moved through the motions, sucking it up and doing my job with all my heartache tucked away in a neat package. I pretended that everything was fine.

On Monday, I arrived home and tracked down Ganga Das. He told me his version of the story. It turned out it was Chun's pot. Ganga Das said he knew how much trouble Chun would be in if Ma found out it was his pot, so he'd said half of it was his.

"You mean it wasn't yours? You took the rap? You went to jail for him?" My voice raised an octave with each question.

Ganga Das nodded. He looked pale. He'd only been out of the hospital a few months. He still appeared too thin to me.

"Ganga Das, what were you thinking? What about your health? The smoke! The doctors warned you, no smoking, and even secondhand smoke is bad for you." I heard myself lecturing and saw his eyes glaze over. He was done with the conversation.

Ma raged on for days. She perseverated, worried the newspapers would find out and write about the ashram.

Ma stared at me. "Your son Ganga Das needs to learn his lesson. He needs to move into the River House and work taking care of the people with AIDS."

I flinched.

"What do you have to say?" she said, daring me to say something. "Tough love—that's what's needed, something you and your mother know nothing about." Ma dismissed my mother and me.

Ganga Das and I packed his things, and I stored the rest of his belongings. The knot in my stomach tightened thinking about Ma's rants. How her face twisted at what she deemed sinful. I always thought the punishments she doled out to the ashram kids were more extreme than the actual crime. This would be no different.

I dealt with Ganga Das's move as best as I could. I was pissed. The final blow came days later when the issue of his scholarship to college came up.

"He can't go. He'll be ruined. This isn't on me—you need to take responsibility. You tell him he can't go. Tell him the scholarship was canceled," Ma said.

I left the room and lost it. "This is fucked and wrong!" I yelled at my mother.

"Ma only has Ganga Das's best interest in mind. You need to trust Ma," she said. Her upper lip quivered.

I didn't believe her.

Still, I stormed off to tell my son he wasn't going to college, explaining to Ganga Das that he wouldn't be going to Manhattanville College on the full scholarship he'd received. I was unconvincing. He knew it was Ma who'd decided his fate and that I was just going along with her. He knew I'd never do this. I knew Ma was wrong. Why couldn't she see how this would jeopardize Ganga Das's education, his life, and his future? Once Ma made up her mind, there was no changing it. I felt powerless. I was unable to fight for my son. I stuffed my pain deep inside. My eyes met my son's. He knew this was all Ma's doing.

My phone rang. My hands shook as I picked up.

"Ma wants you to come over," the person on the phone said.

When I arrived, my mother was on the phone yet again, while Ma screamed at my son.

"Did your mother tell you I canceled your scholarship?"

My mother repeated Ma's words, even though I knew Ganga Das could hear Ma in the background. I shook my head, looked at my mother, and narrowed my eyes.

Fuck me. She can't even keep her own story straight. I bit my tongue. Ma had forced me to say I was the one who thought he shouldn't go to school. At least now he knew the truth.

"Hang up, Shody. I don't want either of them in darshan. I don't want to see either of them ever again."

Ganga Das was remanded to work and live at the River House, where my paternal grandmother, suffering from dementia, was living. I would go over and visit her and see Ganga Das.

After a few long months, Ganga Das was released from his punishment at the River House. Ma remained mad at him. He was finally going to graduate high school. He finished his required work, but Ma forbid him to graduate with his class. His classmates were outraged. One taped Free Ganga Das in white letters on the back of her red satin cap. I sat in terror the entire event. Ma never saw it. The following fall, Ganga Das moved to Gainesville and went to college.

34

I Put a Spell on You

"You are in charge of my words," Ma announced as I went through her messages. My mother placed a tray with a bowl of cabbage soup and a banana on her desk. She peeled the banana and took a hunk, chewing it slowly. The pungent stink of cooked cabbage spread through the office. Ma's latest weight-loss attempt was the Cabbage Soup Diet.

"Thank you. We've been transcribing darshans and I've been editing them. I've gone through much of your poetry for both the autobiography and the yoga teacher training manual. It's beautiful." I told her I was in touch with a cousin of hers who knew someone in the publishing industry to help find an agent to get Ma's autobiography published.

"Does she think she can do anything with it?"

"She's sending it out to people." I chewed on the end of my pen.

"And the *Kali Natha Yoga Manual* is beyond beautiful. I am thrilled."

The yoga teacher training manual was a compilation of years of teachings, poetry, meditations, and yoga asanas[1] Ma had created. It was the most comprehensive collection of Ma's teachings to date.

"Thank you, Ma. It was a team effort."

"I'll mention them on the darshan line."

"That would be great."

"But really, what you and Devi accomplished is one of the greatest gifts to your Ma. Be sure to tell Devi." Devi was the head of the Atlanta ashram. She was one of my closest friends and had helped create the yoga manual and teacher training program for the ashram.

"Yes, I will."

There was so much information that it took two binders to fill. "We have our next teacher training in a few weeks." I crossed it off my list.

"I love teaching yoga. How many people do you have?" she asked.

"Quite a few. We have a lot of interest."

"I want all my kids to take the yoga training. I'll tell everyone tonight in darshan to sign up."

I was glad that Ma was happy about our direction with her writings and the yoga program. She got up to prepare for darshan, and I went out to give announcements. Mata, a sizable and imposing student of Ma's, lumbered toward me. She had been with Ma for a long time and had helped with some editing of Ma's book early on.

"I need to be part of whatever you are working on." She was way too close to me. She didn't like me and was pissed that Ma had given me the boon of editing her work.

"I can't talk right now."

"This is not your job. It's my job. I should be doing this project." She was five-foot-ten, massive, and thick. She bared her yellowed teeth at me and smirked. "I am Ma's editor."

"Mata. I'm working on the book project at Ma's request."

She raised her voice. "You should focus on running the ashram. That's your job. What the fuck do you think you are doing? You know shit about editing. I'm sure I'd find thousands of mistakes in that yoga manual." She was like a grizzly bear on its haunches, mouth opened wide and ready to lunge. I looked out at people coming into the room and asked her to step outside, so we didn't make a scene in the temple. I walked out the back doors, and she followed, storming behind.

She pointed her finger at my chest. "You don't know the first thing about writing. You write like shit. Everything you write grammatically sucks."

I faced off with her. "Why is it you have nothing good to say about anything or anyone? Why is it no one can do anything right except you?"

"Fuck you, Krishnapriya."

"Nice, Mata, nice."

I walked back in a bit shaken and chanted with the satsang.

After darshan, I found my mother at her desk. "Ma needs to deal with Mata. She's like a rabid dog."

"What happened?"

"She's pissed because Ma gave me the book project. Since Ma had her work on the autobiography, she feels entitled to any projects with Ma's writings."

"We can talk to Ma about it."

"You know she won't deal with it. She'll tell us to take care of it."

"She'll at least be aware of the situation. I'll speak to Ma in the morning."

The following evening, I walked into Ma's rooms.

"There will always be a gardener in your midst," Ma said. "You have a lot of power, and you are young. You are close to Ma. People are jealous. Just remember to be kind and listen. You have full control over my writings. I trust you. Remember, Mata has had a hard life."

"Thank you, Ma." I excused myself and went to darshan.

Mata glared at me as I took my seat. I closed my eyes and waited for Ma.

"Namaste, my children. Tonight, I'm going to tell you a story." She often had a few good stories she told over the years. I settled in.

"There once was an old master and his students who lived in a small monastery. The master loved his garden. He and his monks lived peacefully according to their vows. One day, the master hired a new gardener. The master explained to his monks he needed to take a trip and would return in a few weeks. In the meantime, he wanted them to take care of the monastery, continue their practice, and study the teachings. They assured him all would be fine and bid him a safe journey."

I realized that Ma was telling this story for my benefit. I also knew it would be lost on my nemesis.

Ma took a sip of her Perrier and continued her story. "The gardener began his gardening. The monks smiled as they passed by, but the gardener never smiled back. Some of the monks tried to engage him in conversation, but he refused to speak to them. He just continued his work. The day after the master departed, the monks looked out the window to see the gardener pulling out the flowers they had recently planted. The monks became upset. One of the monks decided to go speak with the gardener. He explained to his fellow monks that if he approached the gardener with kindness, surely, the man would understand the monks' concern. He walked down to the gardens and approached the gardener. 'Good afternoon, gardener, a pleasant day, isn't it?' He smiled, but the gardener looked up and glared. The monk was a bit ruffled. He stuttered and in the kindest manner asked the gardener why he was pulling out the flowers.

"The gardener looked at the monk and hissed, 'This is no concern of yours. Go away.' "The monk was shocked by the gardener's response and tried another angle. 'We planted these beautiful flowers for the master. He loves them. He will not be happy when he gets back and sees that you've pulled them out.'

"The gardener ignored him. And with a brush of his hand, he waved off the monk and grumbled on about his business.

"The monk returned to his brothers and relayed the story. The monks were outraged. Long discussions ensued as to how to deal with the situation. The next day, the monks looked out at the garden and saw the gardener had taken out the new trees the master had planted. The monks became irate. They drew straws to see who would go and talk to the gardener.

"The gardener screamed at the young monk who'd drawn the short straw, 'Get out of my garden!' Each day he would gather his gardening tools and head to the garden, and each day he became meaner and nastier to the monks as they passed by." Ma paused and looked around the room. She had the satsang's rapt attention.

She smiled and continued. "Finally, the monks went to speak to the head monk. They explained that the gardener was ruining the master's garden. By the time the master returned, the garden would be a mess.

"The head monk had also been watching with concern and agreed that something must be done. Finally, he went and spoke to the gardener. The gardener and the monk exchanged fiery words. The head monk, exasperated, told the gardener he was fired and to leave the grounds. The gardener threw his tools down and stormed off. The other monks ran down to the garden and happily began to tend it.

"When the master returned and noticed his gardener was gone, he gathered his monks and asked where his gardener went. They explained how terrible the gardener was and how they had to fire him. The master looked at the monks and said, 'You fools—he was your liberation!'"

Ma chuckled and slapped her knee as she finished her story. She looked at me and smiled. "There are many gardeners in your midst. They are here to teach you, my children. I love you. Namaste." And with that, she got up and left.

Great. I thought I would never be free of this woman, and she is my path to liberation. It seemed there were many gardeners in my midst.

While I juggled gardeners and jealousy, Brahma Das resurfaced. He and his wife were engaged in a bitter divorce. She was one of Ma's personal assistants.

Chandra, the ashram attorney, called me to his office. I stepped in, and he put his finger to his lips. I sat down quietly. He scribbled *Brahma Das* on a piece of paper.

"If you go down this road, I'll blow the whistle. I'll expose Ma as a fraud and the ashram as a cult." Brahma Das didn't realize he was on speaker.

I shifted in my office chair. Things would surely spin out of control. He had spent years defending Ma and the ashram against negative press. He would use everything he knew against us. Chandra hung up.

"Krishnapriya, as the CEO, you'll need to act as spokesperson for the ashram," the ashram attorney told me.

We spent hours each day meeting in Ma's rooms, strategizing.

"We need to do everything we can to pray for your Ma and this ashram. He'll rue the day he did this to the ashram. His ego would not die. He's a greedy miser." Ma sat at her desk reading the latest article.

I pulled out my book of spells. We chanted incantations and recited spells for protection. There was a spell for almost any situation, including ones to sway a jury or judge in your favor.

People who had left the teaching joined in his battle. They wrote letters and talked to the press. The court of public opinion was not in our favor. I hated him for what he was doing to Ma and the ashram.

In the end, the case was settled, but the damage would haunt us for years to come.

35

Under Pressure

My brother's fists came down on my desk with a thud. The stapler, pencils, and files bounced; small statues fell like dominos. The veins in Durga Das's temples looked as if they would burst. The pictures on the wall were now crooked, and I knew the rest of the office could hear us. Over the last few months, my small corner office had become the site of a series of showdowns, each increasing to a higher crescendo.

"I want you to understand that we need to move forward with this project, and without your support, it will not work. It's the one and only plan that will save our financial situation. What do I need to do to convince you? The numbers are all here in black and white." Durga Das pushed the financials at me.

I inhaled deeply. "I'm having a difficult time getting behind the plan. You want to develop the property, carve it up, sell lots, and build an eldercare center to fix our finances? Why not just finish one project at a time? The numbers don't add up. We are digging ourselves into a deeper hole. We need to slow down, not speed up." I tossed the papers back at him.

"Goddamn it, Krishnapriya. I can't believe we've come this far and now you are questioning it all."

We'd been fighting for months. And now we were at odds over how to run the organization.

"You're in charge. You need to run the organization," he said.

"What do you think I am doing?" I asked. I felt like a ping-pong ball.

I struggled not only with the difference in philosophy about running the ashram and increasing our revenue streams but also with how thin we were spreading our resources.

"Why do we always go here? Why do we have to always end up in a fight? I don't understand," I said.

"I don't want to do this with you. This is about business."

"I think it's important."

"You're twisting all of this and making it about us. It's not about us."

"Why is it that we can't have a discussion? It always ends up here and you don't want to talk about it." Tears rolled down my face.

My brother jumped up and punched the door in numerous successive strikes. The frame of the door cracked as he landed a fifth-degree taekwondo sidekick. He stormed out the door and slammed it behind him. I sat alone, shaking, and lowered my head into my hands and sobbed.

36

Hare Rama, Hare Krishna

It was 2001, and for once, everything was going well. I was facilitating yoga workshops and intensives and speaking at conferences. I'd practiced meditation and yoga for as long as I could remember, and I loved teaching. Ganga Das had fully recovered from his cancer. He had regained his strength, looked healthy, and was working at a local restaurant in Vero Beach.

In the spring, Ma dropped a bomb. I was in her rooms giving her messages while she was exercising.

"It's time for you to become sannyas.[1] I think you should take sannyas this year." Ma returned from her contemplative moment.

I froze. I held onto my breath as well. I knew I was supposed to be honored and make a fuss. Everyone in the satsang wanted to be one of the chosen. Instead, I wanted to puke.

I kept a straight face, but this was the last thing I wanted. Everyone was clamoring to become a swami. I was fine running the ashram and deferring bullshit matters to the people who were swathed in orange.

"Well? What do you think?" Ma kept pedaling on her elliptical machine.

"What about Tarini? Isn't she taking her vows in a month?" my mother asked Ma. While they discussed my fate, my mind spun. I knew there was no way I could say no. If I did, I'd be revealed. Ma would dig in deep to find out why. I couldn't do that to Sampuran, and I'd be thrown out of the teaching for sure. I was doomed. I was being handed a life sentence. My mind swirled with all kinds of thoughts. Going deeper into my spiritual path was the only thing I wanted. I couldn't care less about a title, the color of my clothes, or the outfit I wore. And the last thing I wanted was people kissing my feet or being relegated to look like a tambourine-beating Hare Krishna at LAX. I did not want to be a swami.

Ma stopped pedaling. She looked at my mother, trying to decide whether she wanted to include me in the upcoming ceremony happening in the next few weeks.

"Let's wait until next May. I want Tarini to have her moment with her Ma."

God, please get me out of this room. My temples pounded. I felt like my lungs were being crushed under the weight of Ma's announcement. I couldn't catch my breath. Becoming a sannyas would mean the end of my relationship with Sampuran. I think we both had been holding out hope that we could find a way to be together.

I finished up messages. As I left the room, I heard the exercise bike resume its revolutions.

That night, Ma announced that I would be taking sannyas with Govinda next year. Mild clapping filled the room. I wasn't smiling.

Over the next year, I tried to ignore the thoughts of my impending vows. I felt like I would lose what little freedom I had. I shuddered at the idea of joining this group of Ma's elite teachers. Running the ashram and being one of Ma's inner circle, I didn't need a title. I thought the swamis were a bunch of bumbling idiots, a group of orange-clad Stepford Wives. They took Ma's words literally and held the party line so tightly, it was as if they'd lost the ability to think for themselves. I thought about Sampuran.

I looked out the kitchen window. Across the pond, the acharya from New York stood in his orange garb in front of the Baba temple. An older male devotee from Atlanta dropped to his knees and then his stomach and kissed his feet. I didn't want this to be my fate.

Sampuran planned a surprise for my fortieth birthday. I snuck off to Orlando for the weekend, where he'd rented a hotel room. He took me to Cirque du Soleil. We drank B&B until our heads swooned. We dined on Café-Tasse Belgian dark chocolate, allowing it to melt on our tongues. And we made wild, passionate love into the evening. Waking late the following morning, I rolled over and burrowed under Sampuran's arm. He pulled me in and held me. He was quiet, pensive, thinking.

"What are you thinking about?" I asked.

He hesitated. "I was thinking, maybe we should take a break. I'm worried you're going to get caught. I don't want to be the reason you get in trouble. We both know what's at stake. I feel a tremendous amount of guilt."

I sat up, pulling the covers up around me. "What are you saying?" I felt like I had been kicked in the stomach.

His blue eyes bored into my soul. "I love you. I don't want you to get hurt."

"It's a little late for that." Tears streamed down my face.

"We can be friends," he said, and pulled me closer.

I sucked in my breath. "Sure, we can be friends." I knew I needed to let him go. How could I expect him to continue our romance without a future? Sneaking around burdened with the fear of getting caught by either of our teachers? I was bound to my life, and he to his. I knew I had to let him go. There was no way this relationship would be sanctioned by either of our teachers. Guilt had finally taken its toll on the romantic part of our relationship.

We would be friends from this point on. No more making love. No more making out. One thing I knew was that his friendship was more important than anything to me.

May arrived, and with it, my day of reckoning. Ribbons of orange and pink hung like wispy curtains above the tip of the temple. Palm trees swayed in the wind and bowed toward the Hanuman Temple. A balmy, tropical breeze brushed through the May evening. I could smell the magnolia blossoms, and the scent of sandalwood was thick. Hundreds of people settled in around the temple; some crammed on the tiered wooden benches, while others sat on pillows on the concrete. The chanting began. Govinda and I sat before Ma. I grabbed his hand, and he gave it a gentle squeeze. We both had prepared ourselves for this moment, but neither of us wanted to do this.

Sampuran sat on the edge of the temple nearby. I glanced over at him. Our eyes caught, and I smiled. He smiled back. I had organized the day's events up until now, but tonight I'd be a participant. I handed off the index cards to my mother.

The bells and conches blared. The fire and warm air merged on my flesh. I felt the love of hundreds of people wash over me as a slight wisp of a breeze whispered through my hair. I focused on Ma. At this moment, a year of anguish dissipated into an abyss of love between the three of us, Ma, Govinda, and me.

"Namaste, my children." Ma's burgundy sari shimmered as thousands of intricate beads caught the firelight. Large jewels sparkled on her fingers and wrists, and long strands of rudraksha bead malas, some the size of golf balls, hung from her neck.

"I'd like to honor Sai Maa[2] for being here tonight," Ma began.

I'd all but forgotten about Sai Maa. She was our humanitarian award recipient this year. Hundreds of her students had come to town with her to witness or be part of the ceremony. Earlier that morning, Sai Maa had called me into her guest suite and offered to take me into the light. Why was it gurus and spiritual teachers always wanted to entice the students of other teachers and gurus? I wasn't interested in her showing me anything.

Ma turned to Sai Maa. "Would you offer a blessing for my children?"

I offered Ma a conspiratorial look and rolled my eyes. *Okay, dolphin energy, here we come.* The corners of Ma's mouth turned up slightly. I had told her about my morning and evading the visiting holy teacher's clutches.

Sai Maa blessed everyone and all entities now and forever and, yes, offered the wisdom of the dolphins to grace us all.

Ma surveyed her audience. "We gather here tonight to share this very special ritual as my two children become sannyasin. My sannyasin serve humanity. They take care of the ashram, and most of all, take care of their Ma. They are married to God and take a vow to always serve. Tonight, you will witness a very rare ceremony. It takes many years to become sannyas, if ever. It is a moment when my children give themselves over fully to this teaching. You will witness this intimate ceremony as they shave their heads. Watch as they dip in the waters of the Ganga, purifying themselves, and Ma covers their bodies with holy ash. Ash, the holiest of substances, has burned in these fires for over thirty years. They will become the son and daughter of the Mother Kali and the great Lord Shiva."

Govinda and I were both lost deep in our own moments. There would be no turning back. I caught a glimpse of my boys in the crowd and wondered what they must be thinking as it appeared I was sinking deeper into the teaching. How many years had I been told I was born to serve her? And that my children were born to serve her? I looked up at my guru and surrendered.

"Are you ready?" Ma asked.

I nodded and closed my eyes. This was it.

"Begin."

Sampuran picked up his guitar, and our eyes met for a moment. A tear dropped onto my white silk gown, and I looked away and shut my eyes. He chanted a soft, melodic chant. His guitar played my heart.

"Sampuran, come sit next to your spiritual sister," Ma said.

I cringed. We were way beyond brother and sister at this point. Ma handed him a pair of scissors, and I felt his hands on my head. He took a gentle hold of a lock of my hair, and I felt the scissors open and close against my head. The stainless steel reverberated in my ear. He placed the pieces of my dirty-blond hair into the hands of a swami who held out an orange cloth.

Sampuran then sat behind me. He was so close, I felt the heat from his body. Here in this moment lay the secret and the lie embodied within even this most sacred ceremony.

Ma signaled to the musicians. The harmoniums whirred to life, the pounding of the drums vibrated in me, and chanting filled the background space. The sound of buzzing clippers closed in. My hair fell to the ground, into my eyes, and onto my clothing. My eyes remained fixed on Ma's. As my hair dropped away, a freeing sensation cascaded over me.

Govinda and I glanced at each other's freshly shorn heads, and I wondered if this was how sheep felt. Ma touched our heads, one in each hand. She gave us each a special mala and a pile of orange clothing.

"I am going to walk with my children to the Ganga. They will purify themselves in our holy waters. Then I will anoint them with Shiva's holy ash. When they return to the temple, they will be sannyas. Remain here and chant to God."

Ma began to rise, and I reached for her hand to help her up. Govinda stood on her other side.

"Come, my children, let us go," she said.

A gaggle of orange-wearing sannyas followed behind. One carried a trident as we walked to the nearby thatched hut. All of the temples twinkled with hundreds of white lights. I felt the eyes of the remaining satsang and guests watch us as we departed.

We reached the edge of the pond. The dark body of water was still. I took a breath. Govinda and I jumped at the same time and swam until we could tread water. I shivered, but I dunked three times as instructed. When I returned to shore, my white clothes clung to my body.

We both lay down on the grass by the shore's edge. Someone handed me a towel to cover my eyes, and Ma dumped a bucket of holy ash over my wet body. I could smell the ash as it dropped onto my body. Dust particles filled my nose and my mouth. Ma placed her foot upon my chest. "Mother Kali steps upon Shiva, her consort. You are Kali's daughter. You are Shiva's consort. Jai Kali Ma!" she yelled.

I sat up and wiped the ash from my head to prevent it from dropping into my eyes.

"Go back into the Ganga, swim across the pond, and meet me by the Baba Temple," Ma said.

The moon was nearly full and created a path of light across the rippling waters. I pushed away any thoughts about the creatures that lurked in the depths. I'd followed the light.

Ma walked around the pond, escorted by a parade of orange and one man in flowing white and a turban. Behind them, a cadre of miscellaneous folks followed.

I swam freestyle to the other side as Govinda swam by my right hand. Every few strokes, I lifted my head to see how far from the shore I was until my feet met the silty bottom. I stepped down into the algae bed and scurried out of the water.

Ma waited by the Baba statue, and Govinda and I bowed. Then Ma returned to the chanting mass, and Govinda and I changed into our orange clothes. Attendants held up sheets for us as a makeshift dressing room. I was helped into a shimmering, light-orange silk Punjabi gown with matching pants. I needed to hurry and get back to Ma at the temple. She'd be getting impatient.

The sandy dirt was cool upon my feet, and Govinda and I walked the short stretch back to the temple. The chanting was frenzied as the satsang, guests, and other devotees stood swaying, clapping, and smiling. Cheers and whoops greeted us as we walked past the stone foo dogs guarding the entrance of the temple.

People reached out to touch us as we made our way to Ma. We bowed before her, and she smiled at us like a proud mother. She dipped a small paintbrush into a container and swirled a circle of red on Govinda's forehead. "I love you, my son." He hugged her and smiled.

She dipped the brush back into the container and lifted it toward my head. A cool swish crossed my forehead. This was about being one with God, I reminded myself.

"And you, my daughter, I name 'Swami Krishnapriya Bhagavati Jaya Sati Saraswati.'"

I repeated the rhyming mouthful.

"You have my name now," she whispered. "Come, let's go to the temple."

We walked up the steps into the smaller inner sanctum, where Hanuman, the monkey god, presided. Ma fed us fresh fruit. "I love you, my swami daughter."

"I love you too, Ma."

The ceremony ended, and the crowd dispersed. I ducked into the bathroom and gazed at myself in the mirror. My head was shaped like an egg. It was shiny, too. There were no nicks. It was a nice-shaped head. Gold hoop earrings would be stunning if it hadn't looked like someone had used my forehead for target practice. A large red circle took up my entire third-eye point. It swished around with a tail. Above my ping-pong-size red splat were three thick white lines smeared across the top of my head.

Sampuran was waiting for me when I arrived back to my room. I curled up in his arms on the floor. There would be no more passionate nights in hotel rooms or heated nights in his Explorer. I fell asleep in his arms on the carpet of my floor.

37

Ashen Lady, Give Up Your Vows

MY LIFE DIDN'T CHANGE DRAMATICALLY after I became a swami. I was still the same person. No one would be kissing my feet or bowing before me. I worked in the office, organized intensives, took care of Ma, and practiced yoga. I continued to figure out creative ways for the ashram to be financially solvent. It was an impossible task, yet I held on to the hope I could change the ashram culture and make a difference.

It was a Thursday night. No guests were in darshan. On the nights when it was only the residents, Ma took us into a deeper space of meditation. The chanting was magical. Ma settled into her seat.

"Tonight, I am going to take you into the space detachment. The emptiness, the place of detachment where the vast silence resides. Close your eyes. Bring your awareness and your breath to the base of the spine."

I began to breathe, concentrating on the space where my seat met the pillow. My body relaxed, and I let go.

"Take a gentle, powerful, silent breath. Remember that pain adheres to pain. If you meet someone in deep pain, it's important to remember it is not about you. Love them. Hold them. But don't take on their pain. Remember to breathe into the heart and out of the top of the head three times. And the third time, you stay there. You stay right on top of the head or slightly over the head. This is the place of detachment."

I could feel myself floating, going deeper and deeper. I longed for these moments.

I continued with ashram business. Ma's autobiography was about to be published. We prepared to celebrate her sixty-fourth birthday. I was planning our trip to Barcelona for the Parliament of the World's Religions. Working at my desk, my computer pinged. It was an email from the publisher. They had been bought by a bigger company. With regret, they passed on Ma's book. Ma was heartbroken. I couldn't believe all the work and this was what happened.

Just after Ma's sixty-fourth birthday celebration, I was getting dressed for the day when the phone rang.

"Krishnapriya. It's Mom." She sounded stuffy.

"Are you okay?" I asked.

"I am here with Ma. She just received a call that Jimmy is dead."

"I'll be right over."

I was the last to enter Ma's rooms. I walked over to Ma and embraced her.

"I am so sorry," I whispered in her ear.

Ma grieved her son. I worked.

My brother continued to work on his plan to develop the property and build the eldercare center. He thought it would solve our financial problems. I thought it was a mistake. It became a source of contention between us.

It had been almost a year since I'd last seen Sampuran. We had spoken occasionally, a few random calls, but he'd slipped away from my life. One evening, he called and wanted to come visit.

We sat on the floor of my room after darshan.

"You know you broke my heart?" I said.

"I didn't mean to hurt you." His white kurta pulled across his chest. I tugged on the edges of my orange top.

"You just walked out of my life and disappeared for a year." I held his gaze as my lower teeth gripped my bottom lip. "Why is it always so damn hard to talk about how you feel?"

"I needed to work some things through," he said.

"I realize you were going through a lot of changes. But it was hard not having any communication."

"I know. I'm really sorry. I care about you and never wanted to hurt you."

"You know I love you, and our friendship is important to me. Please, if you are going to disappear on me, would you just let me know?" We hugged.

Although we were no longer lovers, I was happy to have him back in my life.

Hanuman graduated from the University of Florida and took a job teaching English in Japan. Ganga Das remained cancer-free and was healthy. He finished his two-year degree at Santa Fe Community College and moved to California with his childhood sweetheart, Jaya Ma. Hanuman wouldn't be home for at least two years.

One night after darshan, Sampuran and I were eating dinner in my room.

"I think you should go to Japan and visit Hanuman," Sampuran said.

"I'd love that. I miss him. We talk a lot, but it's not the same."

"I went there when I was a kid; my father was stationed there for a bit. I'd like to go back."

I poked his side and giggled. "That would be fun. I'd love to go with you."

Sometime later, I was rummaging through my drawer and found an envelope from him. My heart thumped when I opened it. I looked at the note.

"Here's your plane ticket to Japan. I wish I could go with you. You'll have fun with your baby boy."

I reread the note and picked up the phone. "You are so sneaky. I am speechless. And excited."

"It will be fun. Ma will be away for the summer. It's perfect."

"Thank you so much."

A few weeks later, I landed in Narita Airport after a fourteen-hour flight. Hanuman stood by the gate. I cried.

"Oh my God, oh my God. You look fabulous." I kissed him and hugged him and cried some more.

"Thanks, Mom. Welcome to Japan." We found our way to the train for a three-hour ride to Mito, the town where Hanuman lived. He pointed out the countryside; farms and rice fields dotted the land as we moved farther away from the city.

"The town I live in is relatively small. Very few *gaijin* live there." He was learning to speak Japanese.

It had been a long time since we'd seen each other. I couldn't remember the last time we'd spent time alone.

"I've planned your trip," he said. "We'll go to the beach Oarai, visit the Great Buddha of Kamakura, climb Mt. Fuji, and if we are up to it, take the bullet to Hiroshima."

"I am so excited." I clapped my hands and jumped up and down like a giddy teenager. He laughed and shook his head.

"Am I going to meet your girlfriend?"

"Yes." He rolled his eyes. He was smitten. "Her name is Chicako. She's going to take you to the mall tomorrow while I work."

"That sounds great. I look forward to meeting Chicago."

"Mom, her name is 'chee-cock-oh.'" He corrected me with a hint of "please don't go there, Mom" in his voice.

Japan was magical, and it was a turning point in our relationship.

Hanuman had grown up. No more smoking, drugs, or unhealthy behaviors. We were both older and wiser. He wanted respect from me, and I was proud of him. We climbed Mt. Fuji, visited the Great Buddha of Kamakura, and swam in the Pacific.

I flew back through San Francisco, and Sampuran planned to meet me there. We'd spend the weekend together before I flew back to Florida.

"*Kanichiwah*!" I waved. "*Arigato su mi san*."

He laughed at my attempt to greet him in Japanese and gave me a brotherly hug. "Welcome back, weary traveler. Let's get your bags. Are you hungry?" he asked.

"Famished. What's our plan?"

"You'll see."

The cab pulled up in front of the San Francisco Four Seasons. "No way."

"Only the best, and since I would never even think of staying in a highfalutin joint like this, I figured this would be a fun experience to welcome you back."

We entered the lobby, and Sampuran checked in. The porter took our bags, saying, "I'll meet you and your lady friend upstairs."

Sampuran turned bright red and stuttered some incomprehensible reply.

We waited till the elevator doors closed. "Oh my God, lady friend? Do you think he thought I was a prostitute?"

Sampuran grinned. I stared back at him.

"No fucking way."

"Come on, lady friend. It's only because you look way younger than me."

"I am way younger than you."

I stopped short before the door. "Are you joking? The penthouse?"

"Come on." He pushed me in. We ordered room service and talked. Both of us were nervous. I suggested a drink to calm our nerves. He told me under no uncertain terms did he intend to do anything that might lead to heartbreak. My drink made me bold. My hand reached for Sampuran. He resisted. I persisted. He relented. It was a moment when I realized just how much I loved him, even at the risk of breaking my vows.

38

R-E-S-P-E-C-T

A FEW MONTHS LATER, I was called to the salon for "hair day." Ma was seated in her salon chair as my mom was mixing a thick, black liquid.

Ma gazed down at me as I sat at her feet. "Do you know how much I love you? I love you as if you were my own blood. I actually love you more than my own blood."

My heart swelled. My skin tingled. I met her eyes.

"My birth children don't have any interest in this teaching. They only care about my money or what they can get from me. Isn't that right, Shody?" Ma looked in the mirror.

My mother remained silent. She turned Ma around and began clipping her hair up.

"We need to have that meeting with Chandra and look at my will."

Ma rewrote her will on a routine basis. It was often based on who in her family was in good standing. Any inappropriate behavior, they'd be removed.

"I need to remove Chun from my will after how he's betrayed me. Tell Krishna Bai to tell him, too. He's no longer my son."

"We meet with Chandra tomorrow, Ma." My mother always had a soft spot for Ma's children. She stood up for them when she felt Ma was being unreasonable. It was a source of conflict between her and Ma.

"Did your mother tell you what I told her this morning?" Ma asked.

"No, Ma," I said.

"Shody, what's wrong with you? I tell you something so important about your daughter, and you don't tell her?"

"I didn't see her this morning," my mother said as she painted the dye over strands of Ma's hair.

Ma leaned forward in her chair. Her face searched mine. "You are going to teach and take my legacy out to the world. I am going to give you a special place in my teaching. And after I am gone, you will help lead this teaching."

"Ma, I don't want to talk about this. I don't want to think about it," I said.

"Oh, don't worry, I am not dying for a long time," Ma said. "But this is an important moment for you. I want you to know how much I trust you. I trust my ashram to you and my teaching. I want you to carry my legacy. Do you understand?"

"Yes, Ma. Thank you. I love the ashram and the teaching. I want nothing more than to see it flourish and grow."

"And another thing I have been thinking about. You know how I have promised to take you to India? I am not sure that my health will stand up to the trip. You know how sick your Ma's been. I am just not sure I can do it. Right, Shody?" Ma turned to my mother.

"It's true. I don't think Ma would do well in India with everything going on with her health. I'm worried it will be a major setback for her." Ma had been ill on and off for years with different ailments. Her back was always a source of pain.

"You understand, don't you?"

"Of course."

"I want you to lead a group there, as my daughter; you go and do yoga and travel to Baba's ashram. Call Sampuran. Ask him what he does when he takes his students and how much he charges. See, Shody? See, this works out way better; your daughter can go."

My mother and Ma seemed relieved.

"I will be with you. You'll take me there in your heart," Ma added. We talked about all the places I would need to visit. Finally, I was going to India.

The people who had been with Ma the longest would only talk to my mom about their issues. They wanted no part of confiding to the sannyas. I couldn't blame them. I didn't trust them, either. If a swami decided a person was doing something that they perceived as wrong or could impact the ashram or Ma in a negative manner, they would not hesitate to tell Ma. No secret was sacred. My mom was the closest person to Ma, and everyone wanted to speak with her about their issues. The satsang trusted her.

I thought it was fascinating and frustrating that some of Ma's students were unable to make the most common sense decisions without asking my mother for fear there might be karmic implications.

"Can I throw away this piece of old chewing gum that was on Ma's desk?"

I had even overheard someone ask if they could throw away a dirty tissue when cleaning Ma's rooms.

There were others who, when left to their own interpretation, did some absurd things. Like the time one of the horses on the ashram died. Ma was joking and said to one of the women, "Go dig up Misty."

She did.

In a fit, Ma once told someone to dip their head in a vat of paint.

He did.

Practicing yoga and hosting retreats and workshops were my

passions. I convinced Ma that we needed to invite well-known yoga teachers and speakers to come to the ashram to teach.

In 2007, we invited renowned yogis and chanting duo Deva Premal and Miten to offer a workshop at the ashram. We rented a tent and sound system and set it up behind the dining hall. Deva and Miten had planned to come to Ma's evening darshan the Friday night before the event, but they arrived later than expected and missed it. After darshan, Ma returned to her private quarters for the evening. We used the term "Ma's locked up" when she closed up for the night.

I went back to my house, where we hosted important guests. Someone had set the table and brought them dinner.

"We are so sorry to have missed Ma," Deva said.

I was disappointed that they wouldn't get a chance to meet her, but what to do? I gave them a short tour of the temples around the pond. They were deeply moved by the ashram's beauty, the temples, and the exquisite stillness. A small group of us had dinner with our guests at Shirdi House and discussed ashram life, being with the guru, and chanting. They seemed thirsty to hear about our lives.

"You don't know how lucky you are to have a guru in the flesh," Miten said.

Deva nodded. Her smile lit up the room. "We miss Osho every moment of our lives. We carry him with us in our hearts."

Miten's depth shone through his eyes. He was an old soul, I thought. I had read several of Osho's books. His teachings were profound and prolific, and his famous discourse on the word *fuck* was hilarious. Osho also had a lot of negative press, and I was familiar with that and the fact that the Western mind had a hard time grasping the guru tradition.

The next afternoon, hundreds of guests arrived on the ashram. They'd traveled from all over Florida to attend the workshop. Men in baggy yoga pants and dreadlocks walked with women in flowing skirts. Flowers floated around the pond. Sampuran and I sat in the back of the tent.

Deva and Miten's chanting permeated the ashram. Participants swooned and swayed. The energy was dynamic. Ethereal voices accompanied by the sound of the flute and a gentle strum of the guitar sent people into a meditative state. In the end, blissed-out yogis found their way to their cars, vowing to return to our lovely sanctuary. We said our goodbyes to the beautiful, chanting nomads.

A few days later, I woke at 5:30 a.m. to attend Dead Dawn darshan. Ma was seated in her chair. She wasn't in a good mood.

"Namaste, Ma."

She sifted through the mail and tossed it aside. "So, the workshop was a success?"

I offered my positive, upbeat report to her. "Yes. It went very well. Thank you. The ashram made some money. We had a number of people who want to come back and spend time here. It was a really wonderful event and a great success."

A shadow passed across her face as she fussed with some papers in front of her. "You know they disrespected me. Not only did they not come to darshan, which I couldn't give a shit about, but they didn't even bring the guru an offering, not even a shitty CD." She turned to me.

My back went vertical. "That is not true. They spoke about you with great respect. They loved the ashram. They were very apologetic. They couldn't make it to darshan and didn't realize that would be their only chance to see you." My hands clenched as I defended them.

"I don't buy it for a second. If they wanted to see me, they would have made it happen. And they know if they come to the guru, they should bring a gift."

"But Ma, that isn't how it happened."

Her brows creased, drawing her eyes into predacious slits. "Why are you defending them?" Her nostrils flared.

I leaned forward, trying to ease her heart. "They are lovely people. They travel the world, and they'll take their experience here with them. It's not what you think."

"I don't want to hear another word about it. End it." She threw the papers down and responded with her glare.

I knew when to shut up. There was no point in pissing her off any further.

"Is there anyone out there I need to know about?" Her tone cut through me.

"No, Ma. No guests. It's just us this morning."

She got up to go to the bathroom.

I turned to my mother. "She's wrong about this and about them. This is fucked up. What is it really about? They come here and bring a ton of people to see the ashram, and she's pissed off that they didn't come to darshan. If we want people to visit the ashram, they are not always going to dance to our tune. It's time we become more expansive if we're going to grow this ashram." I kicked the leopard carpet. I hated the faux animal print. It reminded me of a middle-aged suburban housewife looking to prey on the local pool boy.

The rest of the girls in the room couldn't have cared less. No one was interested in this battle.

Ma walked by me when she returned. A cold breeze followed her. "You are so off," she said.

"I am sorry, Ma, but I just don't see it. I don't agree."

My mother shot me a look.

Ma put her hand up. "End it, I said."

We walked out to darshan, none of us smiling.

Ma sat and ended the chanting immediately. "The guru is to be honored and respected. My Baba is my life. I do whatever he tells me. He is never out of my heart. And when guests come to this sacred ashram, it is up to all of you to teach them how to be with a guru."

I squirmed on my cushion. *Oh, for God's sake. She's going to talk about this in darshan.* I sat on my hands.

"I've never been so disrespected. Those people disrespected your Ma."

Most of the satsang had attended the event and had been talking about it ever since. I wondered if they'd buy it.

"If people come here to this ashram, they need to know how to be with the guru and how to respect the guru."

I pressed my body into the floor. I wanted to jump up and strangle her.

There were those who did not want to share Ma with anyone, and there would be repercussions from the fundamentalists in our teaching, like, "How could you let this happen? We never wanted to open the doors to the ashram. We don't want Ma to get hurt."

The meditation was short, and Ma left with a hasty "namaste."

I stormed out.

The weekly sannyas meetings were a battlefield. Mohan, the ashram's board president, and I sat next to each other. He had been with Ma since he was in his twenties. We despised being inside this building for another dreadful meeting when we could be at the beach ducking waves. Each swami took a turn leading the meeting, and my brother was in charge this Sunday. We commenced with our obligatory spiritual missives. He discussed finances and new construction. I tugged on my short bangs. I knew about the financial situation. It was discussed every day, in staff meetings, board meetings, and executive meetings and privately when people came to my office.

He moved quickly through his list. "In addition to taking care of the ashram, we need to make sure Ma is being taken care of. As swamis, it is our duty."

I flinched.

"As you know, Ma was upset and felt disrespected."

"I don't agree with this at all. They came here to this ashram with great respect." My voice was a bit louder than I meant. "Ma's wrong. This is wrong. I can't believe you can't see it." I surveyed the group.

"Dhumavati, Himalaya, do you believe this?" I looked at them, pleading my case. Both of them had been very positive about Deva and Miten. I was met with silence.

I rolled up onto my knees. "If we can't bring people here without a scene or a drama, maybe we should rethink what we are doing. We might want to reconsider growing and expanding." I glared at my brother. "Maybe we should not let anyone come to the ashram and teach here." I challenged the rest of the group. "So much for being open and loving unconditionally." I rolled my eyes. *What a bunch of crap. What a bunch of fence-sitters.*

The meeting ended, and I bolted out of the door. Mohan caught up to me.

"This is fucking stupid. It's all stupid." I shook my head. My patience for the swamis' antics was waning. I felt internally fractured. Many years before, when Ma felt offended, I would have sided with her. Now it just appeared she was throwing a tantrum. It seemed her insatiable need to be respected was endless.

39

Shattered

"I WANT YOU TO TAPE THE NEW ASANA. It will change the face of the ashram. I need to have it so I can learn it, too," Ma said as she read a piece of mail.

Many of these poses were complex, and it was impossible to memorize them. Some of the practices had fifty to sixty different instructions.

A few days later, I was called into Ma's rooms before darshan.

I entered through the door of Ma's salon. "Namaste."

"Namaste. What's happening out there?"

"It's pretty crazy. A number of guests have arrived, and the energy is frenetic."

"Where's my video?" she asked.

"I'm working on it, Ma." I explained our plans to tape the asana down by the river.

"Did you read my email darshan this morning?"

"Not yet."

"Well, if you're not reading it, why am I doing it? Shody, what am I supposed to do here?" Her voice pitched as she looked at my mom in the mirror.

My mom separated the strands of Ma's hair. She looked back into the mirror at her.

"I need you to read darshan line before you see me," Ma said. She had begun teaching darshan via email so all of her students from around the world could receive her daily teachings. It was coined "darshan line."

"It's karmic, and in your position, you should know better. What is wrong with you? And why haven't you done the video I asked you for weeks ago?"

I froze in place. I saw where the conversation was heading.

"Is your job too much? Do you need me to take it away to make it easier?"

"No, Ma, I'm sorry. The video is scheduled for this week."

She swiveled her chair toward me. "I can't do this. I don't understand. If the guru asks for something, it should be the first thing you do."

I leaned back.

"Just leave. I can't look at you. I can't have you in here right now. You are a swami. You should know better."

"Namaste, Ma." I stood and departed.

I walked to the temple to sit. There was too much to do—I could no longer keep up. I needed to make the video happen right away, so I rescheduled the shoot for the following morning. I'd been excited to do this for Ma. Now, I couldn't give a shit.

The next day, my mother explained Ma wasn't feeling well. "She's unable to teach for a few days," she explained. I was grateful for the time off. My mom delivered the video to Ma.

My cell phone roused me from sleep somewhere around 6:00 a.m. It had been days since I'd last seen Ma. The call was from Ma's rooms, and an early-morning call was rarely good.

"Namaste," I mumbled, wiping the sleep from my eyes.

"Namaste, Krishnapriya. It's Yashoda." My mom was using her formal voice. "I am calling to let you know Ma loves the video. She wanted you to know."

"That's good," was all I could muster. I rolled up to sitting. I wanted to forget the whole damn video thing.

"Ma is teaching tonight. She's calling us in early."

I made sure not to be late, but the swamis from out of town were already in Ma's rooms when I arrived. "Namaste, Ma."

Ma was deep in conversation with both head swamis from New York and LA. I sat in the doorway and looked at the pictures of dead people in the hallway. Hundreds of thimbles and pretty containers of dead people's ashes rested by each photo; people I'd known for years lined the shelves.

"Did you get my message this morning?" Ma asked from the salon chair.

"Yes, Ma. Thank you."

"Why are you making this about you? You didn't put Ma first."

The room turned into a vacuum. The swamis glared at me. The swami from New York appeared to relish the showdown.

"The fact that it took you so long to do the video just shows me where you are at."

I put my pen down. There wasn't much to say without adding fuel to the fire.

"You are a good yoga teacher, and I love the video. So why couldn't you do it when I asked? I'll never understand." She shrugged and tilted her head.

I leaned my head against the glass door.

"Why aren't you promoting yourself? What is this unworthiness?"

My fingers fussed with the collar of my orange top. I needed air.

"Where's Krishna Bai?

"Acharya, find my earrings.

"Shody, get me my meds."

I sat in the chaos. *Breathe*, I reminded myself. Remember Yogi Bhajan's advice—*stay calm in the center of the hurricane.*

"Who's here tonight?" Ma asked, not looking my way.

I recited the list.

"You need to get over yourself and snap out of it. You are bringing a heaviness into my rooms. Do you feel that, Acharya?" Ma looked up at Acharya, standing near her.

"Yes, Ma," he said, as he pulled her hair through the curling iron.

What an asshole. I wanted to cry, but I knew that would just prove Ma right. I looked around the room at all of them. They were tourists. They were clueless about what it was like to live day-to-day with Ma, to live in the fire of our teaching.

"Do you understand? I am the guru. You are supposed to be taking care of me. I am not supposed to be taking care of you, especially in my rooms."

"Yes, Ma." I heard my voice crack. I excused myself and left the room to make announcements.

I hit the hall, gulped in the cool air, and then stopped in the bathroom. I needed to get myself together before stepping out in front of all those people.

I crossed the threshold into the darkened temple, where I was met by hundreds of smiling faces, incense, candles, and flowers. I smiled and choked out the evening announcements.

I had to return to Ma's rooms. She was in the bathroom. The entourage had relocated to the living room, and I was met with twenty pairs of eyes. I glared at most of them.

"Well, what's going on out there?" Ma asked as she entered the room. Her teased hair poufed out around her head, and her cheeks were streaked with brownish rouge and made her look like a strange caricature of herself. What had Acharya done to her? She no longer looked like a spiritual teacher.

"They're ready for you, Ma," I said, attempting to be upbeat.

"Good, you got it. Never again put Ma last."

I nodded.

"Okay, let's go." And that was it. It was business as usual.

A few weeks later, I was called into the salon once again during Ma's weekly dye job and my allotted time to do business with her. I ticked through my messages.

"How's Hanuman doing?" Ma asked.

"He's thinking of going to Thailand to help with the tsunami cleanup, and then he'd like to go to India. I thought maybe I could plan a trip then and take a group to India like we discussed." I was excited about the possibility of finally going to India.

"Let's see. Send your son my love. Tell him his Ma misses him, and he should write more."

I finished up my list of messages.

On my walk home, I started thinking about visiting the Kali temples in Dakshineswar and Baba's temple in Kainchi and that maybe I could even slip down to Tiruvannamalai to visit Ramana Maharshi's ashram in South India. I made a list of people I knew wanted to go to India and pulled out my *Lonely Planet India* book. Sleep came easy. I dreamed of temples and traveling.

The phone rang. I rolled over. It wasn't even 7:00 a.m. "Namaste."

"Namaste, Krishnapriya, it's Yashoda."

Uh-oh. My mother in business voice. "Mom?" I mumbled.

"Look, I need to speak with you about yesterday. Ma is very upset. She's been up all night, sick about the India trip. She really feels it's not time. How can you think of taking people to India when there is so much to do here?"

The tension in my gut moved up to my heart and was about to reach my throat. I had thought the conversation was positive yesterday. I couldn't believe how naive I had been.

"Ma is afraid. And she feels you are bringing too much of you into her rooms. You need to be more present."

The sour taste turned to rage. "I couldn't have been more present and open in those rooms with Ma yesterday. What is it she's looking for? What does she want from me?"

"Well, I think she'd like you to be more present in a bigger way."

"What the hell does that mean? I am being killed why? Because I suggested a trip to India? This was Ma's idea. This is crazy. Tell me then, just how am I not present?"

"Look, Krishnapriya, Ma is afraid. She is worried about you leaving the ashram and flying off to India."

"Yah-shooow-dah." I drew out the syllables of her spiritual name, hearing myself balanced on the edge of sarcasm and defiance. "Which is it? Me going to India or me being present? What does one thing have to do with the other? This is bullshit."

"Krishnapriya. I am not sure what is going on with you. But your emotional state has been seeping into Ma's rooms for some time now, and it's not appropriate."

"I veil my emotions when I am in Ma's space. And you know what? I'm really tired. I am tired of hearing all of the things I am not. You tell me Ma needs me, she can't live without me, and in the next breath, you guys tell me I am negative because I don't want the ashram to be chopped up and pieces of the property sold off. And now I am being told I am not present. I don't do things quick enough. And I bring my stuff into the rooms. I can't take it. What do you guys want from me?"

"You have done so much to move the ashram forward. I just want you to be happy."

"I'm not, and killing me all the time isn't helping. It seems as soon as I begin to make changes that will actually help the ashram grow, Ma kills me for things that don't even make sense. I don't understand."

"You know how much Ma loves you and trusts you."

"Maybe it's time for me to step down. Let someone else run the ashram."

"That is not what Ma is saying. That's just your ego speaking."

"I am burnt out. I know Ma preaches her students never burn out. Well, guess what? I am burnt out." I punched the comforter.

"People look up to you. They need you and count on you."

"Let's face it. I can't talk about the problems of the ashram. It's construed as negativity. And when I do, it's bringing myself into the rooms."

"Ma is okay with you going to India. She's just not okay taking everyone else, not right now."

"'Ma wants you to go. Ma doesn't want you to go. It's okay but just not now.'" I grabbed my pillow and punched it again.

"What do I tell Ma?"

"I don't care."

"Ma loves you so much. You guys are so tuned in to one another, and if you are struggling, of course she is going to feel that. It scares her. I need to call Ma now."

"Whatever." We both hung up. I rolled into a fetal position and wept.

If this was Ma's way of teaching me, I wasn't getting the lesson. Lying there, I thought about the past few weeks.

No matter what I did, Ma got upset.

40

Rat in a Cage

THE HOLIDAYS WERE UPON US, and 2007 was coming to a close.

"We need to have a meeting." Mohan's voice was clipped over the phone. It was Sunday, and I was in my office trying to catch up. He was in his board president mode.

"What for?" I rocked back in my office chair.

"No big deal. We need to discuss the ashram financials." I heard him rustling something in the background.

I flew forward onto the edge of my desk. "You're joking. I am preparing for an intensive. What's so important it can't wait? We just had a board meeting last week and an executive meeting a few days ago."

"I'll be over in a few." He hung up before I could protest.

I slammed the phone down. Mohan and my brother were up to no good. I returned my attention to the blue screen of my computer. Let's see, opening meditation, yoga, and small groups. I typed the beginning of the schedule for the weekend. My extension rang, a flashing red light accompanying it.

"Namaste," I answered.

"We're here," Mohan said.

"Who is 'we'? And where are you?" Spit landed on the receiver.

"I'm with your brother. We're in the conference room."

What could possibly be up? I picked up a notepad and stomped across to the other end of the office. Durga Das and Mohan were seated together at the far end of the conference table. They both offered me a weak smile. I pulled out a chair in the middle of the room a few seats away. It was beginning to feel like a trial.

"What's up?" I asked.

Mohan cleared his throat. "You know the ashram is in a serious financial state. We can't pay the bills. Not enough people pay rent, and we are living on credit. And we have all agreed to move forward with a plan to alleviate some of the pressure with the land development program." He tapped a pen on his paper.

I leaned back and folded my arms. They knew I was opposed to the development plans. My notebook and pen rested in front of me.

"We have sold a few lots already, but we need your help." Mohan paused.

My respiration increased as I stared at both of them. My mouth opened, but nothing came out.

"We need you to get on board with land development. You are connected to everyone in the teaching. You have great people skills." Another pause. They both smiled.

I wanted to rip their saccharin grins right off their faces.

"We'd like you to help sell lots." Mohan smiled at me from across the table.

"You're fucking joking."

Mohan laughed. "I remember the annual Christmas Tree Sale. It was a great public-relations event. It was well known that on your shifts, you'd sell trees as if they were gold. We need your ability to speak with people."

"I can't believe you are both sitting here asking me to do this. I have taken on more than my share here. You beat me up every chance you get regarding my job and role as CEO. And now you want me to sell fucking lots. This is okay to add to my job description, but any talk of the yoga program isn't?" I held my breath. I knew if I exhaled, a torrent of tears would come with it.

"Krishnapriya." My brother interrupted his silence. "People love you and respect you. The ashram needs you now more than ever." His voice oozed like melted butter.

My jaws contracted. I clutched the edge of the table.

"You hired Baba Ram to sell lots and run your development program for thirty thousand dollars a year. The rest of us receive a few hundred dollars a month. This is wrong." I recited my current list of responsibilities. My tears were starting to escape.

"It's for Ma, her legacy, and this teaching," Durga Das said.

I pushed the table away and leaped up. "Fuck you. Fuck you both." I yanked the door open and wrenched my shoulder as I stormed out. In less than twenty steps, I reached my office and slammed the door, shaking the whole building.

Then I left the office to find my mother and collapsed onto her office floor, my hands to my face, my chest heaving. "I can't take it anymore. The land development committee comes up with a plan to reduce the current ashram debt of 1.8 million dollars. They want to build an assisted living facility that won't make any money. They want to rape our land and sell lots for private homes on the north side of the property. And now they want *me* to sell property. This is fucked."

"Krishnapriya! Your brother is working hard to make this ashram work."

I glared at her. "And what does that mean?"

"We've hit a critical crossroads. They know you can make things happen," my mother reasoned.

"I have plenty on my plate already. What the fuck are they paying Baba Ram for?"

"Just look at it. See if you can support them."

I walked the long way through the woods back to my house and called Sampuran. He had listened to me bemoan the ashram situation for the past year. After years floating in and out of our ashram, he was aware of the patterns of it. It was really the same story: Our expenses were greater than our income. The infighting between the board of directors, the office staff, and the swamis had increased. We all disagreed on what was important to the ashram and how to fix a problem that had existed from the time the ashram was established. Supporting Ma and her lifestyle was costly and something we couldn't or wouldn't address.

"Would you be willing to help?" I asked. "Come in as a consultant, and help this group get real? Help us get our arms around what is happening with the ashram and the direction we're heading? I don't know where else to turn." I vomited it all out. "It's all slipping away. It's a disaster waiting to happen. I know in my heart if we move forward developing the land, particularly the assisted living facility, we'll drive ourselves into debt or possibly lose the ashram. I don't know how to prove it or show them it's not a viable plan. I need someone who understands the nuances of the finances and the implications." I sat on the floor of my office and drew my knees to my chest.

"We need to review the numbers on the eldercare project and the land development project. I'm not sure they'll listen, but I'm happy to help," he said.

"Thank you. I'll email you the financial statements." I hung up and rubbed my temples.

I tracked down my brother and told him I wanted Sampuran to attend the next board meeting as a consultant. "I want him to review the numbers with the board before it goes to vote."

"Well, I've invited Vishnu Ram as well." Vishnu Ram was a former member, now an attorney. The battle lines were drawn.

A few weeks later, we were back in the conference room with

financials and spreadsheets strewn across the table. The board members sat around the oblong table.

"Let's take a moment and center ourselves," Mohan said.

Everyone quieted. The tension in the room was as dense as the swamp near my house. Mohan opened his eyes and asked Sampuran to begin.

"I have reviewed the numbers for the project, and it seems that we are about to embark on an endeavor that has great risk." Sampuran proceeded to point out the issues we faced in our financials and the burden of taking on more debt. He was lucid and clear in his delivery. I was relieved that someone else saw the issues.

"I looked at the numbers for landscaping, and they appear unrealistic," he continued. "And there doesn't seem to be a concrete plan for labor. And we have to look at the state of the economy. It does not appear that it is going to get better anytime soon. We must take that into consideration."

Seated to the left of my brother, Vishnu Ram interrupted. "The economy will shift after the New Year. I, too, have reviewed the numbers and the financials, and they are solid." He sounded like he was stating a case for the grand jury. He pounced and pointed out why it worked. He dominated the conversation.

Sampuran's veins tightened.

The board voted to move forward. I was the only one with a dissenting vote.

"They chose financial suicide," Sampuran said as we walked back to my house.

"Thank you for trying to make sense of it all."

He shook his head. "I can't believe they won't listen."

"This is how it's been for the last year and a half. I'm not sure I want to continue to be the CEO."

"Why don't you change it, then? Do what you love. Run the yoga school, teach, work on Ma's books, and focus on the expansion of the teachings." He said it so matter-of-factly. And for the first time in ten years, I realized I was ready to change my position.

I decided to float it to Ma, but I waited for a few days to allow the concept to percolate and first discussed it with my mom to get her acclimated to the idea.

My mom and I were on the back deck with Ma finishing up a new yoga asana.

"Ma, I've been thinking that maybe it's time to shift my job," I said evenly.

She hesitated. "I am not sure that's a good idea."

"I think Mohan would be great as the new CEO. He's got a great business mind. He's one of your swamis, and he's devoted to you."

Ma looked up from her papers.

"I will still be involved. But this will give me time to work on your books, the yoga, and the teacher trainings."

"Do what you feel is best for Ma and the ashram," Ma said.

"Thank you, Ma." I exhaled. For the first time in a long time, I was excited about new possibilities. I hoped tonight's darshan would shift my state of being.

I walked Ma out to darshan. One of the swamis guided her to her chair.

"Namaste, my children. Tonight, I am going to take you deep into the meditation. Baba gave me a new meditation to share with you. It will change the teaching. Each of you will experience what it is to be in the center of the skull."

I followed Ma's instruction. I allowed her words to guide my breath.

"Don't worry, my children. I will do it for you. I am taking you to this space of awareness."

When darshan ended, I followed Ma into her rooms. The girls were finishing up the evening cleaning. My mother was getting Ma's supplements. It was just the two of us.

"Ma, why don't you show us how to get there on our own?"

"I told you I am doing it for you."

"Would you teach me how to get to the space in the center of the skull?"

She leaned over and in a whisper said, "Then you wouldn't need me anymore."

I sat back and saw her—really saw her. It was a moment of pure honesty and said with such innocence, it stunned me.

41

Dream On

The New Year finally arrived. The last few weeks, I had been overwhelmed by the influx of guests, intensives, and holiday celebrations. I was exhausted. With the festivities finally over, I thought things might slow down. I thought that changing my job would shift the unease and confusion I'd experienced for so long. For a while, focusing on Ma's writings and teaching yoga distracted me. But nothing really changed. Something deep within gnawed at me. I wasn't sure what it was or even how to express what was occurring.

Feeling like I hadn't slept in months, I crawled into bed and drifted off.

A blue hue illuminates the stage and radiates out across the bodies of the fans dancing in the aisles. Eminem is singing, and I am there as his guest. I am dancing by the corner of backstage, my head swaying to the beat of his voice, lost in the music, lost in his words.

He finishes his set, invites me to join him in the greenroom backstage, and hands me a check. It's a donation for the ashram. I thank him and excuse myself to go to the bathroom, where I meet my reflection in the mirror. Something's wrong. My breathing is labored. My mouth is filled with a clear, malleable, plastic substance. I look at it in the mirror; it has a slight blue tinge. I try to pull it out. Some of it breaks free while the rest snaps back into my mouth, filling my throat. I am choking. My eyes bulge. I see myself in the mirror; sinewy blue veins throb beneath my skin, pulsing in and out. I put my fingers into my mouth and try to dislodge the foreign substance. My finger pulls out a long, stretchy string of viscous matter from deep in my throat. I free some, but when the substance hits the air, it hardens and part of it snaps back into my mouth. My mouth and throat fill again. My fingers dig deeper.

Jarred awake, I wiped my forehead with my pillow. This recurring dream often replayed itself with the same theme but a different twist. I took a few long, slow breaths and returned my head to the pillow, trying to shake off the dream. My throat hurt. I drifted back to sleep and then back into the dream.

I'm back in my childhood neighborhood, in my old house, walking down the split-level's stairs. My mouth is filled with a sticky, gummy substance. I am trying to get it out.

I am desperate to get somewhere but not sure where I am going. I am burning hot, so I take off my jacket and then my shirt. I have almost nothing on. I begin walking. I am looking to get back to the concert. It's a long walk to Vero Beach. My mouth continues to fill with the clear, sticky stuff. I can't get at it. It fills my mouth, my throat. I need air. I can't tell anyone what's happening. I am afraid. I can't breathe. I am dying.

I jolted upright. My tank top was soaked, my hair stringy and limp. I rubbed my eyes awake, fumbled for the pen and journal resting on the antique cherry nightstand, and scribbled down the dream. My throat felt like sandpaper, as if something had gotten stuck in it, like a pill that went down the wrong way or a tortilla chip that scratched my windpipe on the way down.

I rolled out of bed, dressed, and went to work. At my desk, I couldn't focus. I was itchy and anxious. I pushed papers aside, stacked files, read emails, made lists. I looked around the office—I really needed to dust the shelves. Instead, I shut the door and walked home.

Lying on my bed, I stared at the shapes on the ceiling, and then I rolled over, grabbed my phone, and dialed Sampuran.

"How are you?" he asked.

"Well, I'm not sure. I'm in a state."

"You're always in a state."

"I had an unsettling dream."

"What about?"

"I've had this reoccurring dream for years. My mouth fills with some kind of substance. It reminds me of the scene in *The Matrix* when Keanu Reeves's mouth is shut with a putty-like material. He tries to talk but can't." My eyes were closed while I relayed my story. "I have never told anyone about these dreams." I buried my nose in a tissue.

"What do you think it's about?"

"Something is trying to come out. And I feel like my throat center is stuck."

"What is it you are unable to say?"

Uncontained tears rolled down my cheeks as I contemplated his question. "I think I want to leave." My voice squeaked as the words tumbled out. A dense, dead space permeated the line. I couldn't believe it was out. "Are you there?" I asked.

"I'm here."

There was a long, weighty pause as we both retreated back to our own thoughts.

I'd never thought I'd say those words. I was an ashram lifer. I had always been certain I'd spend the rest of my life with Ma. And there it was. It just came out, just like that.

I broke the silence. "I don't know what I'll do or where I'll go." My throat burned. "Oh God, how will I tell them?" Terror and realization filled me at the same instant. I knew it was true. I knew it was time. "I can't tell anyone. What will Ma say, or worse yet, what will she do?"

"Maybe you should give this some time and space. Maybe you'll wake up and feel differently in a few days."

I cringed. What was he saying? Did he not think I was serious? I felt a slight tremble. "I don't think so." *He thinks I am being rash. He knows how committed I am to the ashram.*

"I'll stay until July when Ma leaves for the summer trip." I was thinking out loud, sensing him listening to my thought process.

It was only a couple months into 2008. July seemed like a long way away. "In the meantime, I can organize my departure. I can put people into place, redistribute my responsibilities; it will take the better part of the year to do this, anyway." I looked around at all the crap in my room.

"And then there's dealing with Ma," I said.

"You need to think this through carefully."

"You know what they say about leaving the guru's feet. No chance of enlightenment. No liberation. Most of the people who've left have been ostracized and labeled betrayers. And I come back up the ass of a cockroach."

"Yeah, we've been told that kind of stuff, too. Well, maybe not the cockroach part. She really says that?"

"Yes, she does—generally any time someone leaves the teaching for sure. I want to do this well. With love and integrity. I love Ma. This is my home."

42

Welcome to the Grand Illusion

The weeks following my epiphany and realization, my deepest fears rose to the forefront of my mind. I lost weight. My hair was falling out. What would happen when I finally told Ma I wanted to leave? Would Ma let me go? Would she freak out? Was I giving up any chance of liberation? Where would I go? How would I make a living? Most students who had left the teaching were shunned. Ma would insist her close students call and harass them with threatening messages.

"They will never be happy without Ma," she told us. "They will live out the rest of their miserable and unhappy lives and never know God."

It was Saturday night, one of the few nights guests were permitted to attend darshan. The curious came. Those seeking came. The lost and lonely came.

I tossed my cushion and sat in my usual seat. I pulled on a loose thread in my leggings. I didn't bother to chant.

"Namaste, my children." Ma put her palms together and tilted her chin. "Welcome to my ashram. We are an ashram of service. I am The Mother of thousands of . . ." She looked down at the curly-haired student seated next to her, who finished her sentence.

". . . gay and lesbian children and everything in between," she parroted on cue.

I cringed. *Oh my God, here we go again*. I pulled on the thread harder, ripping out the hem. Ma smiled and looked into the room.

"I grew up on the streets of Coney Island. I spent my youth underneath the boardwalk. My first gurus were homeless people, drug addicts, prostitutes, and alcoholics. They shared their lives and their dreams. They shared their food. They taught me the true meaning of service. When Chews was dying of an overdose, she told me to pay back. Her voice rides on the winds of my beating heart. I learned one thing that day: There are no throwaway people. Each person is whole, unique, and complete. We are all God's children. This is the essence of my teaching. And this, my children, is what I do. It's what this ashram does. My kids serve and serve and never burn out. This teaching is about unconditional love." She sat back and took in the people sitting before her.

I yawned. How many times had she repeated this story? Ma droned on, and I tuned out. My mind drifted. I was counting the days and calculating my exit.

As soon as darshan was over, I slipped out of the room. I no longer cared to meet the guests who had come for the first time, to ask them what they thought of darshan. I raced to the sanctuary of my room and called Sampuran. He suggested I call Lorraine, a mutual friend. She'd had a similar experience of leaving a community. I trusted Lorraine. Sampuran and I hung up, and I dialed her number.

"Hi, Lorraine. How are you?"

After dispensing with the usual niceties and greetings, I laid out my dilemma. "I've decided it's time to leave the ashram."

"Wow, that's huge." I could hear the surprise in her voice.

"I've not been happy for a long time. I no longer am comfortable with the direction of the ashram. I feel like the teaching has stopped evolving. And I feel like shit. I'm always exhausted. I haven't felt good in a long time."

"There are times in our lives when we realize it's time to move on," Lorraine said. "It sounds like you're clear you want to leave. When I left, it was one of the hardest things I'd ever done."

"When I listen to Ma, I hear her from a different vantage point, one I never fully allowed myself to have before. It's as if something deep inside me has been tamped down and locked away and is now trying to push its way out of me like a painful splinter embedded deep into the flesh. No amount of digging at it dislodges it, and just when you finally catch hold of a small piece of the splinter, the rest of it recedes back into the depths of the skin." I thought about the black salve my grandmother had used when we were kids to help draw out our splinters. I needed a balm for my soul. "My plan is to leave in July as soon as Ma leaves for her summer retreat."

"You may not make it until then. Once you push the button, once you know something isn't working, it's hard to stick around. Living on the ashram with Ma and the teaching has served you, but maybe now it's time to see what else life has in store for you."

"I'm terrified. I have no idea where I'm going to go or what I'm going to do, but mostly I'm worried about what will happen when I tell Ma."

"Write it down. Start with writing her a letter. It will help clarify what you'd like to say."

"That's a good idea."

"Call me anytime. Let's keep talking. Love you."

"Thank you. I really appreciate it."

I stared at the popcorn ceiling overhead as my chest heaved and tears streamed down my cheeks. It was time to call my father. I put on my sneakers, grabbed my phone, and walked around the newly paved roads of the ashram that had once been pristine woods. All around were small wooden signs impaled in the ground with the message Lot for Sale burned into the wood. Imagining what the property might look like in a few years, I walked faster around the loop.

I looked at my watch—Santa Fe was only a two-hour time difference.

"Hey, Dad, do you have a moment?"

"Sure. How are you?"

"Dad, I think I'm going to leave the ashram."

"Are you okay? What's going on?"

"I've decided to leave. I just can't be here anymore. I've been sick the better part of the year. I'm unhappy."

"Well, dear, you know I'll support whatever decision you make."

"I'm a wreck about it. I don't know how Ma will react. I want to take the high road and stay connected, but—"

A red-shouldered hawk shrieked overhead.

"Maybe you could present it to Ma that you need to take a leave of absence, a sabbatical."

"That's a great idea."

"Have you told your mother?"

"No way. She'll freak out. No one can know. I've only told Sampuran."

"I remember when I left the teaching. Ma took my glasses and smashed them on the ground. I snuck off the grounds and started running down Roseland Road. Ma had people chase me down. Your brother and a handful of men raced after me with an axe. I was terrified. I didn't know where to go."

"Jesus. I had no idea." I stopped walking. Could something like this happen to me? "I don't know where I'll go or what I'll do."

"You know you're welcome to come here and stay with me and Elizabeth. You could help with the radio show. I'd love to work with you." Elizabeth was my dad's new partner, and she helped him with his New Age radio show. He interviewed numerous authors, spiritual teachers, and healers.

"Thanks, Dad. I'll think about it. I need to think about a job, though. Do you know anyone in Hawaii?"

"As a matter of fact, I know someone who has a coffee farm on Maui. I could call them."

"Maybe. I'll get back to you on that. Please don't tell anyone."

"Okay. I won't, dear."

"Promise me."

"I promise."

"Thank you."

"Call me if you need anything. I love you. I am here for you."

"I love you, too."

As I walked, I thought about all the things I could do. I had excellent organizational skills. I could run a nonprofit. I had some decent tech skills, too. I toyed with different scenarios: running a yoga or retreat center; doing marketing; becoming a publicist. I clutched at the collar of my ribbed tank top and breathed in the scent of the woods, moist and earthy.

Detouring down to the river, I sat on the bench, watching the mullet jump. As I returned to the main property, I took in the temples and the beauty of the grounds, knowing I'd soon be leaving all this behind.

The next day, Sampuran came to visit. As we sat on my bed, talking, I mentioned my dad's offer of moving to Santa Fe.

Sampuran seemed to be thinking hard before he spoke, as if he was trying to pull his thoughts from some far-off place. "I have an idea. A suggestion. A possible alternative."

I tugged at my bed pillow, waiting for him to spit it out. His hesitancy made me anxious.

"You could come to Orlando. You could work for me." The words came out of his mouth slowly and thick.

I froze.

"I bought a house near the ashram. It's just sitting there. You could move in."

I tried to process his suggestion. I wasn't sure this was the right move for me. What if I moved in with him, and it ruined everything we had? He'd lived alone for so long. He was still deeply involved in running his ashram. Did I really want to work for him? "I'd like to think about it," I said.

"You could live at the ashram while we remodel the house. We could go to Costa Rica. I have a lot there. We could build a house, but living in a foreign country could be challenging. We could go to Japan. We could go to Chile. I'll take you to Hawaii and maybe visit Ramesh in India."

My head swirled at the number of scenarios he'd laid out. I'd never had so many options in my life. Each suggestion could liberate me from my current life. I felt excited about the prospects of a new life. But the fear of stepping into another dependent situation rattled me.

"You could teach yoga and help me with the ashram."

"I . . . I . . . I don't know what to say."

"Just say yes."

I curled up in his arms, confused. I wanted to say yes.

A few days later, I was in Ma's rooms before darshan, where I was having a hard time faking interest or being present. Ma was discussing her schedule. Incense burned in front of Mother Kali, and fresh flowers in a vase and bright-red hibiscus flowers rested at her feet. In a few days, I was leaving for Boulder for an ayurvedic[1] panchakarma[2] treatment.

As I gave Ma her messages, she interrupted me.

"Shody, Denise is planning on visiting the last week of April."

My body stilled. That was the same time I was going to Truckee to visit Ganga Das and Jaya Ma. Their baby was due in early June. I tightened up while Ma and my mother bantered about the details of Ma's daughter's visit. Fussing with my notebook, I waited for my moment.

"Ma, I want to remind you that I won't be here that week," I said.

Ma looked up at me from her oversize, leopard-skinned chair.

"That's the week I'm going out to see the kids."

"Okay," Ma said. No scene. No nothing.

My plan was to leave in July when Ma went on her summer retreat. I just needed to be patient. I began to pack up my things, waiting until people were asleep or out of the house. In the back of the cedar walk-in closet, I wrapped a set of red-and-black sushi dishes in a March edition of the *Vero Beach Press Journal*. The scent of cedar had faded long ago. Newspaper rustled and crinkled as I folded it around each piece of ceramic. The dishes had been a birthday gift from my brother. He would be left to clean up the mess after my departure.

What if someone walked by and heard me in here crumpling paper? I sat cross-legged in the back of the closet, prime real estate I had acquired along with my ashram status as CEO and adviser to the guru. I closed my eyes and followed my breath in and up. The raspy sound of the inhalation rattled in my ears like a wheezing asthmatic's. I prayed. I begged for an end to my suffering, internal conflict, and terror. It seemed only fair that one of the saints, gods, or goddesses I had prayed to with every drop of depth in my being and every ounce of belief I'd come to know should damn well answer me now. I searched the quiet. I drew in another breath, the coolness tickling my nostrils. My breath was warm and moist as I exhaled; my chest expanded with each inhale and then left me deflated. I'd meditated, practiced yoga, lived a life of selfless service, and done all the things I was told to in order to be one with God. But in this moment, there was no message from beyond nor guidance being received—it was just me and my breath. Was I actually throwing away any chance of finding enlightenment?

It was late and dark when I crept down the stairs and opened the heavy, wooden front door. The night sky, vast with stars, offered me no solace. I loaded the car with a few boxes and covered them with a blanket. I would drive them to Sampuran's ashram tomorrow.

43

There Must Be Some Way Out of Here

I WOKE UP EXHAUSTED. I rubbed the knot in the back of my neck. I felt like shit. I had been unwell for months. Ma, along with a handful of students, had begun practicing ayurveda. Gathered in Ma's rooms, we had taken a test to figure out our constitution and eat accordingly. I had decided to embark on an ayurvedic detox.

I'd eaten nothing but mung beans and rice and lost five pounds. My bags were packed. I was leaving for Boulder in the morning for my ayurvedic panchakarma treatment. I closed the door to my room, tossed my keys on the bureau, and noticed the pulsing red light on my answering machine. Setting my bags down, I walked to the nightstand and pushed the button.

"Krishnapriya, it's Yashoda. Please call me when you get this."

I dialed my mother's number. "Hi, Mom. What's up?"

"Look, I need to speak with you. Ma is upset. When she told you Denise was coming and you said you were going to be out of town, she felt you were flippant with her."

I pushed the receiver into my jaw.

"Ma's feeling afraid, and now you aren't going to be there to take care of her."

My body tensed. I couldn't believe I was getting this call now, almost two weeks later and the night before I was leaving. Ma was afraid because I was going away while her daughter visited.

"Ma is worried. Who will she call to find out what's going on?"

"Mom, this is crazy. Ma seemed fine when I told her. And frankly, she doesn't need me to be around when Denise visits; there are plenty of people to support her." I felt myself getting defensive. What mother needs backup when her daughter visits, anyway? "Isn't Denise coming to spend time with her mom?"

"I think you should consider changing your ticket."

"No way. I'm not changing it. It's the only time in the schedule I can go." I ran down a list of the ashram calendar events.

"You need to think about it. Ma depends on you. She feels you've put yourself first, before her, before the guru."

"Bullshit. This is bullshit. And there is no way I'm changing my trip." I slammed the phone down. We were in a stalemate.

I had a small window to visit Truckee after I returned from this trip. I desperately wanted to visit Ganga Das and Jaya Ma and help them prepare for the baby. I flopped back onto my soft bed.

I flew to Denver the following day, then drove toward Boulder. White, fluffy clouds danced upon the tips of a jagged mountain range in the distance. I called Lorraine.

"Hey. How are you?" Lorraine's voice was calming in my sea of crazy.

"I've packed several boxes. I've started clearing out my office. Now, Ma wants me to cancel my trip to see the kids. I am so mad."

"Don't be surprised if you can't stay until July," Lorraine reminded me.

I checked into the hotel and met John Douillard for my first appointment. He prescribed four hours a day of yoga along with more mung beans and rice. Each day, I underwent a new ayurvedic treatment. I was rubbed with raw silk gloves. I inhaled pungent herbs and had hot oil dripped on my third-eye point. Each drip of oil thumped between my brows. I remembered hearing about water torture as a kid and wondered if this was what it felt like. There were days when my body was packed in ice, placed in a tent, and heated to 105 degrees. I hoped these treatments would make me feel better, less stressed out, and less tired and give me more energy.

Each morning, I practiced hours of yoga, ate mung beans, walked to the center for a treatment, walked back to the hotel, ate lunch, did more yoga, walked back to the center for another treatment, did more yoga, ate dinner, and ended the day with an herbal enema. The scent of Indian herbs leaked from my pores. My hotel room stank. The smell made me sick, but I settled into this daily regimen.

On the second day, my cell phone rang.

I looked at the caller ID. It was Amba. She had been one of Ma's students since the early New York days and had recently become an ayurvedic practitioner. This had set off a new phase of eating and dieting on the ashram. Amba helped many of us ascertain our ayurvedic constitution. While Ma wanted to lose weight, I wanted to get healthy. Amba was studying with John Douillard to become an ayurvedic practitioner herself, and here I was in Boulder with her mentor, embarking on a seven-day ayurvedic cleanse.

"Hi, Amba."

"How is it going?"

"I'm doing well." I pulled the pad of paper closer and took up the pen on the coffee table, doodling hearts on the page while I listened to her talk. The point of one heart placed into the top of another until they merged together. The white page disappeared as we discussed the treatments and the herbs John had prescribed.

"Ma asked about you tonight."

My body tensed. "Oh. What did she want?"

"She asked how you were doing. Joked a bit about John. She

asked if you were having fun having hot oil dripping all over your body."

I stiffened. "She did this in the middle of teaching?"

"You know, she mentioned it before she settled in after I stopped chanting."

Ma was up to no good. She wasn't overly enthused about my going out of town for the week. I continued to doodle hearts. The more Amba and I spoke, the more distorted my hearts became.

"On her way out of darshan, she mentioned she hadn't heard from you. She wanted you to call her."

The room closed in and became oppressive. "You've got to be kidding me. I'm trying to take some time to get well and regain my energy. This is supposed to be a silent retreat."

"Oh, no, she was fine. I don't think she was upset or anything."

I wondered if Amba really believed that. I just wanted the space to heal. To be quiet. "My mother's called numerous times now. I really don't understand. It's as if they don't want me to have any space to get well." I tossed the pen across the room.

"I think you're just oversensitive and raw. The cleansing process opens you and makes you more vulnerable."

I pushed down a scream. "Well, thank you for calling. I need to go." I extracted myself from the call, but I'd barely taken a breath when the phone rang again.

"Hello?"

"Hello, Krishnapriya. Durga Das here."

My brother rarely called while I was traveling. I was suspicious. "What's up?" Exhausted, I put my head back on the pillow.

"I need to talk to you."

For Christ's sake, didn't anyone respect what I was doing? I sighed. "What can I do for you?" I was a bit curter than I meant to be.

"I understand Mom talked to you about Ma and the situation with Denise coming to the ashram. It's the same time you plan to visit the kids."

"Yes, Mom and I spoke before I left."

"Well, Ma is really hurt. I'm calling to ask you to reconsider your decision."

I dug my nails into my hands. "No, Durga Das, I am not changing my plans. I explained it to Mom, and I'll explain it to you. It's the only time on the calendar there isn't an event. It's the only time I can visit my son before the baby is born. Besides, I don't have any relationship with Denise. I am not canceling my trip. There are plenty of people who can support Ma and help with her daughter." I dug my nails deeper into the hotel couch.

"I'm sorry that you feel this way. I don't think you realize how much Ma depends on you. She can't live without you. I think you need to reconsider your decision."

"I've made up my mind."

"Well, think about it, okay?"

"I have to go." I hung up and whacked the phone onto the table. I clawed at the couch. *Jesus, this is never going to end.*

The phone rang again. My body tightened.

"Hello?"

"Hi, how are you?"

It was Sampuran. Ahhh, a bit of sanity. I smiled. The weight fell away from my heart and was lifted by his voice.

"I think it may be time to go now," I said. "I can't stay until July. I can't do it."

"Are you sure?"

"Yes. Definitely."

"Did something happen?"

"The phone hasn't stopped ringing. My mother has called continually for the past two days. She wanted to know why I haven't called Ma. She said Ma doesn't have any information about the upcoming Atlanta intensive. Then she asked about Ma's correspondence. I finally told her she needed to stop torturing me."

I propped my feet up on the wooden coffee table. Everything in the room was a varying shade of brown: taupe walls, brown couch, brown carpet, brown paneling, and dark-brown wooden furniture. The room was dark and confining.

"I told John I wanted to leave," I confessed to Sampuran.

"Really? Do you trust him?"

"Yes. He's not going to tell anyone."

"What did he say?"

"He was a bit cautious and very neutral. I thought for sure he'd talk about his experience leaving Sai Maa. He didn't. He said to be compassionate toward my mother and Ma. He told me to stay strong in love, be gentle with myself, and have gratitude."

"Hmmm. That's unfortunate."

"I guess he has too much at stake to be real with me. He makes a lot of money from the ashram. He offered some story about the sun, a seed, and creation. And how it's all about the light." I was paraphrasing his counsel.

"What a wuss. He had a real opportunity to help you. To walk you through what is about to happen by sharing his story. And we know from other people what Sai Maa tried to do to him. Instead, he decided to package it and make it all nice. It isn't nice. This is hard stuff happening to you."

"I guess he can't go there."

"Compassion; it's not time for you to be compassionate. You defied Ma by saying you wouldn't change your airplane tickets. She's mad. She isn't accustomed to being told no." Sampuran breathed heavily into the phone. "What do you want to do?"

"I want to leave when I get back. I'll arrange to have my brother pick me up from the airport. I'll tell him first, and then speak to my mom. There will be no turning back then." I sucked in a breath. "Then I'll talk to Ma. I'm terrified of what could happen. I want it all to be okay. I love her, and I want to stay in touch. I just need to go."

My mind churned with all the things that could happen. Would Ma get angry? Would she forbid my mother from talking to me?

Would she throw me out? Was it possible she would bless my departure?

"Lorraine suggested I write a letter. I have written so many over the last few months, but the one I ended up with is pretty short. It expresses my love and gratitude."

"I'll make arrangements for a U-Haul truck and a few guys to help you move out," Sampuran said.

"Thank you. I would really appreciate it. I can't believe how scared I am. I don't know how she'll react. I've been around for a long time. I've seen so many people leave the teaching and rarely with her blessing. Ma got so angry when Swami Kumara decided to leave the teaching. Every swami was told to talk to Kumara and tell him he was making the biggest mistake of his life. It went on for months. I went to speak with him. I couldn't believe he was leaving The Mother's feet."

I got quiet, playing out each scenario in my head for the umpteenth time.

"When Lorraine and I spoke, she said if Ma is really who she claims she is, if she truly is an elevated being, then there is nothing to worry about."

"But you know what has happened in the past."

"True, but somehow part of me thinks it might be different because of who I am to her."

"You need to be prepared that it might not go as you hope. But if it does, that will be great. On the other hand, if it gets ugly, you just need to be ready."

"Yes, I know." I bit my bottom lip.

"It will all work out."

"Thank you. I'll talk to you tomorrow. I'm winding down here. Only a few more days before I come home." Home; what a joke. It wouldn't be my home much longer.

I opened the computer and wiped the dust off the screen. The beach screensaver beckoned me. Hitting the Skype icon, I called Hanuman. His digital face appeared from across the world.

"Hi, sweetheart. How are you?"

"Hi, Mom. I'm doing great." He was sitting in his tiny Japanese apartment, a shoji screen and a tatami mat visible behind him.

I stared into my Mac. "I need to talk to you about something important."

"Sure, what's up?" He was eating udon from a bowl with chopsticks.

"I'm going to leave the ashram," I blurted out.

"What? Wow, I didn't see that coming. What happened?" He set the bowl down. "I support you and whatever you decide to do, Mom. I totally understand. I needed to go, and it was good for me," he said, still looking a bit unsure.

"Thank you."

"When are you going to tell Ma?"

"As soon as I get back home. I need to call your brother now. I'll talk to you soon, okay? I love you."

"I love you, too, Mom."

I placed my head in my hands and cried. Although there were people around me, I felt so alone. Something Amrit Desai had said while visiting the ashram came back to me: "Walk toward fear with love."

My flight was in the morning. I would start with my brother.

44

Hurts So Bad

I HELD THE PHONE TO MY EAR while I circled the hotel room.

"Namaste."

"Namaste, Durga Das, it's me."

"What's up?" he asked.

"Can you pick me up from the airport tomorrow? I need to talk to you. It's important." I continued to pace. The room was ripe with a mixture of anxiety, mung beans, and nasty herbs.

"Everything okay?" he asked.

"Yes, I just have some things I'd like to speak to you first about."

"Okay, no problem."

I gave him my flight details and thanked him. There was no turning back. I packed. My mind swirled with different scenarios of how I could tell Ma I was leaving. What would I say when I saw her? How could I do it best with the highest intention? I wanted to set a new bar and accomplish what few had in the past—leaving with love and honor and still remain connected.

My heart thumped the entire way to the Denver Airport. I called my dad, wanting advice on the best way to approach my brother.

"Hi, Dad."

"Hi, dear. I'm upset. Why didn't you tell me you told Vicki and John?"

Fuck me. This was the last thing I needed. When I'd told my aunt and uncle I was leaving, I didn't think they'd talk to my dad. They had always been there for me. John had taken me on a father-daughter canoe trip when I was eight when my dad wasn't available. Vicki had helped me give birth to Ganga Das while my mother was living at the ashram.

"Look, Dad, I've always been close to them. They've always been there for me. Both of them are happy I'm leaving."

"You needed to tell me. They say they've known for weeks. You made me promise not to tell Elizabeth."

"It wasn't time to tell Elizabeth. The more who knew, the greater the risk it would leak out." My hands shook on the steering wheel. "If you want to tell her now, go ahead. Please make sure she doesn't tell anyone else, not even her daughter." I was desperate to protect the story until I spoke to Ma.

"Thank you." He reined in the accusing tone.

"Durga Das is picking me up. I'm going to speak to him first. I'm still working on what to say. My guess is his response may gauge how everyone else reacts."

"Good luck, dear."

"Thank you. I'll call you tomorrow after I speak to everyone."

I hung up, and my cell phone rang.

"How are you?" Sampuran asked.

"I'm okay. I just spoke to my dad. He was pissed off because I told my aunt and uncle about my decision and made him promise not to tell his wife."

"Well, that doesn't help really." He paused. " We have a bit of a glitch in the plan. Swarn is coming to Florida next week. We may need to make some alternate arrangements."

I felt my chest tighten. I wondered why it was a problem—he and Swarn had not been together in years.

I rubbed my chest. This can't be happening. I thought I'd have a place to stay, heal, and start a new life. I bit my bottom lip and took a deep breath.

"I can go to my aunt's. They said I can stay there for as long as I need. I'll figure it out."

"It will work out. We'll deal with it."

I arrived at the airport. "I've got to go. I'll call you after I speak to my brother."

I stepped into the long line, waiting to board. Fighting back my heartache, I swallowed the pain. It tasted like nasty herbs. I felt so alone.

"We are beginning our initial descent into Melbourne Orlando International Airport," the pilot announced. Soon, I retrieved my bag and exited through the automatic glass doors. The warm Florida air caressed my skin. There were vibrant shades of pink and orange swathed across the sky as if an artist had swished his long brush back and forth across the universe with abandon. The scent of salt and sea entered my nostrils.

My brother's red Toyota Corolla rolled up to the curb, and he jumped out and gave me a hug. The trident tattooed on his forearm pulsed as he heaved my suitcase into the back seat. "How do you feel?"

"A little tired, but good. I feel cleansed, that's for sure. Can you smell me?"

"You look good."

"Thanks. It was intense. It takes a lot of work to get healthy." I climbed into the car and took a few deep breaths. *Stay centered*, I reminded myself. Although I had played this out in my head over and over, I had no idea what I was going to say. My brother was committed to Ma. He had been on the ashram since he was young. He was trained to take care of her. Once I told him, would he tell

Ma or my mother? Would he try to talk me out of my decision?

"How was John?" he asked.

"He's good. Very helpful."

Dusk settled over the Indian River as we turned onto US 1. Pelicans flew in formation with a steady eye beneath them. I craned my neck out the window to see if any dolphins were jumping. Small dots of islands disappeared and reappeared as we moved toward home. I pulled myself back into the car and rubbed my stomach.

"Durga Das, I need to tell you something. I am asking for your trust and that you promise you won't say anything to anyone about what I am going to say."

He remained focused on the road. "Sure. What's up?"

"I am going to leave the ashram."

There was no reaction. Poker face. Years of training, I figured. Driving Ma and spending summers in close quarters would make anyone an expert in non-reaction. But I saw his body stiffen. The car filled with an awkward silence.

"Is this a fait accompli?" he asked.

"Yes. I've been unhappy for a long time. I can't live the way I'm living any longer."

More silence. He fidgeted in his seat but continued to stare ahead at the road. "Well, it sounds like there is no discussion. It seems you have made your decision, and there is no room here to change your mind. I don't understand. Why are you doing this?"

"I need to do this. I need to take some time. I need some space to figure out my life." I wanted to put my head back against the headrest, but the force field that had taken over my body wouldn't allow it.

"You're stuck in your mind and not in your heart."

"Durga Das, I need to go." A begging need lodged in my throat.

"You are being completely selfish. You are only thinking of yourself. You are stuck and rigid." He turned to me. His eyes accused. "I am so hurt. I can't believe you are going to leave. How can you?

What about Ma? What about your commitment to the ashram?" He fired off his questions with a pinched face.

I thrashed around, trying to explain. "I don't want to hurt anyone. I need to do this. I can't live the way I am living anymore."

A long, uncomfortable silence crowded the front seat.

We turned into my driveway. The front lights were on, but no one seemed to be around. Relief flooded me. I couldn't bear seeing anyone in my current state. I flicked on the hall light, and Durga Das carried my bag upstairs.

I unlocked my room and turned on the light. The smell of essential oils welcomed me into my space. Home.

Durga Das looked pissed. Soon, the familiar comfort of my room had been replaced with a heaviness. For all the fighting, unrest, and disagreements my brother and I had endured, I wanted him to understand, to empathize, to love me. I didn't bother to bring up how many times he'd been on the edge of leaving the teaching himself.

"This is all in your mind. You are stuck in your mind," he finally said.

"Durga Das. I am in my heart."

"Okay then, speak from your heart. Tell me why you are leaving."

"Durga Das, I have been speaking from my heart."

"I'm so hurt. I don't even know what to say." His face turned bright red. "Why didn't you say something sooner? Why not look at alternatives? Maybe you could change some things and still be here."

"Durga Das, I am really unhappy. I have to go." I reached out to touch his arm.

"You'll be unhappy wherever you go. You need to take a deeper look inside. You need to look at what this will do to the family, to Ma. What about the pain this is going to create? Don't you care?"

"I don't want to cause anyone any pain. I am trying hard to do this well. I want to do this with integrity and honesty. I want to maintain a relationship with Ma and the ashram. This is my home. I love Ma. I love the ashram. I love the people here. I don't want to hurt anyone."

"I have to go. I am sick to my stomach."

My bedroom door shut hard.

I wondered if this was an omen of what was to come. I crawled into bed.

45

Sorry Seems to Be the Hardest Word

I TOSSED AND TURNED ALL NIGHT and was still awake at 6:00 a.m. when I heard people getting up for morning darshan. I pulled the covers over my head. There was no way I was going to darshan. I finally fell asleep.

When I awoke, the house was quiet. I crept downstairs. My stomach growled, but I wasn't sure I could keep any food down. I'd lost almost ten pounds in the last few weeks. I made a bowl of oatmeal and returned to the safety of my room.

My mom had left two messages. She was wondering why I wasn't at darshan this morning. Ma had asked for me. I gripped the bed frame as my insides churned. I needed to finish this, even if it meant committing spiritual suicide. It was time to tell my mother. I thought about the years at Ma's feet. The beauty, the love, and the madness. My mind flashed on the hours spent in Ma's rooms rehashing events, whether it was a teen in trouble, a student leaving, or someone speaking ill of Ma.

I moved hangers back and forth in the closet, pushing aside the orange. I never wanted to see the color again. Opening the drawer to my nightstand, I pulled out the letter I had written to Ma weeks before.

I dressed and left to face my mother. The woods smelled earthy. Time was moving fast. Turning the doorknob to the back entrance, I hesitated. Then I went in, knocked on my mom's office, and slowly opened the door. She was shuffling papers at her desk.

She smiled. "Hi, babe, how are you?"

I hugged her. Her body was warm and comforting, and I held on tight. "I'm doing okay. A bit tired. How are you?" I clutched my letter.

"Oh, you know, busy. Packing and getting ready for Atlanta."

I sat on the floor in front of her altar. The shelf was filled with photos of people who'd died over the years. The dead stared back at me. I pulled away and redirected my attention to my mother.

"How was your trip? I missed you," she said.

"It was a lot. There were several intense treatments; I feel a bit raw from it all. I won't be eating mung beans and rice for a really long time. After three weeks, I can't even look at it."

"I don't know how you ate that gruel to begin with. It's so disgusting. I gag whenever I try it." She picked up a glass paperweight and wiped under it.

Okay, do it now, I told myself.

"Mom, I need to talk to you." My voice hiccupped. This was going to be harder than I'd thought.

"Sure, what is it?" She turned toward me and waited.

"Mom, this is really hard." I remained quiet while I searched for my breath. Where was my breath? I needed it.

"Mom. I need to leave. I need to go."

There. It was out.

Her hand went up with speed and covered her mouth. She let out a gasp. "Oh, no. No. Oh my God. No. Oh my God. Poor Ma."

She grabbed at her shirt and made a loud, sighing sound like she was being crushed. The fabric bunched up where she grasped at her heart. "Oh my God. This is going to kill her."

Had I heard her right? Had she actually said that? The room closed in around me. I put my hand to my heart and massaged my chest, attempting to ease my breath back into my lungs. My mother looked as if her best friend had just died.

"I can't believe that's your response." My voice cracked. "Poor Ma?" I grabbed a wad of carpet. "Don't you even care why? Aren't you going to ask me what is going on or if I'm okay?"

"Of course I care. But I am worried about Ma."

I bit my lip. "Of course you are."

She slumped into her chair. "What brought this on?"

"You know I have been struggling for a long time. I'm not happy. I haven't been well for a long time. I don't agree with the direction the ashram is moving." I listened to myself explain my reasoning.

My mother looked like a bear trying to free itself from the metal jaws of a trap. "Why didn't you say something? Why didn't you say it was too much? Ma always said to tell her if it got to be too much. We could have made changes."

"Mom, I've been telling you both for a long time. That's why Mohan is taking over my job. No one listened."

"I can't believe that this can't be worked out. Oh my God." Her eyes dulled. "I can't imagine you not being here."

A large lump lodged in my throat. "Mom, I'm tired. I am tired of being killed. Tired of nothing ever being good enough. I can't do it anymore. I just tried to get well and was harassed the whole week I was away, nonstop. I don't want to do it any longer. I don't want to live this way. I need some space."

"Ma trusts you. She trusts you with her life. She trusts you with the ashram. She thinks the world of you. She always talks about how wonderful you are and what a great job you're doing." She stopped, and I saw her mind whirling. "And the yoga—oh God, you are her yogi. Oh, no."

I set my intention. "Mom. I want to do this well. I'd want to stay connected and still be part of the ashram. I'll take Ma's yoga out to the world. I love her. This is my home. I am grateful to Ma for everything she's taught me. Everything she's given me."

"What am I going to tell her? What am I going to say?" My mother was breathing heavily. "What are we going to say to the community?"

"We can say I'm taking a leave of absence, if that helps. Or I'm taking a sabbatical. Say I'm working on my health."

"Maybe we can tell everyone Ma is sending you out to teach."

We spent the next few minutes running different scenarios. It was as if we were back in our routine, working together for the greater good.

"I'm happy to do what works best for everyone as far as the story we tell. I would like to make it all okay and go as smoothly as possible."

"Good, that is good."

"I wrote Ma a letter. I'd like you to give it to her." I handed her the neatly folded paper. "You should read it."

She unfolded it as if it was a fragile glass. She opened it and read it slowly. She never was a fast reader.

Dear Ma,

After much thought, I've decided it is time for me to leave. I am profoundly grateful for everything you've given me. I love you.

Your daughter, Krishnapriya

"I am not giving this to her. It's not enough." She tossed the letter on her desk.

The love and softening I had felt seconds ago dissipated.

"This is all she gets after all she's given to you? It's not good enough. I'll tell her myself."

I threw my hands up. "Fine, whatever."

My mother's eyes were swollen and puffy. Her mouth turned downward in some impossible upside-down, half-moon frown.

I walked toward her and gave her a hug. I held her for a long time. "I love you, Mom. It will be okay."

She held on tight and sobbed in my shoulder. "I love you so much."

"I love you, too."

You'd think I'd been diagnosed terminal. Maybe it was true, and my prognosis was a slow spiritual death. Back in my room, I waited for the call.

I called Sampuran. "No one seems to really care what I'm saying or feeling. They're only worried about themselves. My dad was pissed because I told my aunt, my brother was hurt, and my mom only cared about Ma."

"Sounds like the same old ashram victim mentality."

My phone rang. It was Rudra Das. My mother had spilled the beans.

I heard the phone downstairs ringing off the hook.

"Rudra Das is trying to hunt me down. My mother must have told him."

"Get ready. There will be more of this."

Five minutes later, there was a knock at my door.

"I need to call you back." I hung up the phone.

Rudra Das stood at my door rocking back and forth. "Can we talk?"

"Sure. Let's sit in the room next door." I didn't want him in my room. I wanted to leave the conversation as quickly as possible.

He leaned back against the wall-to-wall mirror. The house had mirrors everywhere. I sat across from him, my reflection gazing back at me. My eyes were puffy and pink.

He pulled at his eyebrow. "Yashoda told me."

"I figured as much."

"Look, I have been here before. I almost left. You don't have to do this. All you need to do is surrender, and it will all be okay."

"No, that's not true. I have spent the last twenty years surrendering. I need to go."

He'd never understand. It was a fucking epidemic.

He rocked back and forth. "This will pass. All you need to do is wait it out. What makes you think you'll be any happier if you leave? Happiness comes from within." He was using the tired old rap I had used on others who had left. "How can Ma live without you? She depends on you." He pulled on his brow with greater aggression, his body twitching. "Please don't do this."

"Look, I have made up my mind. I'm leaving." I stood up, ending the conversation, and slipped back to the safety of my room.

I phoned Lorraine. "Hi, it's Krishnapriya."

"Hey there. How are you?"

"Hanging in there." I imparted what had occurred thus far before I heard the click from another incoming call.

It was Ma.

"Lorraine, I'm sorry. I have to go. I'll call you soon."

46

Helter Skelter

"NAMASTE," I ANSWERED EVENLY. My body already felt heavy—the real show was about to begin.

"Namaste, Krishnapriya, it's Yashoda."

Ma was screaming in the background. "How could you? How could you do this? You of all people? You've betrayed me!"

I stiffened and adjusted my seat on the bed. Her voice sliced through me. My mother remained silent as Ma's voice shattered the safety of my space.

"You've cut the guru's heart out. I am devastated. I don't want to live."

Just sit still, I told myself, *and breathe. Do not react.* I reached for the yellow legal pad on the table by the bed and began to write.

"I trusted you. I'll never trust anyone ever again. This is the worst thing anyone has ever done to me. You . . . you did this. This is worse than losing my Jimmy."

Had she actually just told me this was worse than her son killing himself? *Keep breathing*, I reminded myself. I scribbled down each allegation and offense. My chest and lungs felt crushed as she threw up litany after litany in her accusatory diatribe. I had always known that her reaction might be bad, and I thought I'd prepared myself, but this was worse than expected. While her chaos attacked my soul, I kept writing. I wasn't sure what made me write down the conversation, but somehow, I thought it might be important. It also helped me focus on something other than her screaming at me.

"Why didn't you come to me? Why didn't you tell me? Why this way?" she yelled. "Talk to me!" She hadn't taken one breath yet. "I can't live. I'll never be able to live. I raised your kids. I saved Ganga Das's life. I was the one who called Hanuman when he was depressed and suicidal. I prayed for him when he went to jail. I called him home. I saved your whole family.

"You need to get over yourself," she ranted on.

I wanted to cover my ears, yet I didn't want to miss a word.

"I can't believe I was stupid enough to trust you. You have no balls."

Tears fell, and the blue lines on the paper bled beneath me. I couldn't see what I was writing, but I didn't dare remove the pen from the yellow pad.

"This is worse than what Brahma Das did to me." Now I was being compared to the man who'd tried to destroy the ashram when he left.

"Why didn't you talk to me? We could have figured it all out."

Ma stopped.

I took a breath.

And then she started up again. "So now your kids are gone, and you are out of here. Is that what it is? I knew it when you wouldn't change the airline ticket."

I pressed my fingertips into my temples. This was how it was to be.

"You should just die. You are ruining the lives of hundreds of people."

Did I hear that? Did she just tell me I should die? I felt a wall build around my heart. I could not believe it had come to this. In my heart, I'd believed that truth and unconditional love would guide my departure.

"I don't want to teach. I don't want to go to Atlanta. What about the yoga? Yoga is your life. I put you in my will. I took out life insurance. I am such a fool. I always say, 'What can I do for my Krishnapriya?' I gave you too much. I fucking knew it."

I had yet to utter one word.

"You are a coward. Do you realize your Ma could die? You'll rue the day you did this. Do you care if I die? You were born to be at my feet; it's the only reason you are alive."

I heard shuffling on the other end of the receiver.

"She wanted titles. She wanted sannyas. I don't know what to say."

My mother attempted to calm her down. "Ma. Ma."

"Look, Shody, she came back from John just as sick."

They began speaking to each other while I listened, remaining conscious while rendered immobile. I needed to do something to save myself. I began a silent mantra of protection Sampuran had said was useful to ward off psychic attacks or negativity. He had warned never to repeat it more than three times, or it could backfire on you.

"*Ah, Lakh Baba Siri Chand Di Rakh.*" I repeated it three times.

Ma turned her attention back to me. "You left to get healed, and you are just as sick as when you went. Is there someone else? Do you even know what you are doing? What about your children? She owes me, Shody. I gave her life. What about your grandchild? How could you steal that joy from us? You are so selfish. Do you even care?" She started screaming louder.

Then it all stopped. There was a calm that came over the vicious storm. I thought of the eye of the hurricane: The wind stops, the sun comes out, but the next set of storm bands is imminent. They warn you not to go out during the eye of the storm.

"Okay. Do it small. You owe it to me. We can work it out. Maybe we can get back to center, resolve it, and reason it through." Ma's voice had calmed. "You had your tea party with John. Oh, poor me. You are supposed to love the guru more than yourself, but no, you love yourself more than the guru. What's physically wrong with you?"

This time, she waited for an answer.

"I am burnt out," was all I could say.

"I can fix that. Ma can fix that. How can you walk away? I gave you everything. I gave you my heart and soul."

There was a long, silent pause. I could feel she was working up to her next outburst. I took a breath and thought, *Just stand your ground. Don't say anything. It won't matter. She just wants to win, get her way, and save face.*

"You will be a tortured soul for the rest of your life. Shody, there is no chance to help her."

Was that true? If I walked away, would I be unhappy forever? Doubt fogged my senses.

"Do you know the karma for betraying me? Do you understand? You can't finish what you started. I don't trust anyone. You've taken my joy. I have taken care of every member of your family." Ma listed all of them, alive and dead.

"Why don't you think I can help you?" She was asking, but she didn't want an answer this time. She whispered to my mother, "You know, Shody, I'm saving her life. Okay, we can do this gradually." In a calm voice, she said, "You need to stay here for a year. You owe it to me and this ashram."

"No." I snapped as an overwhelming sense of guilt filled me. I loved my home. I loved the people.

"You have to," my mother begged.

They both negotiated for a time, but I knew I couldn't stay for a year. I could barely stay another minute. Time stretched slowly during the negotiations. There was more yelling. More begging. I shut down. I knew I needed to protect my heart or what was left of it. Ma and my mother discussed how my exit wouldn't be viewed negatively or reflect poorly on Ma.

We agreed to hang up and rethink how to do this in the best possible way to make my departure okay for Ma and the ashram.

I was worn out, exhausted, and pissed off, but still I was trying to smooth out the situation. I wished it hadn't gotten to this point. I loved Ma. I didn't love her behavior. I was hurt that she would do this to me after all of the years I'd devoted to her.

I leaned back on the headboard while I replayed the last hour, Ma's accusations tumbling through my aching head.

The phone rang, jarring me.

"Namaste, Krishnapriya. Ma would like you to come over to her rooms."

I envisioned my mom's pursed lips. I'd known I'd get this call, and I knew what I was about to walk into—more yelling and more of what I'd just experienced. Ma was playing to win. Time was their bargaining chip.

I pulled myself up and dragged myself to the car. I had no doubt this was not going to end well.

47

Stand by Me

I WALKED INTO MA'S ROOMS AS I HAD thousands of times before, only this time it would be different. In a pair of red-plaid flannel shorts and a T-shirt, Ma sat coiled in her chair. Her eyes were crimson. Her face was drawn and off-color.

"Namaste, Ma," I said respectfully. I sat down on the floor across the room, facing her. For the first time in many years, I was sitting across from Ma, not next to her. My mother was to my left, close to Ma's chair. She didn't look well.

"You are so selfish. You have broken this Ma's heart. Why can't you open your heart? You are going to hurt thousands of people. Why are you doing this?"

I didn't move. "Ma, I need to take some time. I haven't been well for a long time. I don't want to do this any longer. The job has become too difficult."

"You are making yourself sick. It's all you. Why don't you just suck it up? Others will leave the teaching because of you." Her voice rose as she pointed her crooked finger toward me.

I watched her and said nothing as she searched, looking for a vulnerable spot. She wanted to break me.

"You owe me. I made you."

I felt caught in a time warp as Ma kept repeating her accusations.

My mother finally interjected. "How do we make this work?"

I began to spin my own story of why I was leaving. "I think we should tell the community I am taking a sabbatical, a leave of absence due to my health."

My mother looked at Ma. "Maybe we should say Ma is sending you out to teach. We can do this slowly. I think you should stay at least until Ma's birthday. Until the end of May."

I choked. Another six weeks. Surely I'd wither and die.

Ma jumped in. "It's the least you can do."

My mother agreed. "Really, we need you to do this."

Defeated, I relented. "Fine. I'll stay for a little while." I was too tired to fight, and at this point, I thought, what's a little more time? Maybe it would smooth things out.

"You can train Mohan to take over your responsibilities, and you can work from home and continue with yoga and the teacher training," my mother continued.

Dead. I felt dead. There was no life left in me. I wondered if this was what they meant when they said, *I am a shadow of my former self.*

Ma glared at me. "I am beyond ruined. I am beyond hurt. This will help with some of the karma, but you will be a tortured soul until you're ninety-nine."

My anger finally began to bubble up. I bit the inside of my cheeks.

"You'll still be welcome on the ashram."

"Thank you," I said weakly.

"You are so selfish. Stealing my joy with Ganga Das and Jaya Ma and their unborn baby. I gave him life. This baby is a miracle baby. He wasn't able to have children, after all." She waved her hand through the air.

Now she was using my unborn grandchild.

"And what about your vows. Don't they matter? You became a sannyas."

"I never wanted to be a sannyas. You made me a sannyas." I rolled my shoulders back and sat up.

"How fucking dare you?" Her eyes grew big. There was fire dancing in them.

"Krishnapriya!" My mother screamed my name.

"Have you told anyone else you're leaving?" Ma asked.

"Yes, Sampuran and the boys," I said, and even as it slipped from my lips, I knew telling her would be a mistake.

"How dare you? How dare you tell my spiritual son?" She uncoiled from her pose. "You told your sons." Spit ejected, and she began foaming at the mouth. "Your son's sperm had cancer in it. I fixed that! Who else knows?" She wasn't going to stop the new interrogation.

"Only them," I lied, but it was too late now.

"Call them. Tell them you've changed your mind."

I unfurled my hands. I needed air. I needed out of this room. I was in the jaws of a viper that was swallowing me whole. I nodded.

We finished the negotiations. I would not go to Atlanta this weekend. I'd call Devi and explain I was sick. I'd stay on for a while and help with the transition. I thought this might possibly repair and ease my relationship with Ma in the future. She could easily forbid my mother and the community from ever speaking to me again.

"The first thing you do when you leave these rooms is call Sampuran and those boys. Do you understand? It's karmic."

"Yes, Ma." I clenched my teeth and left the room.

I had been captured. I was a prisoner of war. Back at my house, I curled up on my bed. There were no more tears. I felt empty, and not the good kind of empty I sought in meditation. This empty was a hollowness.

A slideshow of the last few hours flashed over and over in my mind, continuing to show the scenes. All the years I had dedicated to Ma and the ashram had come to this.

All I wanted was to leave honorably, with love and integrity.

The phone rang.

"Hi."

"Hi, how are you?" Sampuran said gently.

"Well, it didn't go so well. It was pretty awful." I told him everything, including that I had agreed to stay a little longer.

"If things get too crazy, you can leave—just leave. Leave everything. Don't worry about your things. You can always get other things. It's just stuff, right?"

"It's true. There isn't much I want here any longer. I'll pack a suitcase of clothes and put it in the car."

"That's a good idea."

My throat was sore. "I can't believe it's come to this. I can't believe the things she said.

All these years, my love, devotion, and dedication, for what? I spent twenty years serving her and my home and everything I loved. She told me the only reason I was born was to serve her. She said I would be better off dead."

"Holy shit. That's pretty horrible." His voice was strained. We talked for a long time about spirituality, gurus, and finality.

"You know she is going to try to break you? She'll continue to use everything against you, including your family."

"It seems like it. She asked me if there was someone else. I lied and said no. She would make that the reason I was leaving. I know she'll come back and ask again. I want to tell her the truth."

"I am okay with that. There is some wisdom in telling the truth. At this point, it doesn't matter anymore. They say the truth will set you free."

"Thank you. I was worried about you and the fallout if I tell her." My body sank into the comforter. For the first time in hours, I was able to take a breath.

"I don't care. It's fine with me. I can handle myself. Don't worry, okay?"

"At this point, I want it all out on the table," I said.

"Good. I think that is a good plan."

I felt eased by his presence on the phone. "I better go and pack. I'm not sure when the next call will come. They're leaving for Atlanta on Friday. The plan is to talk when they get back on Monday."

"Call me if you need anything. Okay?"

"Yes, I will. And thank you for being here for me." I pulled out a suitcase and packed a few things. When I was finished, I looked around my room. My books were the only things I was really attached to. But like Sampuran said, I could always get new ones. The rest of it didn't matter. All I knew was that there would be no sleep tonight.

48

Everybody Wants to Rule the World

THE NEXT MORNING, the sky was a brilliant April blue. Billowing, white, cotton clouds drifted by. It was a beautiful day except for the ominous internal dread that rumbled inside me. I sat up, my pillow damp, my flesh heavy with the weight of my aching bones, and I got up and walked to the closet.

In the kitchen, I made coffee, leaned on the counter, and took a big gulp. It would give me the strength for the next task on my list. I refilled my cup, returned to my room, and punched in the numbers by heart.

"Namaste," Devi answered. "How was your trip? How was the panchakarma with John? Don't you love him?"

Devi and I had been close friends and confidants for many years, but I knew I could only reveal part of my unfolding story. "It was a good trip. I'm a bit worn out." I shared my stories about therapies, diet, and nasty enemas, but I was anxious to get to the business at hand.

"How are things going? Are you ready for Ma this weekend?" I asked.

"We are so excited. We've been cleaning for weeks now. We're ready to receive The Mother. It's going to be a great weekend. We have lots of new yoga students coming," she bubbled, with bright enthusiasm. "Will Ma be visiting the houses?"

"Um, I'm not sure. But I have to let you know, I won't be coming on this trip. I'm not feeling well." I paused.

"But you always attend and help guide the intensive retreats with Ma." I could feel her calculating what this might mean.

"I've never missed guiding an intensive. But you guys will be fine. It sounds like everything is together. Maybe we could go over the schedule and talk about some things that need to happen in my absence."

"Sure."

I heard myself slip into business tone. "You'll need to make sure Ma knows everyone coming up to her."

"You mean, I get to be you." Her voice raised an octave, and I could feel her excitement over the phone. In the midst of business, I realized she was eager to fill the role.

"Yes, you get to be me. Call me if you need anything. Shody will help you, too. I'm sure you'll have a great intensive. I'll talk to you soon. Love you. And thank you."

The first chore of the day was done. I grabbed my car keys to go to the bank and to get more storage boxes.

Back upstairs, I packed another emergency suitcase. Somehow, I'd managed to avoid any of my housemates. My cell rang. My mother. I swallowed, almost choking on my own saliva.

"Namaste, Krishnapriya. I am here with Ma. We are in the salon," she said perfunctorily.

"Namaste." I walked outside and sat by the fence near the pond, where the gators croaked out their mating calls.

"Ma wants you to know she is devastated."

"I am sorry. I never meant to hurt her."

"You have a responsibility to Ma and this ashram."

I could hear Ma in the background. I knew her so well, I could tell her mood through a third person holding the phone. Her anger leaked through.

"Ma would like to know if there is someone else."

Okay, there it was. I had been waiting for this line of questioning.

"Yes." There. It was out.

My mother's voice gagged. "Who?"

"Sampuran." I paused. "I love him."

I heard Ma shout, "Why didn't you tell me? We could have worked this out! I would have married you!" Then her tone shifted. "Have you had sex with him?"

Really, we are going there? A bitter, nasty taste rose up in my throat. I visualized Ma in her salon chair, her hair matted with jet-black dye.

"Did you have sex with him on the ashram?" she continued. "Where have you had sex with him?"

I felt violated. Raped. My palms dampened. "I am not going to answer these questions," I said to my mother. "And if Ma continues down this road, I am going to hang up. Do you understand?"

Ma continued firing questions for my mom to ask. "Where? When? How often have you had sex with him?"

I hung up and looked at my phone. Not bothering to brush off the cut grass that adhered to my wet body, I stomped across the yard. The ringing telephone jarred me, and I answered it. Why I answered, I am not sure; maybe I still held out hope that all of this nonsense would blow over and it would all end up okay.

"Krishnapriya, how could you be so disrespectful? What's happened to you? This is totally unacceptable. You need to write Ma an apology," my mother reprimanded me.

I was five years old again. "I am sorry, but I told you I was going to hang up if Ma continued to ask questions about the details of my relationship." My mouth and jaws tightened.

"Ma is the guru. You don't hang up on the guru. It's completely disrespectful. You need to write an apology. Do you hear me?"

I leaned back against my car, looking at the suitcases. I just wanted to bring an end to the perversion of questions.

"Fine. I'll write an apology."

I heard Ma in the background. "Hang up, Shody."

I decided I needed to go to Orlando for the weekend. Then I'd come back on Monday and see if we could figure out any of this. I found a crumpled tissue in my pocket, blew my nose, and ran upstairs to grab my last bag and my computer. I needed to get out of there. Tucking the remaining things in my back seat, I lifted my head to see my brother running toward me. He was charging toward me full force, like a bull facing off with the red cape. His eyes blazed. I turned, and he was on me before I knew what hit me. He grabbed my wrist.

"No! Don't. Get off me!" I yelled. He pushed me. I moved toward my car. He flipped me around in a bear hug. Grunting, he pushed me away from the car and toward the pavement.

"Get off me! Get the fuck off me! You are fucking hurting me!" I sobbed and screamed at the same time. I writhed, trying to extract myself from his grip, but he tightened his hold. I couldn't breathe. He was crushing my ribs.

"Krishnapriya! Krishnapriya!" he yelled, spitting out my name.

"Let go of me!" I screamed.

"Stop it! Stop, Krishnapriya."

I grabbed his shirt and pulled on it, hearing a ripping sound. He let go.

I fell to the pavement, sobbing.

"I just wanted to talk to you," he said, breathing heavily.

"So you attack me?"

He gave half of a laugh. "Give me a break. I didn't attack you."

"And what would you call that then?"

"I didn't want you to leave."

I stood up and brushed myself off.

"I just wanted to talk."

"Fine, then let's talk."

We walked across the driveway and sat on the grass in the same spot where I'd just had my last showdown.

"How are we going to best take care of Ma? You can't leave it like this."

So, he'd just come from Ma's rooms. They'd sent him over. They were worried I'd leave. This was a mission to stop me.

"I'm going to Orlando for the weekend. I'll be back on Monday."

We discussed what would happen after I left, and then his phone rang. He handed it to me, and I sighed and took it.

"You really need to write Ma an apology letter. Your behavior is totally disrespectful." My mother was like poison ivy; no matter how much you scratched, it still itched. No matter how much pink shit you put on, there was no relief. I explained again to her why I'd hung up, but no one was listening.

"I need to go to the office," I said to my brother, handing him his phone, and then I wrote a short apology note and emailed it to Ma. Not wanting anyone to see me in my current condition, I slipped out the back door, drove out of the driveway, and headed to Orlando.

49

You Don't Own Me

TWO HOURS LATER, I WAS AT SAMPURAN'S DOOR, and I fell into his arms. My pain, sorrow, and fear were erased in his embrace. I was safe for the moment. He microwaved Amy's Bowls for dinner, and we sat in his living room.

He pushed the bowl closer. "Eat something. It will help ground you."

"I'm not very hungry." I picked at the rice. His ashram was so quiet. There were only three people living there. The walls of his room were taupe and the carpet beige, but a splash of color from the Persian area rug helped. The rooms screamed of masculinity, heavy with wood and muted colors. The only room that hinted at any femininity was the bathroom. Even his altar was stark, a photo of his teacher, a mala, and a dagger.

My phone rang. It was my mother. "You need to come home. You can't stay up there."

"Mom, I am staying up here for the weekend. I'll be home Monday."

"It doesn't look good. What will people say?"

"I don't care what anyone says."

Her voice pitched as she tried to cajole me into going back to the ashram. "Ma is so hurt. How can you do this? If you come back, it will all be okay."

"You leave for Atlanta in the morning. I'll be back on Monday. I gotta go." I hung up.

Fifteen minutes later, she called back. "Pleeeeeassse, you need to do this. It will make it all better. Please help me." My mother sobbed. She choked out her words. "Ma's devastated. What are we going to do?"

"Mom. I'll talk to you after the weekend." I ended the call, but the calls continued, and so I stopped answering. Each message was increasingly more desperate and intense and unhinged.

A stranger in a strange world, I laid down on Sampuran's king-size bed. This unknown place offered me no rest. I had nothing to hold on to.

I dozed off in Sampuran's embrace, and the following morning, there were ten unanswered voicemail messages.

"Please help me. I don't know what to do." Every message my mother left was more hysterical than the last. I heard people talking in the background. They were on the bus driving to Atlanta. After listening to each and every call, I finally put the phone on silent, laid out a yoga mat, and stretched.

Sampuran came into the room.

"I need to leave. I can't stay until May. They'll never stop." I showed him the voicemails.

"They are gone. You can go and get your things. I have the guys on standby and the truck reserved."

"I'll make a few calls and see if I can get Tara and Shanti to help me pack some things. I can go back tomorrow and be done."

"I'll call Ramon."

"Thank you. I can't believe it's come to this. I can't believe how crazy they are."

"It's how it's always been. This is the way it is. Ma pulls no punches when she doesn't get her way."

"I can't do it. They won't stop. And if I stay, I will be brutalized. I know it."

Sampuran left for work, and I sat by the pool. I called Shanti, whom I'd lived with for the past twenty years, told her I was leaving, and asked for her help. She promised not to say anything to anyone. Then I called Tara. I had known her since she was a little girl when she had come to the ashram with her mother, aunt, and younger sister. Now an adult, she was a bit prickly and generally unhappy. She agreed to help me. I stuffed some things in a bag to drive back to the ashram. For the last few months, it had seemed as if I was forever packing and unpacking.

I hugged Sampuran and headed back to the ashram, my hands trembled on the wheel. The sound of the coquina crunching beneath my tires rattled me as I turned down the long driveway. The house stood quiet, just as I'd left it.

I unlocked my room and went in. Boxes were leaning up against the wall, and there was crap everywhere. I heard a light tap on the door.

I hugged Shanti. "Hi. Thank you for helping me."

"Could we talk? I would like to hear what is going on."

"Of course." I moved a pile of clothes so we could sit on the rug.

She picked at the carpet. "I can't believe you're going."

"I need to do this. I haven't been well. I need some time."

"But . . . but what about me? What if I want to leave?"

"You need to look and see if that's what is in your heart."

"How will I know?" Tears brimmed in her eyes.

Another knock interrupted our conversation, and Tara opened the door. I was grateful for her arrival and thanked her for coming. We began packing like we were on a joint mission. Tara labeled each box with precise efficiency. Shanti asked questions.

I began letting go. Purging. "Tara, you can have my bedroom set if you'd like. I'll take my books and a few other things. Shanti, here, take this bust of Baba." I handed it to her.

She looked at me like I had just given her a priceless Smithsonian artifact. "I . . . I can't take this." She thrust the heavy head my way.

"I want you to have it." I pushed it back toward her. Then I carried out armfuls of orange clothes and dumped them in a pile in the guest room next door. When I was finished, a mountain of silk and satin towered over me. Thousands of dollars of orange. I never wanted to see the color again. I handed Tara bags and boxes of orange jewelry. "Here, give it away."

I told the girls to take whatever they wanted: clothes, TV, furniture, shelves.

Hours later, after the bulk of packing was complete, they said good night.

I sat down on the floor and labeled special things for some other people I cared about. Then I noticed the message machine flashing. It was my mother. She suggested I call and check in to see how the intensive was going for Ma. I listened to the message again and scratched my head. The message was just another emotional button, pushing me further away. *The ridiculousness of it all*, I thought. After everything that had happened, my mother was calling with a nonchalant, business-as-usual message. I wanted to scream.

I didn't call back. I finished packing in solitude and slept in my bed one last time.

50

Follow the Sun

THE RAYS OF SUNLIGHT STREAMED THROUGH my window. It was dawn.

I carried one last box out to my black Honda Civic. The ashram grounds were eerily quiet. It was eighty-nine degrees at ten in the morning. Humidity pressed on my chest. The moving truck arrived at noon, and I rubbed the sweat from my hands onto my khaki capris. A hefty guy named Ramon, whom I'd never met, and three strapping young Hispanic guys hurried as instructed. In under an hour, they loaded my thirty boxes of books, a few random pieces of furniture, and my clothing.

"You must be smart," Ramon said as he carried three boxes of books, bulging his biceps.

"Not really." I offered a weak smile. None of the books on my shelf told me how to do what I was doing. Nope, the books being carted down only explained how to get here, how to be a better yogi, how to find enlightenment. None of my books explained how to leave.

Ramon shut the back of the U-Haul truck and departed for the two-hour drive to Orlando, where my things would be dropped off and stored in the garage of the lake house where I'd eventually live.

I rearranged the Office Depot boxes in the back seat of my car so I could see out the back window. Some of the boxes held a few leftover items from my life at the ashram, last-minute things I'd decided to take. One box contained Hindu statues of gods and goddesses, which I had once dusted, oiled, and prayed to. I would eventually give them away. What was left behind of my ashram existence now lay crumpled in a towering pile of orange swami clothing in the guest room next to my old room.

Before I departed, I hugged Usha and Shakti, who were now also privy to my departure. The news would spread.

I opened the driver's door, and it whined a loud, oil-less whine. My hands shook as I clenched the steering wheel. I stepped on the clutch and shifted into reverse. Waving one last time, I put the car into first and eased down the long, sandy driveway that ambled alongside the adjacent cow pasture. Taking care to avoid the familiar dips, I rounded the bend toward the main road. I'd gotten away mostly undetected, or so I thought.

I'd assumed leaving the ashram might be different for me because of my close relationship with the guru. She'd called me her daughter, told me how special I was, kept me close. I had run the ashram as if it were my own. The community was part of my heart. The guru, the satsang, and the teachings coursed through my veins. I had grown up there. What had happened?

Adjusting the rearview mirror, I caught a glimpse of myself, gray circles puckering beneath my glassy, brown eyes. My skin, which was usually sun-kissed and freckled by this time of year, was the color of yellowed spinach forgotten in the back of the fridge. I looked away and turned up the air conditioning.

When I passed the Palm Bay rest station, the ashram was already seventeen miles behind me. Palm trees, grazing cattle, and vast tracts of open land dotted with scrub oak and saw palmettos stretched out on both sides of the interstate.

I've heard it said that during the dying process, our lives flash before us. I imagined my beautiful guru gazing at me, cross-legged on her love seat, her back resting upon a large black sheepskin, her mare-like, ebony hair cascading around her face and down her back, the trademark red dot swirled on her brow between piercing, dark-brown eyes. Her smile materialized in my mind's eye, along with her conspiratorial glance that I knew so well. Her infectious love swirled within me. How often was it that she and I would think the same thought at the same moment? Would I miss that depth of connection and knowledge I had shared with her? Would I miss the people I'd come to love? Would I miss the drama of this life?

In a way, I *was* dying. The guru's last words to me were like a death. I wondered if the tone of her voice would forever be seared into my soul. I was walking away from everything I believed in.

A convoy of tractor trailers rumbled by. Pressing my palm to my chest, I tried to rub away the weight that had moved in like an unwanted guest who never stopped talking. I read an article once that said you could actually die from a broken heart. I wondered whether that was true.

While I drove, I made a few calls to tell my coworkers about my departure.

"I need to take a sabbatical." I heard myself spinning my own demise with each call I made. Too many years of public relations, marketing, and sales, I suppose. For those I considered friends, I walked a little closer to the truth.

"It is time for me to go," I told them. "I need a break. I'm unhappy. I need to get well."

I plugged my cell phone into the cigarette lighter as the reverberation of the tires trembled beneath me, jarring my internal organs.

I read once that we think seventy thousand to eighty thousand thoughts a day. Surely this number was wrong. It was as if a thousand thoughts a second crowded my brain. I clutched the steering wheel as if that would help my current state. I didn't need to be this way. I had thought that if I listened to my guru, meditated, and led a life of service, I would realize liberation in this life.

The phone on the seat next to me rang again, and I jumped. It was Sampuran, the man I'd fallen in love with. He wasn't the reason I was leaving, even though that's what the guru would tell everyone. I reached over the computer bag and flipped open the black Motorola Nokia.

"Hi."

"Where are you?" he asked.

I looked up to see what exit I was passing. The flat, swampy stretches of land were yielding to cookie-cutter homes and strip malls that housed Best Buy, Michaels Crafts, and Ross Dress for Less.

"I'm on 95, passing through Melbourne. The moving truck should be there in half an hour."

"I know. I spoke to the guys. How are you?"

"I'm okay," I said. But I wasn't. Part of me felt lost and adrift, and the other part longed to be in his arms and start our new life together. Years of guilt and secret meetings were over. His ashram was different from mine. The members practiced Kundalini yoga, and life there seemed much less rigid than at my ashram. Non-celibate marriage was permitted in his ashram, which was quite different from our intense ashram rule that being celibate was the path to enlightenment. Our relationship would no longer be taboo. His teacher was dead, and he was free from being told what to do. Still, it was strange moving into another ashram, even if only temporarily.

"Hurry up and get here," he said.

I smiled. He always knew how to make me smile. "I'm driving as fast as I can."

Another call came in. "Oh my God. It's my mother," I said. "She's left at least twenty messages."

"Don't answer it," he said. "Your leaving isn't going to look good no matter what you do. It's only going to get uglier."

I picked up my water bottle and took a sip.

"They'll keep trying to break you," he reminded me.

"I know," I said. "I'll see you soon."

There had been times in my life when I'd felt as if my skin didn't quite fit, and I yearned to be complete. I thought enlightenment meant I'd become more than who I was. I'd be free from my pain, my feelings of unworthiness, inadequacy, and imperfection. Some greater force would subsume me. I'd thought that by attaining this state of being, I would be different, somehow wiser, and deeper, with Yoda-like knowledge.

I leaned my forehead on the steering wheel and pressed hard on the same point between the brows my guru had touched numerous times to remind me who I was. Then I quickly lifted my head, so I didn't careen off the highway and kill myself before my new life began. *Focus on the road*, I told myself, and wiped the cloudy film from my eyes.

Drawing in a deep breath, I let it expand in my lungs, holding the breath for as long as possible. I held it until it hurt, and then I exhaled a long, slow, methodical breath out. I exited off I-95, whirling around the curve and merging onto The Bee Line and shifting into fifth gear.

In all of my uncertainty, I did know one thing: I was free.

51 (EPILOGUE)

What a Long, Strange Trip It's Been

I LIVED A REAL-LIFE SPIRITUAL FAIRY TALE. Part Cinderella, I worked tirelessly to serve the guru and the ashram. Part Merida, I was a warrior pursuing my spiritual liberation, battling my ego, and defending the realm. Like Rapunzel, I was trapped, not in an isolated tower but in a bubble of belief. In the end, I'd become Sleeping Beauty. Who knew that after all the years of spiritual practice, I'd find myself deeply asleep trying to awaken from a worldly dream.

For twenty years, I yearned to know the secrets of the universe. I wanted what the saints, sages, and yogis promised. I wanted what my guru promised. I wanted liberation, nirvana, enlightenment. I wanted God. I worked hard to attain these things. I meditated, practiced yoga, and served my guru and the ashram.

When I finally woke up, no one told me it would be one of the hardest things I would ever experience or that it would hurt so badly. I thought the process of awakening would be different. I thought I would attain a level of oneness, awareness, and state of consciousness that would make me different.

What started as a beautiful love story, one where Ma would guide me to the doors of enlightenment, ended in a nightmare. The realization I needed to leave happened gradually. It was a series of slow shifts and small incidents that culminated over time and inevitably woke me up to the internal knowing it was time to go.

It was only after I left that I realized I had excused away Ma's behavior, and I was complicit. Leaving stripped me of certainty; I no longer knew who I was or what I believed. It took four years to feel whole again and years of rebuilding the remains of my life.

While Ma's teaching helped thousands of people, myself included, I think I was fortunate that it ended the way it did. It allowed me to walk away knowing I'd done everything to exit peacefully.

Hanuman was a touchstone after leaving the ashram, helping me question and face what I'd once embraced. When I look back, I sometimes question whether I failed my children. There were times I imparted my spiritual ideals like a fundamentalist holding up the poisonous snake of redemption.

After I left Ma, I lived with Sampuran at his ashram, teaching yoga and hosting cooking classes and wellness retreats while working as the director of marketing for his commercial landscape company. I worked on finding myself, figuring out who I was, what I thought, and what I wanted. We traveled. I found a therapist. I explored ayahuasca and psychedelics as part of my healing journey.

Sampuran and I eventually broke up. He remains an important and trusted friend in my life. I moved to Northern California, not far from Ganga Das and his wife, Jaya Ma, and their two children, India and Lakshman. Hanuman lives in LA with his wife, Jordan, and son, Wyatt. Both of my sons are kind and beautiful people, as are their partners and children.

My relationship with my mother is open and loving. Her commitment to Ma and the teaching remains strong. My brother and I are on good terms. My father died of ALS a few years ago.

Ma died in 2012, four years to the day after I left the teaching. We never spoke again.

ENDNOTES

Chapter 1: The Sounds of Silence

1. *Shakti* means spiritual energy.

Chapter 8: I Got You Babe

1. *Chela* is the Sanskrit term for a person following a guru. It means one who is eager to learn, a disciple.

Chapter 13: Dancing in the Dark

1. A puja is a religious ritual, and Durga Puja is a festival in honor of Durga, the goddess of war, strength, and protection.
2. *Brahmacharya* means to stay in conduct within one's self, a concept often characterized by sexual abstinence.

Chapter 18: Losing My Religion

1. In Kundalini yoga, *satnam* is the mantra most used. It can be translated as "true name" or "truth is my identity."
2. A *dhuni* is a sacred firepit in Indian religions, particularly Hinduism, where a fire is kept burning continuously. \
3. A *gurdwara* is a place of worship.

Chapter 21: Wake Up Dead

1. Malas are beads used for meditation.
2. Samskaras are mental impressions left by life experiences.

Chapter 23: Baby, Who Hurt You?

1. *Pranams* are respectful greetings.

Chapter 24: Black Magic Woman

1. *Pujari* are responsible for performing temple rituals.

Chapter 28: Say a Little Prayer for Me

1. *Prasad* is a devotional offering.

Chapter 29: Paint It Black

1. *Vibhuti* is holy ash.

Chapter 30: I Need a Dollar

1. *Mamaluke* is Italian American slang for someone who's done something silly.

Chapter 34: I Put A Spell on You

1. Asanas are yoga positions.

Chapter 36: Hare Rama, Hare Krishna

1. Sannyas is a vow of renunciation of worldly life.
2. Her Holiness Sai Maa Sai Maa Lakshmi Devi.

Chapter 42: Welcome to the Grand Illusion

1. Ayurvedic is a form of traditional Hindu medicine.
2. Panchakarma is a detoxifying and purifying treatment.

CHASING NIRVANA BOOK CLUB QUESTIONS:

1. *Chasing Nirvana* explores the allure and dangers of charismatic leaders. Why do you think communities like this one are so compelling?
2. How does Priya's story reflect the universal human longing for belonging and meaning? What does belonging mean, and when does it become dangerous?
3. In what ways does this memoir challenge or affirm your own ideas about spirituality?
4. What strategies did the community Priya joined use to keep members loyal, and how does this echo other systems of control you've seen in life or society?
5. Was there a moment in the memoir that made you pause and reflect on your own life choices or beliefs?
6. How does this story illustrate the fine line between devotion and manipulation?
7. How does this story resonate with contemporary conversations about freedom, personal agency, and the search for truth?
8. What do you think nirvana, liberation, and enlightenment mean to Priya by the end of her journey?
9. How did the memoir leave you feeling—hopeful, unsettled, inspired, or something else?
10. If you could ask the author one question, what would it be?

GRATITUDE AND ACKNOWLEDGMENTS

WRITING THIS BOOK HAS BEEN AN EXTRAORDINARY JOURNEY, one I couldn't have traveled alone. It wasn't easy. To those who stood by me, supported my vision, and offered guidance along the way, thank you from the depths of my heart.

My deepest gratitude to Brooke Warner and the She Writes Press team for believing in this project and guiding me through the publishing process. Brooke, your insight and support have been invaluable. Special thanks to Sheila Trask, Lorraine Fico-White, and Shannon Green.

To my sons: Hanuman, thank you for all the conversations about our lives and for helping bring this book to life with your humor and revelations. Ganga Das, thank you for your wisdom, depth, and perception. You are both incredible humans.

Sampuran Khalsa: I am deeply grateful for your steadfast friendship, the light you bring to my life, and your belief in the book. Thank you for years of deep conversation about it all. More to come.

To my mother: I love you. And to my aunt and uncle, Vicki and John: Thank you for always being there to catch me when I fall. Lorraine Weiss, thank you for your wise words during some very difficult times.

Kat Terry: Your workshops inspired and supported my writing journey. Thank you for helping shape my story early on. You are the consummate poet, and good friend.

Katherine Hill: I have so much gratitude for all the years of writing for the *Tahoe Guide;* they were invaluable. Thank you for your encouragement in writing this story. Here's to the future fostering the literary arts through our collaborative events, the Tahoe Literary Festival and Truckee Literary Crawl. What fun.

Alyssa Ganong: Thank you for your creative insight with all of my artistic endeavors. Our phone conversations and friendship are priceless.

My dearest Silk Sisters: Jani Osborne, Kath Irwin, Molly Knickerbocker, and Moni Monteverde, your wisdom, honesty, and laughter have lifted me time and again. You've listened to and held me through many ups and downs.

My community of friends who have surrounded me with love and support on this writing journey: Alison Bermant, Nicole Dreon, Wendy Wright, Eric Petlock, Adrian Hex, Jeff Brunings, Karen Barchas, and Melissa Williams, who have read my pages and offered feedback along the way, I love and appreciate you.

A big shout-out to the Tahoe writing community: Sue Norman, Eve Quesnel, Wendy Voorsanger, Liz Tucker, Bridey Thelen-Heidel, Tim Hauserman, each of you shared a piece of yourself and your writing journey, offering me perspective on this literary ride. Thank you. Your thoughtful feedback and keen eye helped refine and deepen this work.

Andrew Lawler: I appreciate the calls and time while navigating the publishing world. Gerard Bocaccio: Thank you for opening doors. And Rhonda Hayter: Thank you for the early editing.

Julia Drake of Wildbound PR: Thank you for your guidance walking me through the literary world. I look forward to what unfolds next.

Finally, to the readers: Thank you for walking this path with me. May this story touch you, inspire you, and remind you of the strength we all carry within.

With heartfelt love and gratitude,

Priya Hutner

ABOUT THE AUTHOR

Photograph: Nicole Dreon

PRIYA HUTNER is a writer, teacher, and cofounder of the Tahoe Literary Festival. The owner of The Seasoned Sage catering company and the arts and culture editor for *The Tahoe Guide*, her writing has been featured in *The Tahoe Guide*, *Moonshine Ink*, and *Muse Magazine*. She also facilitates writing, breath meditation, and self-discovery workshops. When she is not writing, cooking, or teaching, Priya enjoys skiing, hiking, and biking in the Sierra Nevada. She lives in Truckee, California. Follow her at www.priyahutner.com and on Instagram @priyahutner.